THE AWAKENING OF ISLAMIC POP MUSIC

Music and Performance in Muslim Contexts

Published in Association with the Aga Khan University Institute for the Study of Muslim Civilisations and the Aga Khan Music Programme

Series Editors: Theodore Levin and Jonas Otterbeck

This series presents innovative scholarship in music, dance, theatre and other performative practices and varieties of expressive culture inspired or shaped by Muslim artistic, cultural, intellectual, religious and social heritage, including in new creative forms. Bringing together outstanding new work by leading scholars from a variety of disciplines across the humanities and social sciences, the series embraces contemporary and historical cultural spheres both within Muslim-majority societies and in diasporic subcultures and micro-cultures around the world.

Published and forthcoming titles

The Awakening of Islamic Pop Music
Jonas Otterbeck

From Rumi to the Whirling Dervishes: Music, Poetry and Mysticism in the Ottoman Empire
Walter Feldman

edinburghuniversitypress.com/series/mpmc

THE AWAKENING OF ISLAMIC POP MUSIC

Jonas Otterbeck

EDINBURGH
University Press

IN ASSOCIATION WITH

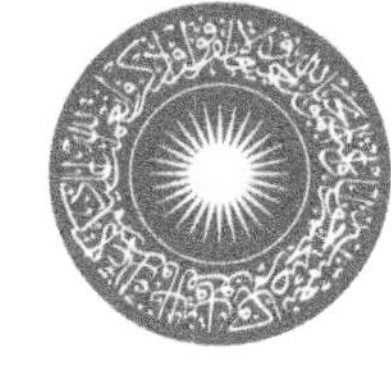

THE AGA KHAN UNIVERSITY
(International) in the United Kingdom
Institute for the Study of Muslim Civilisations

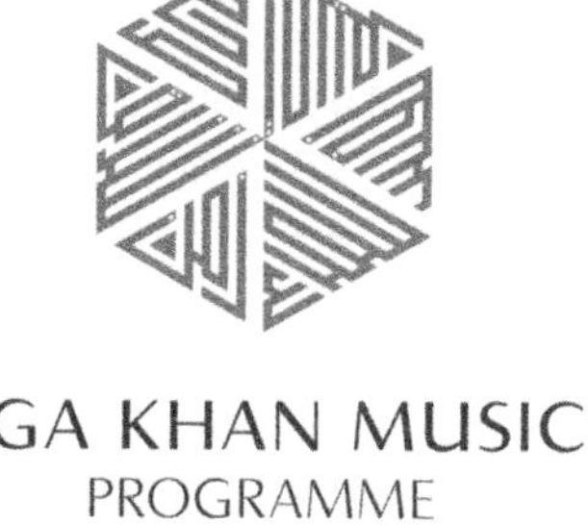

AGA KHAN MUSIC
PROGRAMME

Edinburgh University Press is one of the leading university presses in the UK. We publish academic books and journals in our selected subject areas across the humanities and social sciences, combining cutting-edge scholarship with high editorial and production values to produce academic works of lasting importance. For more information visit our website: edinburghuniversitypress.com

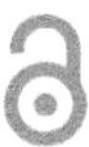

Edinburgh University Press Ltd
The Tun – Holyrood Road
12 (2f) Jackson's Entry
Edinburgh EH8 8PJ

First published in hardback by Edinburgh University Press 2021

Typeset in 11/15 Adobe Garamond by
IDSUK (DataConnection) Ltd, and
printed and bound by CPI Group (UK) Ltd, Croydon, CR0 4YY

A CIP record for this book is available from the British Library

ISBN 978 1 4744 9042 9 (hardback)
ISBN 978 1 4744 9043 6 (paperback)
ISBN 978 1 4744 9044 3 (webready PDF)
ISBN 978 1 4744 9045 0 (epub)

CONTENTS

PREFACE

Over the years, many people have provided input on how to perform this study, from advice about individual sentences to inspired ideas at seminars, conferences or in conversations. This book is what it all boiled down to. Thank you all, especially my students, the higher seminar of Islamic studies at Lund University and the research seminar at the Aga Khan University Institute for the Study of Muslim Civilisations in London. I would also like to thank the two anonymous reviewers of the manuscript for encouragement and good ideas. I hope you will all read it and continue to have opinions about the project.

I would like to single out a few who have been particularly important in different ways. My thanks go to: Mark LeVine for sharing your energy and emboldening me to take on this project; Annemette Kirkegaard for all the years of collaboration and for giving me the chance to become a part of Nordic (and British and US) musicology and ethnomusicology environments; Karen van Nieuwkerk for your inspiring research and for connecting me to anthropologists of the 'Islam and Popular Culture' field; Anders Ackfeldt for having opinions about, well, basically everything and struggling with similar problems as I in Islamic studies; Johannes Frandsen Skjelbo for co-writing an article with me partly reused in this book; Göran Larsson for co-writing another article partly reused in this book and for being so easy to work with; Martin Lund for the many ideas about popular culture; Johan Cato for covering my back; Anna Otterbeck for compiling a Spotify playlist (titled as the book) containing most songs mentioned; Marie-Louise Karttunen for the elegant proof reading; Russell Harris for many detailed and initiated comments on my manuscript; Stephen Lyon for listening and advice-giving; and finally, Leif Stenberg for encouragement and decades of discussions.

Let me collectively thank everyone at Awakening and all the other people with whom I have been in contact during tours or when interviewing. Thanks for sharing. I genuinely hope you will find my analyses fair, but also thought-provoking. Let me single out Sharif Banna for a very special thanks for allowing me access and generously giving me room in his busy schedule.

I would like to acknowledge the following for economic support: the Center for Middle East Studies (Lund University), Oxford Centre for Islamic Studies, Istituto Sangalli (Florence), Vetenskapsrådet (Sweden) (2015-02163), Oscar och Signe Krooks stiftelse (Lund) and, of course, my employers, the Centre for Theology and Religious Studies (Lund University) and the Aga Khan University Institute for the Study of Muslim Civilisations (London). Finally, I would like to thank Firoz and Saida Rasul and Jim and Lynn Walker for supporting and encouraging my research.

Some arguments, texts and ideas that this book draws on have been published previously. I am grateful to the co-authors, peer-reviewers, proofreaders and editors who have helped me sharpen arguments. The following texts in particular must be acknowledged:

(2014): 'What is Islamic Art? And What Makes Art Islamic? The Example of the Islamic Discourse on Music', *CILE Journal*, 1(1), 223–47.

(2015): 'Maskuliinisuus ja islamilainen popmusiikki', in R. Hämäläinen and H. Pesonen (eds), *Kohtaamisia: Kirjoituksia uskonnosta, arjesta ja moni-kulttuurisuudesta*, Helsinki: Helsingin Yliopisto, pp. 80–9.

(2016): 'The Sunni Discourse on Music', in K. van Nieuwkerk, M. LeVine and M. Stokes (eds), *Islam and Popular Culture*, Austin: University Press of Texas, pp. 151–69.

(2017): (with Göran Larsson) 'Islam and Popular Music', in C. Partridge and M. Moberg (eds), *The Bloomsbury Handbook of Religion and Popular Music*, London: Bloomsbury, pp. 111–20.

(2018): 'Den nya islamiska popmusiken och Maher Zain', in Jenny Björkman and Arne Jarrick (eds), *Musikens makt*, Göteborg: Makadam, pp. 233–48.

(2018): 'Beautiful (Pop) Sounds', *Critical Muslim*, 27 (July–September), 84–96.

(2020): (with Johannes Frandsen Skjelbo): '"Music Version" versus "Vocals-Only": Islamic Pop Music, Aesthetics and Ethics', *Popular Music and Society*, 43(1), 1–19.

1

HI AND WELCOME TO THE FIELD

Slough, UK, 29 October 2014, at an Islamic charity concert arranged by Human Appeal. The American comedian Preacher Moss, once in the Muslim stand-up comedy group 'Allah made me funny', has for a short while entertained the young, mostly female, seated crowd. He is smartly dressed in a beige blazer, a beige cap of a slightly darker shade, black trousers, a gleaming white shirt and a turquoise and white striped bow tie, clearly a connoisseur of the trendy Muslim dandy fashion (Khabeer 2016: chapter 4). The audience has already heard a couple of warm-up acts; now it is time for the star. The band starts playing a tight, seventies soul-flavoured intro like those of James Brown. Preacher Moss's soft voice changes, becoming more intense, as he intentionally mimics introductions of the American funk star. 'All right! Star time! Are you ready? Are you guys ready? You? You? You?' He rushes towards the crowd. 'I think we are ready! But I can't hear you!' The crowd screams. Preacher Moss turns around and walks back to the band. 'Ladies and Gentlemen. This is star time! He is ready to come to the stage! You've been waiting all night; he's here; he's in the building. But he can't hear you though. Can I hear some noise?' Again, the crowd willingly screams. 'This gentleman is a multi-platinum recording artist. You know his songs: Thank You Allah, Forgive Me, You are Number One, without further ado, welcome to the stage – My man! Your brother! Maher Zain!!!!' The crowd roars. A smartly dressed young woman in the first row screams at the top of her voice, 'I love him!' as

Maher Zain enters; her male friend films her self-conscious fan-girl scream with his mobile phone, while I shoot them with mine.

Maher Zain takes the stage, leisurely clad in dark trousers, white sweater, black baseball cap and plaid neck scarf, and starts to sing one of his popular songs, 'Radhitu Billahi Rabba' (I've accepted Allah as my Lord), from his second album *Forgive Me* (2012). It is rhythmic, but the enthusiastic audience remains seated and will do so throughout the concert, apart from the children who run back and forth in front of the crowd or sit on the floor singing the lyrics to some of Maher Zain's most accessible songs. Few men show the same fervour as the female majority – a few sing or clap hands at times and a foot might tap the rhythm. The women are much more active. Some even practice what, for lack of better words, I call seat dancing. As standing to dance is not considered morally acceptable, they simply remain seated and move the upper part of their bodies. The day before, in Bristol, the crowd is different, with more female students and not so many families, and some young women grasp the opportunity and stand: swaying at least, although not really dancing, if I may draw a line. At the Bristol concert, I also see cases of self-consciously ironic fan-girl behaviour, my personal favourite being a young woman who pretends to faint when Maher starts to play 'Insha Allah' (Allah willing) and incidentally waves in her direction. She holds her hand to her forehead and falls back in her chair while her two standing girlfriends laugh at her pose, crying out 'Oh, come on'. Mild mannered and handsome, Maher Zain is a regular poster boy for these Muslim women, have no doubt about that.

Something has happened to Islamic charity gatherings and conferences in the last two or three decades. Music performances have become part of what is expected, or even what is most anticipated; they appeal to youth, who will do voluntary work to get a free ticket: having an evening of fun and doing good at the same time. A fair deal.

While on tour with Awakening in the UK, I have met many star-struck and smiling fans. Some can afford the meet-and-greet tickets giving them a chance to chat with the stars before the show, maybe get a compact disc (CD) signed and take the obligatory selfies. However, most experience the singers on stage when being larger than life, amplified and elevated. Even when arranged as charity events, these concerts are also part of a consumer culture logic surrounding staged performances by recording artists.

The old taboo against music – certainly popular music and bands playing all kinds of instruments – in Islamic movements has been partly eroded by the emergence of a new genre of popular music often marketed as nashid or Islamic music, one legitimated by Islamic scholars calling for purposeful rather than immoral art. It has opened the way for a variety of acts covering several different styles including, especially, hip-hop (Khabeer 2016).

Awakening is one out of many Islamic media companies that has sought to meet the challenge of modern popular culture by appropriating it and transforming the content. Over the years, Awakening has emerged as one of the most important global corporations in terms of pop music inspired by Islam. The following are some figures built on Awakening's own estimates: as of autumn 2018, the nineteenth year of its existence, Awakening had produced more than 400 songs and some sixty music videos which, by 2016, had been viewed more than 1 billion times on Awakening's official YouTube channel, and in early 2019 Awakening reached 3 billion views[1] and in July 2021, 4.4 billion; it has sold more than 5 million albums and received forty platinum records, raised more than £21 million in charity concerts and arranged more than 1,500 concerts all told.[2] In short, Awakening has been busy. And music is not Awakening's only trade.

The halal market is a growing economic sector. With an expanding Muslim middle class worldwide, Islamic consumption increases (Janmohamed 2016). The *State of Global Islamic Economy Report 2019/20* estimates the Islamic consumption market at 2.2 trillion dollars (for 2018) with an expected yearly growth of 5.2 per cent (p. 2). Regardless if these figures are entirely true or too optimistic, it is significant that Islamic market stakeholders (and there are several) present the field in such ways. The message is clear. The Muslim consumers are here, ready to spend: provide them with opportunities.

Many consider singer-songwriter Sami Yusuf one of the first global Islamic pop stars – starting his career in 2003 when he signed to Awakening – while,

---

[1] When counting user-generated content (UGC) viewing, using a technique allowing the tracking of views of items you have produced, Sharif Banna claims Awakening videos have been viewed almost 7 billion times. Adding to this, Awakening songs were streamed online roughly 100 million times during 2018 alone.

[2] Information from https://www.awakening.org/ (last accessed 29 October 2020).

at the time of writing, Maher Zain is the company's biggest star. One of his popular songs, 'Ya Nabi Salam Alayka' (Oh Prophet, peace be upon you), passed 200 million views on Awakening's official channel on Christmas Eve 2018, and 400 million by May 2021. Awakening have found more than 300 cover versions of the song on social media. Maher Zain is followed by more than 29 million users on Facebook and by 5 million on Instagram (2021). This can, for example, be compared to Justin Timberlake (both born in 1981) who is followed by 42 million on Facebook. When Maher Zain launched the song 'Antassalam' (You [Allah] are the peace) on 2 May 2020 (during Ramadan), it reached 100,000 views in two and a half hours, 200,000 in seven hours and just less than 500,000 in twenty-four hours. A year later, the video had 12 million views.

The concepts used above to describe the music need defining. What is Islamic pop? What is popular music? In this context, Islamic pop is shorthand for music made with the goal of being perceived and accepted as Islamic, often with the specific intention of celebrating Allah, Muhammad, Islam or Islamic values and lifestyles in lyrics, images and, at times, sounds. Not all music that carries references to Islam fits such a description, something which has been pointed out by Ackfeldt (2019) in his study of US hip-hop and its use of semiotic resources perceived as Islamic in hip-hop culture. Instead, some artists signal political resistance, African American political awareness or simply drop references to Islam because it is considered cool or provocative (Ackfeldt 2019; Aidi 2014; Khabeer 2016). In this case, however, as we shall see below, Awakening is explicitly claiming to produce music that is 'inspired by faith' (Awakening 2014: 2, hereafter '*the Awakening book*') and thus, in my theoretical understanding, has 'the goal of being perceived and accepted' as Islamic.

Popular music is a widely debated, notoriously slippery concept, but once again, in the context in which I am writing, not very problematic. In the first eight chapters of the book, the term 'popular music' refers to music that is composed, recorded, marketed and likely to be consumed in ways enabled by technological developments since the first sound recording in 1878. Contemporary recorded popular music has a regular form in terms of length (often 3–5 minutes) and elements (intros, verses, refrains, bridges, etc.); it is produced with an 'even' volume in the sense that it does not fluctuate much and with a steady tempo without losing the rhythm, and is marketed as singles and albums with accompanying videos, photos, launches, posters and other advertising tools and channels. The artists perform, amplified, on stage to an audience according to a certain protocol that includes concert length, identifiable songs, clapping and applause, the artists' communications with the audience between songs and the overall staged situation. To simplify, I refer to this as Islamic pop or pop-nashid, nashid being a term I examine more extensively in Chapter 2. Here, it suffices to say that it is commonly used in relation to a type of traditional, devotional, Islamic song genre that is now used as an overall genre label for a wave of new Islamic popular music, at times abiding by the form of older nashids, but often not. Nashid is also a general Arabic word for song, for example also applicable to secular songs. I develop my sketchy description of the popular music elements of Awakening in greater detail in the course of discussion.

Since I concentrate on Islamic pop and pop-nashid, I leave aside other genres and trends in contemporary Islamic music (for these areas, see Aidi 2014). Only when there is a clear relation to the music I am writing about will I make references to hip-hop, qawwali and other Sufi music. Gnawa is not even mentioned, even though it is popular as both Islamic music and as world music (Aidi 2014: chapter 7; Kapchan 2007).

Indeed, this book tells the story of Islamic popular music, centred on Awakening. It is divided into nine chapters. Chapters 1 and 2 introduce the study and the third chapter Awakening and its artists. The fourth deals with the growth of the new pop-nashid and the development of Islamic pop. Chapters 5–8 look into the music and artistry of Awakening. The final chapter consists of a discussion of Islamic discourses on popular music over time, a fairly neglected topic as much discussion, both by Islamic intellectuals and researchers, has centred on the legality of instruments as such or on *sama'* (listening) as a ritual in Sufism.

As this book is written by a scholar of Islamic studies, one of the key issues throughout is how the making, marketing and performance of a particular new Islamic music genre relate to Islamic discourse (in its diversity). This should not be understood as a claim that Islamic discourse simply sets up limits for Islamic pop and pop-nashid; my interest is rather to research how Islamic discourse and the music in question challenge and change each other. It is not a relationship isolated from everything else but, rather, one that takes place in several different contexts of socio-economic and political change. Both music and Islamic discourse are diverse and processual, and must be understood in relation to the actual people envisioning them. In order to express this organic relationship, I have focused on how Islamic beliefs are represented in songs and music videos; I have also paid special attention to the importance of performed masculinity to the Islamic pop star persona. A third topic of study is the actual engagement with Islamic discourse by a commercial company. Discussion of these three elements makes up the major part of Chapters 5–8. Awakening and its artists are thus situated in context but with retained agency. Due to their popularity, Awakening's artists potentially assert influence over a wide range of people, more than most Muslims, making an examination of Islamic pop and pop-nashid urgent and important.

When reading this book, I strongly recommend listening to the songs I discuss and taking breaks to watch concert clips. It will make everything I write about more real. When trying to describe sound, one may instigate a certain level of understanding with the reader but there 'ain't nothing like the real thing' to quote Marvin Gaye and Tammi Terrell. Titled as the book, there is a Spotify playlist of more than 100 songs, almost all mentioned songs in the order they appear in this book (https://open.spotify.com/playlist/6ay5kGjZA gpA1aX1YzvbDX?si=RpFvVzJOQlC9Cl9v3zHuQA). Further, I recommend Awakening's official YouTube channel (www.youtube.com/user/awakeningrecords), which, by the way, has more than 11 million subscribers (July 2021).

My approach and analysis draw from anthropology, ethnomusicology, religious studies, Islamic studies, visual studies, musicology and culture studies to name a few fields. There is consequently an overwhelming risk that the rich abundance of overlapping concepts deployed in these different traditions might flood the text instead of helping the reader to understand. Because of this, I have chosen to discipline the prose, keeping it communicative. Regardless, quite a few theoretical concepts and models are exercised, have no fear.

Finally, this book is not a study of the reception, use and appropriation of this music by its consumers, fans and hecklers. I hope to find an opportunity to make more of this aspect in the near future. In this book, the focus is somewhat different; I aim to analyse the contemporary development of possible Islamic expressions.

2

AWAKENING TO THE MUSIC

How do you find a field? Here I take some space to sketch how I came to research pop-nashid and Islamic pop and say a little about the awareness processes that marked that journey; I especially want to discuss some of the pitfalls in Islamic studies. I then introduce the reader to the field and the material before discussing my failed attempts to leave it behind. At the end I discuss the terminology of the music. In a way, Chapter 2 is a prolonged argument about why this new Islamic music genre matters, why an anti-essentialist understanding of Islam is beneficial and why fields no longer behave.

This is the Way! Step Inside

The second undergraduate project I wrote up at university was on Islam and music. Written in 1985, it is a terrible read with no connection to the urban music of the day and little understanding of the Islam part of the title. Instead, it follows the use of Islam as a generic word for any historical, political, cultural or intellectual expression stemming from areas where some form of Islamic tradition dominates religious life, but not necessarily all aspects of social life: rather to the contrary. That kind of usage is strange to secular religious studies today and difficult to reconcile with more complex social theory. It leads to awkward constructions like 'Islamic swords' to refer to military equipment that is neither shaped according to Islamic legal advice nor decorated with Islamic symbols, but simply forged to maximise performance as deadly weaponry or display items. My project work thus placed all kinds of tonal expressions from the so-called 'Islamic world' within the discursive frame of Islam.

Of course, such usage of the word Islam was not unique. As young as I was, aged twenty, my writing was already intertwined with an age-old discourse common in historical studies and, not least, in studies of Islamic art (see, for example, Brend 2005; Irwing 1997; Rice 1985), of which I have since become highly critical: not only because the usage is impractical and imprecise, but also because it leads perception astray. It implies that Islam is a category of interest in all situations when dealing with this so-called 'Islamic world' or 'Muslim world', in themselves problematic categories. It clearly is not. Still, Islam might actually have something to do with things said and done or how they are said or done – it often has. For example, perceptions of Islam can legitimate action, mobilise people and be used as the basis of an appeal to act morally; they can structure gender, space, time and so much more. Yet it would be utterly detached from reality to presume that all aspects of economics, politics, love, lust, greed, emotions, compassion, scholarly logic, wars, military tactics and the development of stirrups in any Muslim context are always best understood through the discursive frame of Islam. Rather, it is wise to assume that people act in a way they believe they have reason to; most people make sense, if they are not off the rails, emotionally or mentally. Then again, few are completely rational, always behaving strictly according to logic or carefully researched plans. Rather, most people have a remarkable capacity to compartmentalise life, to use different rationales in different situations, to make mistakes that would have been seen – quite obviously – as mistakes if the minimum thought had been applied to the situation (that certainly applies to me, at least), and to live with contradictions and ambivalence without any great problem (Schielke 2015). To put it differently, rather than rejecting the category of Islam as valuable in analyses, Islam (in all its multiplicity) has to be repositioned and understood as performative, always in context and always in relation to individuals, structures, discourse and power relations (see Waardenburg 2007). The diversity of Islamic discourses form and mobilise – and are formed by – action, something typical of long enduring religious traditions.

Between 1987 and 1994 I periodically lived in Egypt, working as a tour guide for Scandinavian tour agents. The experience gave me a better understanding of music in that particular society and, of course, of Egypt more broadly. Pop music was everywhere. It was shallow and its stars, both male and female, were sexualised. This was a period when the Egyptian state still controlled television, radio and all major broadsheets, and the intelligentsia and artists of the secular elite decided on and provided media content, amply self-censoring to avoid unnecessary trouble. It was also before satellite television programmes brought new taste cultures from the Gulf to Egypt during the latter part of the 1990s (van Nieuwkerk 2013; Sakr 2001). I came to love some pop music of the day, but also grew tired of the formalistic commercial pop that dominated the scene, with its lovesick lyrics dwelling on words like (*q*)*albi* (my heart) and *uyunak* (your eyes).

I knew that Islamic scholars did not approve of singers lustfully chanting '*ya habibi*' (my darling) every second phrase. Ever since music became a commodity in Egypt in the 1930s, relations between commercial popular music and Islamic scholars had been tense. The national icon, Umm Kulthum (d. 1975), seems mostly to have evaded criticism by Islamic clerics, but then she was known for her piety and for being schooled in Qur'an recitation (Danielson 1997). She also had many religious songs in her repertoire; for example, she recorded the well-known song 'Tala'a al-Badru 'Alayna', later to become a favourite among pop-nashid artists. Nonetheless, towards the end of her life, the Islamist preacher Abd al-Hamid Kishk (d. 1996) had begun to target even her in his preaching, scorning her for the inappropriateness of her love songs (Hirschkind 2006a: 42). I never personally encountered this condemnatory attitude but personal experience is often limited and misleading. One tends to move in circles of like-minded people and, as a Swede in my twenties, I seldom socialised with the religiously devout, or maybe they simply did not express such views when with me. I certainly did not know that precisely during that period, a new discourse on the legality of 'purposeful music' (music promoting Islamic values) was forming sporadically among so-called *al-wasatiyya* (the middle way) scholars, an important theme to which I return in Chapter 4.

In 1992, I enrolled as a PhD researcher in Islamic studies. My topic was not music, but Islam in Sweden. I still travelled occasionally to Egypt and also started to travel to other countries in the eastern Mediterranean world, such as Syria, Turkey and Lebanon. Random incidents kept my interest in Islam and music alive. A poster pasted to a wall close to Damascus University, ripping off Motorhead's famous snaggletooth logo, caught my eye in 1995. It advertised an event called 'Love Desco' and promised 'Metal', 'Rook' and 'Ray'. I snapped a photo and remembered thinking that the quaint poster was probably saying something important about changes in society. At the time, I had never really encountered any metalheads or metal music in the Middle East, apart from seeing audio cassettes with European and US metal bands for sale. The metal scene was eventually to become really interesting, with fine bands like The Kordz (Lebanon), Hellsodomy (Turkey) and al-Namrood (Saudi Arabia), to mention three, but would also clash with public morals informed by Islam, causing a lot of commotion; accusations were made of Satanism and there was moral panic over the assumed connection between crimes, suicides and metal music (Crowcroft 2017; Hecker 2012; LeVine 2008a; Otterbeck, Mattsson and Pastene 2018). A fast track to knowledge about the metal bands of the Middle East is available by conducting country searches on www.metal-archives.com/. Enjoy!

In a hotel room in Cairo in the late 1990s, I switched on the TV and found a music channel. A fit Arab woman clad in something black, shiny and so tight it would have made Catwoman uncomfortable, was kicking, martial-arts style, towards the viewer, singing a type of harder Arab club pop that I had not heard before. Satellite TV had brought something new to Egypt. Suddenly there was an abundance of young, new, women artists who were so profoundly sexualised in the videos marketing them and their music that religious scholars felt it necessary to comment. This led to, among other things, the famous media row over Egyptian singer Ruby's dancing in her videos (Comer 2005).[1] I was gradually made more aware of the Islamic discourse on both music and pop music and started to collect books and articles about it.

In 1998, I got in contact with Marie Korpe of the newly formed Freemuse (an equivalent to PEN but working, at the time, explicitly with music and

---

[1] A typical Ruby video, or Rouby as it is transliterated at times, is 'Eb'a Abelny', 'Come on, kiss me!'.

censorship issues; www.freemuse.org). I have since felt somewhat obliged to provide Freemuse with a solid understanding of what Islamic scholars have had to say on music that is relevant to censorship. Over time, I authored a couple of articles on censorship issues and on music and theology (see, for example, Otterbeck 2004, 2012a), but I was looking for something else, something different.

Entering the Field: Material and Method

In the mid-1990s, the new discourse on purposeful art started to get responses from artists, polarising artistic expression: on the one side, hedonistic, sexualised pop stars and the metal bands, and on the other, pious artists catering for a taste community that believed the others had lost their way but who still wanted to consume modern music (or art generally). Some artists (singers, film stars) actually left the first scene only to re-emerge in the second a couple of years later (van Nieuwkerk 2013). This development boomed in the first ten years of the twenty-first century.

On 12 October 2008, I was invited to give a talk in Rotterdam on Islam and music at a conference arranged by, among others, the Dutch research group ISIM. The well-known Islamic thinker Tariq Ramadan and his entourage were at the same venue, but so were a couple of people from a company called Awakening, among them British singer Hamza (now Tom) Robertson, who performed some songs, and Sharif Banna, CEO of Awakening. We traded cards and courtesies and I took some notes during a short question-and-answer session that Awakening had arranged. I also made a few notes about Hamza Robertson's performance and the behaviour of the almost all-Muslim audience. I especially noted a couple of hijab-wearing, teenage girls who tried out the screaming fan-girl role in an otherwise completely quiet, seated audience in the rather small theatre. After being stared at in a most disapproving fashion by several members of the audience who turned towards the shrieks (I was sitting right behind them), the girls made their way out of the theatre, giggling. Incidentally, those were my first field notes, although I did not know it at the time.

Much to my surprise at the time, the development of new devout musical expressions informed by Islam was taking place under my nose in Europe. It turned out that Awakening was a leading company in the development.

Sharif Banna was to become my key to the field. Our contact has endured over the years and his vouching for me has enabled me to get to know artists, musicians and the other founders of Awakening, for which I am grateful.

The amount of different data available in the field is overwhelming. There are texts (digital and in print) produced by Awakening, a YouTube channel where official music videos are posted, fan videos of live shows and unofficial music videos made by fans, often spelling out the lyrics and at times translating them between different languages. Accompanying the music videos and concert clips on YouTube and other channels are comments from fans and trolls. There are the song lyrics, the recordings and the marketing of the recordings. Further, there are the live shows, audiences, backstage areas, the tour bus, the meetings between artists and fans and TV, radio and magazine interviews. There are the nashid websites, the artists' personal webpages, the Twitter, Instagram and Facebook accounts and all the other social media communication. There is the discourse on music, both historical and contemporary.

Then there is *the Awakening book*, a 176-page book issued by Awakening in November 2014. At the start, the intention was to produce a periodical magazine, but as the volume of text grew, the Awakening leaders made the decision to turn the project into a book. In one sense, it is not: the publication does not have an ISSN or ISBN. It is rather a presentation folder in the guise of a book. It is printed both in a hardcover binding and a less expensive paperback. I use the hardcover version. It is laid out as a glossy, costly magazine, edited by experienced editor Remona Aly, meant to be handed out as an introduction to the Awakening company to future business contacts and so on. It contains a detailed presentation of Awakening and its artists, filled with quotations from different people. Very similar versions of the Awakening history have been repeated to me in interviews; however, I have also confirmed the information through different media that have reported on Awakening over the years. Counter-narratives that I have encountered mainly stem from critics and previous collaboration partners. I will return to that later.

If reading *the Awakening book* carefully, you will find an article by me on page 152. I am not part of Awakening and have no economic interest in it (and was not paid for the short text). I was simply asked in 2013 by

Sharif Banna to contribute an article to the new magazine (that became the book), and I wrote one to be helpful and because I hoped it would open doors. It did.

The Awakening book, which is how I refer to it here, suggests a number of interpretations of the Awakening phenomenon. It includes sentences like the following: 'It is due to globalization that identity has now become something that is conflated – Muslims in the West are not as dissimilar to those living in Muslim countries'; 'People's "Muslimness" is being expressed through popular culture'; or 'The spirit of Islam has always been a flowing, dynamic one, that didn't seek to eradicate local cultures, but rather embraced them, producing a colourful hybrid of Islamic cultures across the world' (p. 34). It is written in an educated, analytical language, albeit in the positive tone of an apologia, and I often quote from it, but also comment on it, throughout this book.

When doing fieldwork, being a scholar of Islamic studies was an asset and I think it made it easier for the Awakening people to have me as a guest (Harvey 2004). They did not need to explain behaviour, views, restrictions or expressions to me and simply presumed I got it. In fact, when on tour with Awakening in autumn 2014 in the UK, I ended up sitting in the tour bus with a non-Muslim musician who had recently joined the tour explaining Islam and Muslim practices to him; a similar situation occurred in autumn 2017.

It also proved valuable that I am an amateur musician myself (mainly drums, guitar and singing) with a lot of experience playing live. I know how to chat about paradiddles, guitar chords and the pros and cons of a six-string bass, and be appropriately impressed by pricy, customised, digital, wireless, in-ear monitors. Understanding yourself as a guest when doing fieldwork implies that you will be prepared to accept the rules of your hosts. Yet, as a guest, you will also have to bring something to the table: a tale, a joke, a point of view, a helping hand, a piece of yourself; you are in a special relationship with the people you are visiting, one that is not really covered by the insider/outsider dichotomy (Harvey 2004). In my discussions with the band's drummer, we sometimes bonded over being drummers; in relation to Maher Zain, at times that we were Swedes; in relation to some musicians, I and they were the non-Muslims in the crowd; when killing time playing Mafia on the tour bus, I was one of the players; and in relation to the audience and the volunteers, I was one of those envied people who could go in and out of the backstage area.

In short, this study is built on fieldwork, visual and textual analyses and interviews, which makes a description of the material used in the book difficult to narrow down. As a general principal though, I have gathered everything available: listened to every song, read all the lyrics and all the promotional material, watched all the official music videos and tried to keep up with the constant flow of fan clips posted. I have participated in Awakening arrangements in Rotterdam 2008 (a day), the UK 2014 (ten days), Malmö (one concert in 2015), the UK 2017 (ten days). I have also been at other numerous nashid concerts with artists not signed by Awakening. Further, I have interviewed singers Maher Zain, Mesut Kurtis, Raef, Ashar Khan, Zain Bhikha, Dawud Wharnsby and Sami Yusuf, Awakening founders Sharif Banna, Bara Kherigi and Wassim Malak, director Lena Khan, communicator Naeem Raza, Islamic scholar Abdulallah Al Judai' and conversed with several others who will not be quoted, like musicians, comedians, bus drivers, fixers, charity volunteers, fans and many more who have helped me understand and contextualise Awakening and its artistry. I did not formally interview singer Harris J due to his young age when I started this study, but I have chatted with him. All through the process, I have made extensive field notes, often at the same time as watching the artists and audiences at concerts.

Leaving the Field: a New Beginning

I decided to end field studies after following Maher Zain's 2017 UK tour. Yet, as is often the case nowadays, you cannot really tell when you are in or out of the field due to social media (Stjernholm 2011: 32). You get Facebook and Instagram updates, the odd email and telephone call, and Awakening continues to produce material. Some interviews conducted after the 2017 UK tour were actually made possible because of contacts gained during the tour. Already, new artists that I have never met have been launched, one after I finished writing the book, but before it was out.

In fact, the very company I am writing about reformed its structure late in 2018. Awakening had grown out of all proportion so the four founders created the Deventi group, which has six companies below it, to enable diversification and make the structure manageable according to Sharif Banna.[2] Consequently, from 2019 onwards, Awakening Music is the correct name of the company engaged in producing music and arranging concerts. The other five companies are engaged in books (Claritas), fashion (Ziryab), movies (Black Swan Pictures), social influencing (Global Muslim Influencers) and media products for children (Sunduqkids).

Therefore, the study can be located in the field of contemporary history, the value of it being its analysis of Islam and artistry, with Awakening as an example of something that has happened, something crucial.

Traditional Nashid, Islamic Pop and Pop-nashid

Before continuing, a few things about nashid, Islamic pop and pop-nashid need to be sorted. This new pop music inspired by Islam goes by different names but one of the most frequently applied is nashid (pl. anashid)[3] or one of many spelling versions of those words. 'Nasheed' is a common spelling for the genre. In Indonesia and Malaysia, the music is called *nasyid*. In Turkey, the phenomenon is often known as either *ilahi* or *yesil pop*, green pop, green being the symbolic colour of Islam. As noted in the previous chapter, in this book I refer to the music as pop-nashid, marking a difference between nashid as a classical vocal genre and modern associations with the word, but I also write 'Islamic pop'; below I discuss the different implications.

Nashid is a very old generic Arabic term for song, appearing, for example, in the work of philosopher al-Farabi (d. 950) on music theory. The Arabic root *n-sh-d* carries connotations of poetry in expressions such as *anshada al-shi'r* (reciting/singing poetry)[4] or *nishida* (a type of poem; see Jargy 2002: 664).[5] As a generic word for song, sometimes narrowed down to a specific meaning at

---

[2] http://www.deventi.com/ (last accessed 28 December 2018).

[3] For the sake of convenience, I will use nashid and nashids (English-styled plural) throughout.

[4] Nelson (2001: 36) argues that the line between reciting and singing is best kept blurred because historical textual evidence often makes it difficult to discern the kind of tonal framing in which a poem was performed.

[5] The word nashid is not listed in either 'Abd al-Baqi's (1986) Qur'an concordance nor Wensinck's (1967) hadith concordance; the closest to a musical connotation is when verbs formed from the same root are used in connection with reciting poetry in different hadiths.

a certain time and place, it is not exclusively associated with Islamic-themed songs, and might refer to Christian or worldly songs, the latter exemplified in the title of the 1937 Umm Kulthum film, *Nashid al-Amal* (Song of hope). But in an English-speaking context, and definitely within the framework of this book, nashid most often refers to an Islamic music genre; further, the term is firmly established in contemporary Islamic discourse. In Arabic, at times this is specified as *nashid dini*, simply translated as religious (i.e. Islamic) song.

The singers (*al-munshidun*) of traditional Islamic nashids – in Egypt, Tunisia and Syria, for example – have often been professionals who are important at Sufi rituals, family celebrations, *mawlids* (i.e. the celebration of the birthdays of holy persons including the Prophet Muhammad) and even in the rituals before morning prayers (Frishkopf 2002; Shannon 2006; Waugh 1989). Some women have risen to fame as religious singers (Danielson 1997: 23; Hoffman 1995: chapter 8) although men have formed the majority.

A *munshid* (fem. *munshida*) ideally must have 'an excellent memory, clear diction, a deep feeling for poetry, and the ability to express this feeling vocally' (Frishkopf 2002: 167). The *munshidun* are expected to improvise and therefore must master traditional modes (*maqamat*) and have a broad knowledge of poetry. The most appreciated skill is the ability to instil energy and a sense of uniqueness into every live performance through improvisation. Although a particular nashid always retains the same semantic, melodic and structural elements in different renderings, the aim of the traditional *munshid* is rarely an exact reproduction of a reified composition or work. As Amnon Shiloah (1995: 61–2) puts it, much vocal music from the Islamic tradition 'blurs' borderlines between re-creation and creation, between composition and improvisation.

As in most musical traditions, there are several different words for overlapping but separate genres, like *madih* (praise), *qasida* (ode) or *latmiyat* (Shi'i laments). Historically, nashid may be synonymous with *istihlal*, a vocal prelude in free rhythm (see Guettat 2002: 447; Sawa 2002: 388), but the music I address is most often simply referred to as nashid or Islamic pop music, therefore I will often leave out the nuances of different traditional genre names that musicologists and expert musicians might expect.

Traditionally, Islamic nashid has been sung without 'instruments' with the possible exception of percussion accompaniment – sometimes specified as a *daff*, a frame drum mentioned in *fiqh* (Islamic jurisprudence). Percussion instruments have a special place in Islamic music theory and jurisprudence because the *daff* is implicitly accepted in one of the very few hadiths to address directly what is called music today.[6] At the same time, musical instruments have repeatedly been considered problematic in *fiqh*, especially string and wind instruments. The logical terminological solution has been to exclude percussion instruments from the category of instruments.[7] The most restrictive Islamic legal experts have limited legal tonal expressions to the call to prayer, melodic Qur'anic recitation, songs for specific occasions like pilgrim chants and family celebrations, working songs, military music and caravan songs. Celebratory songs praising Allah and Muhammad have also been considered halal (legal). Some restrictive Islamic legal experts have imposed further rulings on these expressions in terms of the topics of lyrics, instrumentation and – particularly in regard to Qur'anic recitation – the degree of elaboration of tonal expression (al-Faruqi 1985; Otterbeck 2017; Shiloah 1995). The description 'restrictive Islamic legal experts' is deliberately chosen to signal that there is no consensus in Islamic thought on music and other tonal expressions, and that there are far more flexible interpretations. In fact, music is among the issues that have raised debate throughout Islamic intellectual history and continue to do so (Alagha 2016; Otterbeck 2016; see also Chapter 9, this book). It is important to remember that while Islamic intellectuals and legal experts have aspired to control the social and cultural sphere of other Muslims, this influence has not been in any way absolute or very efficient. A rich vein of popular music, at times actively relating to Islamic topics, has coursed throughout history.

During the twentieth century, nashids started to be recorded for documentation purposes but also for radio, and eventually for commercial and political use, and the recordings of some *munshidun*, like Egyptian Sheikh Sayyid al-Naqshabandi (d. 1976), became quite popular. The mass manufacturing of musical instruments, and the later electrification of performances, also changed the nashid genre, introducing, for example, the violin as a common

---

[6] See for example *Sahih Bukhari* vol. 4, part 56, chapter 14, hadith no. 730; for a discussion, see Farmer [1929] 2001: chapter II.

[7] See, for example, Otterbeck 2004; Rasmussen 2010: 10.

instrument at professional *munshid* performances in Egypt (Hoffman 1995). The brilliant Egyptian *munshid* Ahmed al-Tuni (1932–2014) most often performed accompanied by violin, flute, assorted percussion instruments and at times an *'ud* (lute), and did so throughout his long career (Hoffman 1995; Waugh 1989). Frishkopf (2000) stresses that a hierarchy of instruments exists. The *daff* is almost always accepted, followed by the *nay* (the reed flute), certain local stringed instruments, then the violin. At the bottom lie so-called Western electric instruments not at all associated with Islamic music genres. This also affects style, as slower tempos, the *daff*, clear diction and a 'liberal use of the reed flute' together make the music sound Islamic.

Developments took different directions in different locations, however. In Malaysia, a commercially successful, often fully orchestrated nashid (or *nasyid* in Malay) developed, with both male and female singers (Matusky and Beng 2017). In Tunisia, the Sufi ritual tradition called *al-hadra* (the presence) generally includes performances in large vocal groups, with handclapping, drums and Sufi and folklore dancing, but seldom violins. At times the music part of it was (is) labelled nashid. In an analysis of *hadra* in Egypt, Frishkopf (2014) lists heterodox but fairly recurrent traits, one of them being the use of secular melodies and lyrics and instruments associated with secular music. Frishkopf (2000, 2014) and van Nieuwkerk (2012) have both demonstrated how secular melodies and lyrics influence, are borrowed by and affect some nashid performances.

During this commercialisation, a number of *nashids* and *munshidun* became well known and listened to outside the rituals at *mawlids*, in Sufi orders and other Islamic contexts. Some forms of music, like the Pakistani qawwali, an Urdu-based cousin to nashid but owing much to Indian classical music, were embraced by music connoisseurs worldwide, successfully blending with and giving rise to the peculiar, but commercially functional genre, 'world music' (Bohlman 2002). Qawwali musicians make use of a number of tonal instruments, especially a very typical harmonium whose sonar texture is a trademark of the genre. In the 1990s, master musicians from Pakistan like the Sabri Brothers and the incomparable vocal equilibrist Nusrat Fateh Ali Khan (d. 1997) found their way into many record collections, including mine. To my discomfiture, I only recently discovered the talents of 'the queen of Sufi music' Abida Parveen.

Yet the changes sketched above have not taken place in every context; instruments may still be a contested issue when singing nashid and the parallel genre *na'at* is to my knowledge never instrumentalised. For example, the Pakistani Sufi Zindapir (d. 1999) prohibited the playing of instruments at his centre, Ghamkol Sharif (Werbner 2003: 8), a prohibition still adhered to judging from the many films of the main rituals at the centre to be found online – provided a microphone with extensive use of echo is not considered a musical instrument. Likewise, Cairo-based al-Ja'fariyya, a Sufi group studied by Frishkopf (2014), never allows instruments at performances. In a somewhat similar fashion, Saudi scholar al-'Uthaymin (d. 2001), the Saudi mufti Ibn Baz (d. 1999) and the hadith scholar al-Albani (d. 1999) – all dead for almost two decades, but enjoying a revival with the help of eager, Internet-savvy Salafis – were all highly negative about instrumentation, but not about meaningful, mobilising nashids without instruments (Baig 2011: 281; Lahoud 2017; Otterbeck 2004, 2012b).

New Trends and What to Call Them

The new wave of pop-nashid and Islamic pop is not self-evidently a straightforward continuation of classical nashid. Rather, certain stylistic elements from the genre, certain popular melodies and lyrics, and certainly the name itself, are intermingled with pop music genres, commercial marketing techniques and influences from the halal consumption trend and world music, especially Sufi versions. In the booklet accompanying Sami Yusuf's CD *al-Mu'allim* (2004), a proud proclamation is made that the aim was 'to produce an album that is equal if not better in sound quality than albums produced by the Western music industry'. The challenge is ironically met by adopting the song form of 'the Western music industry'.

A typical novelty of pop-nashid, compared to the classical type, is the three- to five-minute limit on song length, so common in popular music, originating in the technical time limitations of records when distributing recorded music (Byrne 2013: 98). Furthermore, the focus on the recorded and distributed song switches the old order in which the live performance is primary and the documented performance is secondary. Typically for pop-nashid and Islamic pop, the recorded, studio-produced song becomes primary and the performance secondary, as with most commercially sold music.

Not all Awakening artists are comfortable with the nashid label or with concepts like 'Islamic music' or 'Islamic pop'. Raef, for example, refrains from calling his music nashids or himself a nashid artist even though others are swift to label him in this way. To him, nashid implies a different attitude to music and tradition. He writes his own songs about things that engage him; for example, a song to his wife entitled, 'You Are the One' (2014), is hardly an 'explicitly Islamic song' even though reference is made to Islamic discourse in lines such as 'I ask Allah to bless you every day'. He is not fond of the expression 'Islamic music' either, feeling that it is too pretentious. Raef would prefer 'Islamically inspired music' since there are many Muslims who do not consider what he is doing Islamic. Claiming to make Islamic music becomes 'arrogant', and that is one thing that Raef is not. Yet, as we agree when discussing this, 'Islamic music' is reasonable shorthand, if not entirely satisfactory.

After studying the music that was, at the beginning of the research process, so easy to call nashid, I confessed to Sharif Banna during our final interview that I no longer knew what to call the music of Awakening. He laughed and said, 'We are in the same boat then.' The first album by Sami Yusuf was launched as a nashid album by Awakening – on posters, for example (*the Awakening book*, p. 24). However, the word nashid is actually not mentioned in the CD folder. During Sami Yusuf's first year as an artist, Awakening reconsidered and started to asked Arab concert organisers to change '*al-munshid*' to '*al-fannan*' (the artist) when referring to him. The reasons were many, but included the association with the classical genre to which they (founders and artist) felt that they did not pay sufficient respect, and the fact that their vision was to produce something new, something else. By not labelling the music nashid, they felt they gained the licence to engage in any kind of music genre. Sharif Banna argues that it is not the music but mainly the 'substance of the lyrics, the image of the artists and how the artists are presented that is "Islamic" or "value driven"'.[8] He has some reservations, however, but I will return to those later.

To complicate things further, some artists refer to Islam without necessarily wanting to be classified as making music inspired by Islam. Such

[8] Interview with Sharif Banna, 11 December 2018.

semiotic references pass unnoticed by most. Many languages normalise a presumed transcendence, a practice incorporated in the lyrics in American soul or country, for example. But if we 'overstand' the text,[9] as Jonathan Culler (1992) phrases it, and ask 'why Islamic references?', we find that these signify an Islamic context and also normalise an Islamic framing of everyday life, believed in or not. Obviously, some songs are not Islamic in any usual sense of the word (neither the lyrics, sounds, genre or performance have that ambition – at times rather the opposite). Still, it is reasonable to contrast a more atheistic language consciously excluding references to Allah, Muhammad or Islam (or other religious words) to a language that does not. Such juxtaposition stresses the religiosity of the taken-for-granted language use.

A fairly new phenomenon in Arab pop is to make the conscious decision to legitimise yourself by recording a religious song now and then, the rough equivalent of recording Christmas albums. This need stems from the repositioning of the status of Islamic morals in public. Once, an open flaunting of such morals would have been considered inadvisable; now, in many contexts, it might be the way to create legitimacy for an artistic persona normally connected with love songs and flirtation. The discursive positioning of the identification as Muslim must be understood in relation to the revaluation of Muslim identity and Islam in relation to public status. In the past, when a secular elite ran the entertainment industry, devout artists often supressed their Muslim identity; now, in some contexts, they are encouraged to take one on.

So, what to call the songs? The Awakening's solution is the formulation 'faith-inspired', but fans and others tend to call the artists' songs nashid regardless, as this has emerged as an all-embracing, popular genre name. In this book, as noted in the previous chapter, I generally use the terms Islamic pop (which is shorthand for pop music made with the ambition to come across as Islamic) or pop-nashid when referring to a very specific form of pop music that has developed since the mid-1990s. I have the ambition to make a minor division between Islamic pop and pop-nashid. The former has generally little musical connection to classical nashid, while the latter pays homage to it. Nashid will be used when referring to music that is closer to the more traditional expressions, making it possible to refer to songs like Mesut Kurtis' 'Burdah' as nashid as well

---

[9] Culler distinguishes between 'understanding' and 'overstanding' texts. While the former is about understanding the text on its own premises, the latter is a technique of asking questions not implied by the text itself.

as Islamic pop or pop-nashid, while 'Medina' by Maher Zain is rather Islamic pop, having dropped the traditional element, even if there is part of a traditional nashid inserted in the middle. Both Islamic pop and pop-nashid are shorthand for music produced in an environment that takes Islam seriously and sees it as an ethical order, a guideline and a path to follow and be inspired by; further, when marketed, the music references both the nashid heritage and general contemporary consumer culture logics.

Finally, pop music is also a vague and changing genre. By Islamic *pop* and *pop*-nashid, I refer to commercially marketed music, not a genre delimitation separating pop from reggae, for example. I beg the reader's indulgence for any minor inconsistencies in this, as being too exact would complicate sentences and overshadow more important messages.

3

AWAKENING TAKES TO THE STAGE

Awakening is a pioneering global Islamic media company that has achieved outstanding success in music production and publishing. They seek to educate and entertain within a framework which is innovative, inspiring and influences social change. The *Awakening* team are committed to a vision that fuses creative flair with Islamic values and which promotes entrepreneurship in culture and arts in a contemporary and dynamic manner.

the Awakening book, p. 1

This rather bold presentation features on the first page of the promotional book issued by Awakening in 2014, effectively encapsulating the ambitions of the company's founders. This is how they would like to see themselves. Yet it holds some truth. They have been successful. The importance to them of 'Islamic values' is often captured in a phrase – frequently repeated in the company's self-descriptions – claiming that Awakening productions are 'faith-based and value-driven' (for example, *the Awakening book*, p. 35).

Below, I review the history of Awakening as a background to the more analytic parts of this study.

Ready, Set, Go!

In 2000, two young London-based men, Sharif Banna and Wali-ur Rahman, decided to try to get a book on Muhammad's life published. Written in 1994 by the then sixteen-year-old Sharif Banna with the encouragement of his father, a Hanafi scholar and *tafsir* expert, Sheikh Muhammad Abdul Qadi, the book's target audience was teenagers. After failed attempts to get it published in the mid-1990s, the plan resurfaced in discussions with Sharif Banna's friend Wali-ur Rahman. The idea to publish it themselves led to a hectic period of typesetting and design. In 2000, 5,000 copies of *The Sirah of the Final Prophet* were delivered and all of them sold within twelve months (*the Awakening book*, p. 22). Since then, the book has been printed in four editions and can still be purchased.

As the book started to take off, they were joined by two more young men: Bara Kherigi, a student friend of Sharif's, and Wassim Malak, an American-Lebanese engineer working with software at the time, who made friends with Sharif after having noticed his book. The four of them registered Awakening and went into business together. All of them had a background of being active in Sunni Muslim circles.

The name Awakening was suggested by Wali-ur Rahman. It was a translation of the word *jagoron* used in a Bengali nashid that he liked. The graphic designer Robert Hopkins designed the Awakening logo, which has been retained. *The Awakening book* (p. 83) explains the choice:

> The logo moved away from stereotypical designs that were typically associated with Islam – like images of a dome, a crescent or a minaret. 'Faith doesn't need to be presented by "holy" signs,' says Wali-ur Rahman. 'The Awakening logo was more in line with modern trends and had universal appeal.'

This idea of being (Sunni) Islamic but in a new way permeates the strategies of Awakening, as will become clear.

From the beginning, a key idea was to increase the quality of Islamic media products. Better paper, better print, nicer covers, more considered lay-outs and production values, and so on. Having read a wide range of published Islamic books, pamphlets and other media since the early 1990s – I wrote my PhD thesis on the subject of Islamic booklets and journals (Otterbeck 2000) – I can confirm that the Awakening products really do appear more well-conceived than most.

The First Years: 2000–8

The company struggled in the first years. The second product it put out was *al-Ma'thurat* (2001), a popular, pious booklet by Imam Shahid Hasan al-Banna,[1] founder of the Muslim Brotherhood movement (on *al-Ma'thurat*, see Roald 1994: 136f; Stenberg 2012). The company issued a sixteen-CD lecture series, *The Life of Muhammad* in 2001, and in 2003 produced the lecture series *Mothers of the Believers* by Suhaib William Webb and made a CD featuring the American Muslim stand-up comedian Azhar Usman, called *Square the Circle: American Muslim Comedy of Distortion* in 2002/3.[2] Together with Preacher Moss, in 2004 Azhar Usman would develop the highly successful act *Allah Made Me Funny*, started on a smaller scale by Preacher Moss. The idea of Muslim stand-up comedy was hard to stomach for some shops which, finding it inappropriate, returned the CD to Awakening.

None of these products secured the company financially even though *Mothers . . .* sold respectably. The company was run either from home or from a phone in one of the offices where one of the founders happened to work. Nonetheless, the company rented a warehouse and set up an online store to facilitate sales. Meanwhile, Sharif Banna and Bara Kherigi were engaged in community work of various sorts, including working with youth, and, according to them, acquiring an understanding of what young people lacked and wished to find in 'the Islamic community'. In the process they set up the Islamic Institute for Development and Research (IIDR). IIDR is now thriving and arranges lectures and courses on a variety of topics.[3]

In 2003, as a result of discussions with Bara Kherigi's childhood friend Siamak Radmanesh Berenjan – now known as Sami Yusuf – Awakening's first music project became Sami Yusuf's debut album *al-Mu'allim* (2004), 'the Teacher', that is, Muhammad. The son of Iranian composer, poet and

---

[1] Imam Shahid means 'leader and martyr' and is added to stress the importance of Hasan al-Banna.

[2] It says 2002 in *the Awakening book* and 2003 on Azhar Usman's webpage http://www.azhar.com/bio/ (last accessed 11 February 2019).

[3] Please explore IIDR on https://www.iidr.org/ (last accessed 11 February 2019).

musician Babak Radmanesh,[4] Sami Yusuf learnt to play a variety of instruments from an early age and later underwent formal training. The CD was recorded in a small studio in Manchester to which Sami Yusuf had access through his father. Bara Kherigi recalls Sami Yusuf recording upstairs while 'I would be writing lyrics downstairs', pressed for time (*the Awakening book*, p. 25). In fact, while Sami Yusuf wrote the music and the lyrics to the title song, Bara Kherigi wrote the lyrics for six of the eight songs, and one together with Sami Yusuf. That pattern of work has been repeated since, both with Sami Yusuf and with later artists.[5] I know that other artists also discuss formulations of their lyrics with Bara Kherigi, who has become director of Awakening Records, the part of the company eventually formed to take care of releasing music. Apart from a Bachelor of Arts (BA) in law from the School of Oriental and African Studies (SOAS) in London, where he and Sharif Banna studied together, he also holds a BA in Islamic jurisprudence from Al-Azhar University, Cairo; he is credited for the most English Awakening lyrics of all those involved.

Sami Yusuf's debut CD went on sale early in 2004 and quickly sold far better than expected – 30,000 copies in the first year.[6] Anticipation had been raised by the skilful strategy of managing to have Sami Yusuf opening for the Malaysian Muslim superstar group Raihan (see Chapter 4), on tour in the UK in the summer of 2003. At that time, Raihan was king of the new pop-nashid trend.

Word spread fast. For example, according to Awakening artist Raef, then in his early twenties and living in Washington DC, he had become aware of Awakening through the book *al-Ma'thurat*, by Hasan al-Banna, a print favoured by many at the time because of its better quality and design than

---

[4] Sami Yusuf's father provided some Persian lyrics for his son and also sang a duet, 'Dryer Land', featuring on Sami Yusuf's album *Salaam* (2012). Sami Yusuf also appears on his father's recordings, for example 'va inak 'eshq' (and now love) (2016).

[5] Bara Kherigi is called Bara al-Ghannouchi in the credits to Awakening's first CD, Sami Yusuf's *al-Mu'allim* (2004). Both are family names.

[6] This figure is from *the Awakening book*. The Awakening webpage states the record sold 65,000 copies in three months. That figure includes sales by distributors in Egypt and in Saudi Arabia. http://awakeningworldwide.com/02_aboutus/02_companymilestones.htm (last accessed 17 November 2015).

previous editions. When Sami Yusuf's album was released, he immediately picked up a copy and played it again and again, fascinated by the quality of production and songs, as he thought there had been nothing comparable around before. At that time, Raef had not heard of Raihan.

In a similar vein to Raihan's recordings up to that point (with a few exceptions), *al-Mu'allim* was recorded using only vocals and percussion. To record 'vocals-only' has been the dominating trend in the pop-nashid genre ever since its slow emergence in the 1980s and gradual blooming in the mid-1990s (Otterbeck and Skjelbo 2020), a trend I discuss in greater detail in Chapters 4 and 5. By using the latest digital production techniques, *al-Mu'allim* was given a complex texture and rich, full production values comparable to non-Muslim commercial pop songs.

To promote the album further, a decision was taken to make a high-cost music video of the title track 'al-Mu'allim'. The Awakening founders invested all the money they had, borrowed more and sold off their possessions to add to the pot (two actually sold their cars). Egyptian director Hani Osama shot the video on location in Egypt. In the music video, Sami Yusuf is portrayed as an affluent, devout photographer, helping others, educating children and paying respect to his mother; in other words, living Islamic ethics on the screen while singing a vocals-only song to the effect that Allah has offered us the best of teachers yet we have strayed from his path. Lyrics are in English with frequent words and phrases in Arabic.

Awakening managed to convince the successful Egyptian satellite music channel Melody Hits (launched in 2002) to air the video when it was ready for the market in autumn 2004, about the time when Arabic music channels really took off. Kraidy and Khalil (2009: 58–62) divide music channel growth in general into three periods, the first of which lasted from 1992 until 2001 with a rather inefficient pay-television system and labyrinthine legal structures, making production and consumption difficult. By 2001, several countries were liberalising media legislation leading to a period when channels established themselves as competitive; this lasted until 2005 when the market became commercially viable and Gulf capital helped to make expansion possible. The timing of Awakening's first music video could not have been better. Faith-based art was being promoted by new Islamic channels, but Melody Hits was a secular channel showing ordinary, often sexualised pop music videos, so the move to have Melody Hits broadcast Sami Yusuf was bold and taboo-breaking; it produced the expected criticism, but also the intended effect.

The song hit a chord and Sami Yusuf became a superstar more or less overnight. Sales skyrocketed. The prestigious Cairo Opera House invited him to sing at the *mawlid al-nabi* celebrations (the birthday of the Prophet Muhammad) on 20 April 2005. Further, Islamic superstar televangelist, Egyptian 'Amr Khaled took the music to heart and promoted it on his programme *Sunna' al-Haya* (Life makers) and his webpages (Armbrust 2005; Kubala 2005).

Some time had passed since *al-Mu'allim* had been recorded and Sami Yusuf could, in timely fashion, feed new material to his fans in the shape of his second CD, *My Ummah* (2005). This album featured a full band and Sami Yusuf playing a variety of instruments, both on the record and in music videos. To cater for a presumed audience abhorring musical instruments, in line with some interpretations of Islamic jurisprudence, a 'percussion version' was issued the same year (percussion not being counted as instruments).[7] For a discussion of Islam and popular music, see Chapter 9.

At about this time, Zain Bhikha, one of the pioneers of pop-nashid, went on a charity tour with Islamic Relief and Sami Yusuf in the UK. Zain Bhikha told me in an interview:

> [T]his young guy [Sami Yusuf] comes up and kind of changes how concerts are held and how business is done, and the business comes into music, and we were, actually, as artists, like, shocked but also a little in awe . . . 'Wow! This is where it is going.' By then I'd been singing for almost twelve years, but I'd never seen that aspect of it.

Part of 'that aspect' was the reaction of the audience that started to relate to Sami Yusuf as fans in accordance with consumer culture logic. Young people came to the charity events to see the Sami Yusuf act, and also to concerts, buying tickets to experience him live.

---

[7] Instruments are valued differently in various contexts and while percussion is seen as primarily innocent in Islamic thinking, Christian discourse in Nashville kept Hank Williams from recording with drums (until his last recordings); see Brackett 2000: 82.

New music videos were made, but now Awakening had money to invest. The third video, 'Hasbi Rabbi' (My Lord is sufficient for me, 2005),[8] also shot by Hani Osama, was as ambitious as it was expensive (200,000 USD, *the Awakening book*, p. 99). It was filmed on location in several different cities including Istanbul and Agra, once again showing Sami Yusuf as a well-off man, this time working, rehearsing with a string orchestra and teaching and playing games with children (I return to the content of music videos in my analysis of Awakening's ideas in Chapter 5 and 6). To address the success in the Arab world, a Cairo office was opened in 2006 that since has served as the main office; the headquarters had previously been in London.

At the peak of all this attention, Sami Yusuf starred at a benefit concert for Darfur at the time of *Id al-fitr* (21 October 2007), held in Wembley Arena in front of more than 10,000 people (Butt 2007). The concert was a joint arrangement with the aid organisation Islamic Relief, and featured acts like Danish Outlandish (who had recorded the song 'Try not to Cry' with Sami Yusuf for his second album)[9] and American Muslim country singer Kareem Salama, then a new act in search of a form. This was not the first Awakening concert; indeed, the year before, the company had celebrated its one hundredth live concert arrangement. Between 2004 and 2008, Awakening arranged over 250 concerts in thirty different countries, and in the process another sub-branch, Awakening Live, had been created (*the Awakening book*, p. 27). The Wembley charity concert temporarily erased the perceptual barrier in UK mainstream media, which reported enthusiastically from the event, amazed by the initiative, the status of the star and the 2.2 million pounds raised.[10] The day before, a similar line-up including Sami Yusuf, Hamza Robertson, Mesut Kurtis, Hussein Zahawy and Nazeel Azami from

---

[8] The central part of the refrain consists of lyrics from a well-known nashid.

[9] Outlandish and Sami Yusuf also collaborated in 2005 on Outlandish's album *Closer than Veins* (2005). Outlandish is not an 'Islamic' band, although the group keeps appearing at Islamic conferences and have a few songs that can be called Islamic pop. Isam B, the main singer, has produced an Islamic pop solo album, *Lost for Words* (2018).

[10] For example: *The Guardian* (https://www.theguardian.com/uk/2007/aug/21/sudan. musicnews) and BBC (http://news.bbc.co.uk/2/hi/uk/7054948.stm) reported from the event. Both last accessed 27 January 2017.

Awakening, and artists like Aashiq Al Rasul (from Meem music) and Poetic Pilgrimage, the British hip-hop duo (one of the few successful female Islamic acts in the UK), had been part of 'Eid in the Square' arranged by the Muslim Council in Britain in cooperation with Islamic Relief and Awakening.

In 2008, Sami Yusuf left Awakening for new challenges. The reasons for this seem to have been many, especially a craving for creative freedom, but also financial and contractual friction. In 2009, some recordings by Sami Yusuf were released by Awakening as Sami Yusuf's third album, *Without You* (2009), causing the artist to call for a boycott of the company. On 14 January 2009, he wrote on his website:

> Consequently, for me to hear these incomplete and low-quality recordings, that only represent a sketch of what I would wish to release for my discerning supporters, is painful beyond description. I therefore wish to make it perfectly clear that an album comprised of any such recordings could only be put on to the market against my wishes and without my approval.[11]

A Facebook page was set up, Boycott Awakening Records, that documents the conflict from a Sami Yusuf fan perspective. Awakening also put out two DVDs in 2008 'Sami Yusuf On: Camera' and 'Sami Yusuf Live at Wembley Arena' and later the CD *The Very Best of Sami Yusuf* (2011). Sami Yusuf has been quite harsh in his condemnation and very public about it, but, according to Sharif Banna, Awakening has refrained from rebutting accusations despite disagreeing with Sami Yusuf's framing of the matter. At its heart seems to be a conflict over the five-record contract initially signed by Sami Yusuf, but as it plays little role in my scholarly work, I will leave it there.

Sami Yusuf has since produced a number of records and continues to be among the most well known of Muslim artists. In 2009, he established Andante Studios to give him complete artistic control over his music. The company has since grown and, among other things, has specialised in animation.[12] In recent years, he has developed his passion for traditional music and frames his performances in a high-cultural style, rearranging his old pop songs to fit a

---

[11] https://samiyusufofficial.com/boycott-the-fake-new-album/ (last accessed 11 February 2019).
[12] https://www.andantestudios.com/ (last accessed 11 February 2019).

classical Persian music frame. He has also recorded an album, *Songs of the Way, Volume 1* (2015), on which he puts to music poems by Seyyed Hossein Nasr, the Washington-based, Iranian-born academic scholar and Sufi sheikh of the Maryamiyya Shadhiliyya order. In a short interview with me, Sami Yusuf confirmed his interest in Sufism and said that Awakening was more commercial and political, describing the founders as 'Muslim Brotherhood',[13] a description I have never heard from any of Awakening's staff or artists, but that has been echoed a number of times by people outside (I return to this in Chapter 7).

With Sami Yusuf gone, the situation became desperate. What had been built up was about to crumble. But Sami Yusuf was not the only Awakening artist. Back in 2003, the company had signed Mesut Kurtis, a singer from the Turkish minority in the Republic of Macedonia.[14] When Awakening made contact, Mesut Kurtis had been studying Islamic studies and Arabic at the European Institute of Human Sciences in Wales since 2001, from which he graduated in 2005. Mesut Kurtis had a genuine background as a singer, performing as a *munshid* in Skopje since he was about twelve. He had already recorded two albums with local nashid groups, singing solo on three songs and had toured locally and internationally, for example to Turkey and the Balkans. He had also made some television appearances. This was all in the 1990s. Towards the end of the decade, he almost started a solo career as a singer with the help of Turkish contacts, but it never transpired and Mesut Kurtis opted for an academic career instead. During his study period in the UK, Mesut was approached by a number of companies trying to convince him to join them, among them Yusuf Islam's Mountain of Light (see Chapter 4), but he wanted to concentrate on his studies. Awakening was different, however, according to Mesut Kurtis. He felt they shared the vision that there was a higher purpose to making music than money or fame.

Awakening released Mesut Kurtis' debut album *Salawat* (Prayers) in 2004 and it was doing well but not on a scale that could support the recently expanded company. Nazeel Azami, who had been singing backing vocals for Sami Yusuf, released his debut album *Dunya* (World, 2006), but eventually left Awakening and took a break from making music.

---

[13] Sami Yusuf, interviewed in Malmö 4 April 2015.

[14] Mesut Kurtis comments that it was Sami Yusuf who tipped off Awakening about him. Sharif Banna is of the opinion that it was another mutual friend. This section on Mesut Kurtis draws mainly from my interview with him in October 2014.

Hamza Robertson joined Awakening in 2006 and released the album *Something About Life* (2007) with them. Hamza Robertson had a background playing pop and rock music with minor bands. He was also trained in the performing arts and popular music. When he embraced Islam around 2004, he changed his lifestyle, but Awakening gave him an opportunity to resume playing and performing. After Sami Yusuf left, Hamza Robertson too split from Awakening and eventually joined Sami Yusuf's Andante Studios, making an album in cooperation with Sami Yusuf under his given name Tom Robertson. It is called *What You've Become* (2014).

Another artist who was never signed but who cooperated through his own agency with Awakening for a short while was Hussein Hajar Zahawy, an Iraqi-born Kurdish percussionist who has been living in Britain since the age of ten. Apart from being an artist, he is a trained ethnomusicologist, something that stands out compared to other Awakening artists. He frequently performs in Kurdish folk dress and generally plays instrumental pieces, better fitting the genre of 'world music'. At one point he was part of Sami Yusuf's band and he also issued an album, *One Word* (2008), with Awakening. On tour with Sami Yusuf, he was at times given a solo act in the set. After the break with Sami Yusuf, the collaboration ended although he retains an international career as a percussionist.

What Awakening needed was another success, so the founders started to scout for new artists.

Entering a New Phase: 2008–18

Awakening wanted to secure its finances and decided to find an investor ready to give the company the necessary risk capital, eventually closing a deal with Saudi Arabian businessman Sheikh Sultan al-Turki, who became chairman of Awakening in the process. Two other Saudi businessmen are both shareholders and board members (*the Awakening book*, p. 45). The search for new artists paid off and Maher Zain, Irfan Makki and Hamza Namira were all signed in 2007/8.[15]

---

[15] It is possible that Hamza Namira was already signed in 2007 as is claimed in *the Awakening book*, p. 61.

While 2008 was a year of dramatic changes, the coming year was to be productive and creative. Awakening was ready to launch Maher Zain's first album, *Thank You Allah* (2009), and, soon after, Mesut Kurtis' second CD, *Beloved* (2009). This was the year when social media boomed and was immediately adopted by the company. Now in a better financial situation, Awakening hired a Saudi Arabian PR agency, Phenomenal PR, to promote Awakening artists in the Middle East. As an early result, Mesut Kurtis' album was launched at the Virgin Megastore in Jeddah in November 2009;[16] his first album, *Salawat* (2004), did well and he has continued to produce solid recordings. In 2014 he released *Tabassam* and consolidated his reputation as a highly appreciated singer, especially in the Balkans and in Turkey. His latest full-length CD is *Balaghal Ula*[17] (2019). During 2020 he started to release new single tracks, meanwhile continuing to pursue higher education and being awarded his master's degree in political science.

It was, however, Lebanese-Swedish Maher Zain's debut album that took the fans of pop-nashid by storm. Maher Zain's music video to 'Insha Allah', by non-Muslim director Mike Harris, had soon been viewed by millions on YouTube. Maher Zain outsold everything else, especially in Malaysia and Indonesia – even Malaysia's Raihan on their home turf! For the second time, Awakening had managed to produce a star, and the crisis of 2008 was over.

Maher Zain was born in Lebanon in 1981, moving to Sweden with his family when eight years old. His father had been a musician in Lebanon, playing at weddings and trying to compose songs of his own. Maher Zain himself was an aspiring musician when he came into contact with RedOne, a Moroccan-Swedish producer of some fame who became a mentor to the nine-years-younger Maher Zain. In 2007, Maher Zain joined RedOne when he moved to the USA to seek new opportunities, but returned to Sweden after a short stay, disillusioned with life in the States although very happy

---

[16] View interviews in Arabic with Sultan al-Turki (https://www.youtube.com/watch?v=bYT-zEK_mWQ) and with Mesut Kurtis (https://www.youtube.com/watch?v=ZOBYAbIwoDQ) from the occasion (both last accessed 11 February 2019).

[17] The title refers to the first words of the first line of a *ruba'i* (a four-line poem) by the Sufi sheikh Sa'adi Shirazi (d. 1291/2). The first line goes: 'He attained exaltation by his perfection'. The poem is the lyrics to the refrain of the title song.

to have worked with RedOne, who is still a friend. Back in Sweden, Maher Zain became active in a local mosque, also working as a lorry driver; the solitude gave him the opportunity to sing and compose, and many of his most famous songs, for example, 'Insha Allah' and 'Thank you, Allah', were composed while driving. He also started to sing nashid with a vocal group in the mosque, where he was scouted by Zana Muhammad, a Muslim entrepreneur living in Gothenburg, Sweden, who knew Sharif Banna. A demo was sent (including among other songs 'For the Rest of My Life'), and after a few telephone calls, Maher Zain was invited to the Cairo office late in 2008 where, after a week of mutual inspection, a deal was signed. Maher Zain pointed out to me that Awakening had been very interested in his character: was he the genuine Muslim guy he said he was? At the same time, one of the first things Maher Zain himself took the initiative to discuss was Awakening's understanding of Islam's position on music.

Maher Zain has released three albums with original material – his debut, *Forgive Me* (2012) and *One* (2016) – and a number of other songs including signature melodies for two TV shows presented by Egyptian superstar *da'iya* (public promotor of Islam) Mustafa Hosny:[18] *'Aish al-Lahza* (Live the moment) and *Uhibbuka Rabbi* (I love you, my Lord). All Maher Zain albums are released in several different versions, including in different languages and vocals-only production. Awakening has also issued compilations and a live album with Maher Zain. Apart from singing and composing, Maher Zain has taken on the role of arranger and producer and is obviously an asset in the studio according to credits from album covers and other artists I have talked to.

Hamza Namira (already contracted in 2007/8) is an Egyptian artist who made three albums for Awakening: *Ehlam ma'aya* (*Dream with Me*, 2008), *Insan* (Human, 2011) and *Esmaani* (Listen to me, 2014). Working in accountancy with music as a hobby before being signed, he was the first artist at Awakening who was neither brought up in Europe or North America nor

---

[18] In a study conducted in 2015 among university students in Egypt, Mustafa Hosny was declared the most popular media *da'iya* of all, 'followed' by 36 per cent of 400 students (Alazrak and Saleh 2016: 226). Mustafa Hosny has also promoted Hamza Namira on the show.

had gone there to study; his songs are in Egyptian Arabic. His first album sold reasonably well in Egypt and Hamza Namira quit his day job to become a full-time musician and singer-songwriter. He rose to fame during the so-called Arab Spring, since when he has had massive success in Egypt; his second album, *Insan*, for example, was the best-selling album in Egypt in 2012. Over the years, Hamza Namira has been a great resource for Awakening, writing and arranging songs, singing duets or choir parts and helping out in the studio.

Due to Hamza Namira's songs on freedom and human dignity being used by those favouring the Egyptian revolution, his music was banned on Egyptian radio as of November 2014. Both Sharif Banna and Bara Kherigi emphasise that he has never supported the Muslim Brotherhood; Hamza Namira has said the same himself in articles.[19] Rather, it has been the other way around: Muslim Brotherhood supporters have appropriated his music. The artist has lived in London since 2015, leaving Awakening in 2018 to release his first album on his own label, Namira Productions, *Hateer min Tany*.

Things had changed for Awakening. The company was famous and with fame come fortune seekers. In order to maintain their ethical profile, the artists taken on board would have to fit the part, and Awakening has negotiated with artists who have not sent the right signals, according to Bara Kherigi. If the artist is not the real deal in terms of good Muslim character, then there is no contract – but Awakening was still learning the trade and made mistakes.

One example of this involves Ashar Khan, a Swedish-Pakistani soul singer and producer,[20] who released one EP, *If You Only Knew* (2008), with Awakening. Ashar Khan had already recorded this in Sweden in 2005, producing 1,000 copies for promotional use. At that time, he had been in and out of the music business for more than ten years, starting as a teenager. According to an interview in 2001, he had fairly recently begun to take Islam seriously.[21] The Awakening album is a remixed re-release of the EP with two tracks added and

---

[19] See for example *The New Arab*, 9 February 2018, https://www.alaraby.co.uk/english/news/2018/2/9/hamza-namira-im-not-a-politician-or-activist (last accessed 11 February 2019).

[20] Where nothing else is stated, the section below is built on an interview with Ashar Khan, 20 April 2016.

[21] Larsson 2004: 87.

two taken out because the lyrics could be understood as referring to making love and going clubbing. The two added tracks were also recorded earlier, in this case for a Swedish Muslim project called Fredsagenterna (Peace agents) run by, among others, Zana Muhammad. This was someone Ashar Khan had known earlier, but with whom he became friends during the recording process; incidentally, it was also Zana Muhammad who connected Maher Zain with Awakening.

According to Ashar Khan, he was never signed to Awakening due to differences in how to proceed with the collaboration and therefore the record was never properly released but, rather, merely distributed by Awakening. Discussions about joining the company started in 2007 after Zana Muhammad had handed a copy of Ashar Khan's EP over to Awakening. Ashar Khan was called to Cairo for five days during the summer of 2007, but by early 2009 a final deal had still not been negotiated because of differences both in artistic vision and in the terms of the contract. Awakening wanted to sign Ashar Khan for several records, but Khan was more interested in making one record at a time for them. Further, Ashar Khan was not particularly interested in recording nashids; he would rather do clean pop. He had worked in a secular market with events and clubs which he felt was probably a bit over the top for the Awakening staff, even though they were not saying so outright. Soon after the printing of the EP in 2008, Awakening and Ashar Khan parted company without any hard feelings. Today, Ashar Khan performs live from time to time, for example during the outdoors 'Id celebration in Malmö, Sweden, in the summer of 2015. In 2018, he released new material under the name Amerykhan.

It is obvious that during the period from 2007 to 2009, when there were financial problems and Sami Yusuf left the label, the company struggled to find a way forward, and not all the artists with whom they were in contact were satisfied with the relationship. Response from the company was slow and its direction was too uncertain judging from the comments of some of the artists who were signed or almost signed but never produced much with the label.

Over the years, there were also a number of artists who were contracted but who did not stay with the company for long. For example, Canadian Irfan Makki was approached by Awakening records after he had initiated a career on his own account. In 1999 he had sung a duet, 'Light upon Light', with pioneering Canadian nashid artist Dawud Wharnsby (see Chapter 4), on an album compilation of the same name that presented new Muslim talent introduced by Dawud Wharnsby. Irfan Makki had already released an independent album called *Reminisce* in 1997 and in 2006 he made an album with Sound Vision called *Salam* that featured the 'Light upon Light' duet and yet another collaboration with Dawud Wharnsby. Awakening signed Irfan Makki in 2008 and made the album *I Believe* (2011) but after a while, Irfan Makki decided to leave the company, amicably according to Raef.

One of the songs on the *I Believe* album, 'Waiting for the Call' (2011), has had the strange destiny of being hijacked by people arguing that Michael Jackson became Muslim towards the end of his life, as Irfan Makki's voice is quite similar to one of Jackson's many singing styles. Sometimes the song is retitled, 'Islam in My Veins'. Saad Chemmari and Mohammed al-Haddad are other artists who joined Awakening but did not stay.[22]

One artist that has remained with Awakening, is Washington-based singer-songwriter Raef (Haggag) who was signed early in 2012. He has an Egyptian family background, a devout upbringing in the USA and has lived for a short period in Saudi Arabia. He started to sing and play the guitar in public around 2007, when he was inspired by, among others, Dawud Wharnsby and Sami Yusuf. His first major experience of giving concerts was touring as an opening act to Outlandish in 2008 after winning a nationwide song competition for the best Islamic song. Before Awakening, he worked as a software engineer, and for a while as a teacher. During the following five years, he was part of a network of independent artists, Poetic Visions, playing hundreds of smaller gigs; Dawud Wharnsby was part of the same network and they became friends, with Raef claiming he learnt much of his understanding of song-writing and guitar playing from the Canadian nashid artist. After a Princeton University gig attended by a friend of at least one of the Awakening founders, Raef was offered the opportunity to join Awakening.

---

[22] Muhammad Al-Haddad features on the Awakening compilations *The Best of Islamic Music, Vol. 2* (2013) and *The Best of Islamic Music, Vol. 4* (2019). He also released an album with Awakening that I have only found online, *Malak Ghair Allah (You have no one except Allah)* in 2011.

At first rather hesitant to sign with them, due to a negative idea about big corporations stifling creativity, he realised after a series of Skype meetings that he wanted to join the company, which had promised not to take creative control of his work. Rather, as Raef described it, he is now in a creative working group with resources like Hamza Namira and Maher Zain, who are skilled at producing and arranging music, and Bara Kherigi with whom he can test his lyrical ideas. His debut album *The Path* was released in 2014. During autumn 2017 he was writing songs for the next album. Early in 2019, 'All About Me', a duet with his old friend and mentor Dawud Wharnsby, was released to promote the album *Mercy* (2019) that was released in May. A few months later, Raef launched a project close to his heart called MiniMuslims, recording positive songs for the littlest Muslims. Songs are either newly composed or old ones with rewritten lyrics.

Londoner Harris J was the winner of an Awakening talent contest launched on social media in 2013. The fans of the on-line community following Awakening and its artists in different media were encouraged to upload films of themselves performing a song and the contest, it was said, was 'open to all regardless of faith, gender, age and background' (*the Awakening book*, p. 123). Ultimately, 755 (120 women and 635 men) uploaded videos that were viewed some 4 million times (*the Awakening book*, p. 126). The winner Harris J, who was only sixteen years old and still at school studying performing arts and singing, was awarded a record deal with Awakening in early 2014 and started touring as an Awakening act. His debut album was *Salam* (2015). Due to his youth, I have refrained from conducting interviews with him. Harris J has tried acting, playing himself in an Indonesian soap opera called 'Salam' (2016). He is also a competent Qur'an reciter, and can be heard and seen doing this on YouTube. In autumn 2017, he started recording his second album and a single has been released. In September 2018, Harris J signed with another company, Winfinity, where he can experiment with new forms of artistry outside Awakening's vision and values, but he still remains with Awakening.

Humood AlKhudher, an artist from Kuwait, was signed to Awakening in 2015 and quickly released the album *Aseer Ahsan* (2015). He had been on the radar for a while and has already featured on the Awakening compilation *The Best of Islamic Music Vol. 1* (2012). Sharif Banna told me in late November of the same year that this was, in a way, new ground. Humood[23] is not an artist with an outspoken Islamic message; rather, he sings about everyday life and the importance of a smile or about being true to yourself, a so-called clean pop artist. He has a background as an amateur singer, active since his early teens when he had the chance to record a song, 'Ummi Filistin' (My mother Palestine; 2002), with the *munshid* (singer) Mishari al-'Arada, also from Kuwait, and releasing an album in 2013. According to Sharif Banna, the company wanted to sign a Gulf artist to 'connect with local audiences' and increase visibility in the region. The song 'Kun Anta' (Be yourself) from the debut album immediately made it big in Malaysia where Humood became in demand. Since his debut album, he has released a number of new songs.

As the perceptive reader has noted, all the Awakening artists mentioned are men. Up until late 2017, Awakening had not signed a single woman artist. I will return to this issue towards the end of the book, but in Chapter 6, I analyse Awakening's artists through the prism of masculinity.

Awakening Books and Other Media

My focus is on music but it should be mentioned that Awakening has continued to issue other types of media, such as audio recordings, DVDs, an app and, primarily, books, of which there were ten by 2004. By autumn 2018, there were twenty-seven, which included almost all the back catalogue, and at least eleven titles on CD with Islamic lectures.[24] While not a focus, some of these provide crucial background material; I do not reference all titles, but I take the pulse of this other output to clarify the main ideas promoted by Awakening. To this end, I have grouped the messages they deliver into two themes important to Awakening: integration and contribution, and ethics and other theological reflections.

Integration and Contribution

An important book on integration is *The Art of Integration: Islam in our Green and Pleasant Land* (2008), an exclusive, high-quality photo book by

---

[23] Humood AlKhudher is known as Humood when performing and recording.

[24] Recently, Awakening has rebranded its book production enterprise. It is now called Claritas Books, https://www.claritasbooks.com/ (last accessed 11 February 2019).

Muslim photographer Peter Sanders. In it, a number of skilled and interesting Muslim individuals are portrayed in their roles as professionals, artists, or simply engaged people, and importantly, historical buildings connected to British Muslim history are depicted. The message is clear. Islam has long been in Britain. Some Muslims are immigrants, others the children of immigrants, yet others have converted to Islam as adults out of conviction. All approach Islam in different ways, meanwhile contributing to the society in which they live. Together they form the plural tradition of Islam in Britain and give Islam British colour. Peter Sanders is a well-connected senior Muslim artist living in London and probably the most well-known photographer of the Muslim world. Please check out his webpage: peter-sanders.com.

The Art of Integration also addresses the issue of creative new interpretations, something that the introduction to *Western Muslims: From Integration to Contribution* (2012), by Oxford professor Tariq Ramadan, makes its central message. Ramadan claims that it is 'imperative that we [i.e. we Muslims] rethink our discourse, our rhetoric, and our partnership. Ultimately, we must refashion an education about ourselves, about the environment, and with others.' He warns against withdrawing from society and calls for an engagement built on participating without 'de-emphasising our Muslim identities', which implies a reflexive rather than static state. Thus, the booklet repeats some of the most important ideas from Ramadan's main book *Radical Reform: Islamic Ethics and Liberation* (2009),[25] while taking one step further in his discussion of the arts. In a section on 'Recreation and Leisure', Ramadan writes:

> If there is an area in which we have difficulty in providing an alternate project, it is recreation and leisure. When we examine the activities that we tend to propose, we note three major faults: we focus almost solely in identifying what is forbidden rather than looking positively at all that is allowed, we perpetuate activities that are from 'over there' however unfit they are for 'here', or finally, we propose activities that are infantile and patronising in relation to the targeted age group. If we treat our adolescents as if they were perpetually eight or ten years old then they will look elsewhere for activities that they see as pertinent and that respect their expectations. (Ramadan 2012: 29)

---

[25] For a thorough discussion of Ramadan's *Radical Reform*, see Hashas 2019: chapter 2.

In this harsh reproach, Ramadan indirectly supports and provides legitimacy and urgency to Awakening's media products. Be creative, think anew, but do it while acknowledging your Islamic rationale and ethics. Symbolically, Ramadan calls for a move from a debate on integration to one on contribution, the later implying competence, creativity and a new, but not compromising, understanding of Islam.

Ethics and Other Theological Reflections

The books and audio CDs on general Islamic topics are interesting in themselves; here, however, I concentrate on publications with relevance for Awakening's music production and who the authors are. Awakening has released a book version (2001) and an audio book on CD (2004) of Hasan al-Banna's *al-Ma'thurat*. The book contains the *wird* (litany) compiled by the founder of the Muslim Brotherhood, which is meant for daily reading (Stenberg 2012). The company has also developed an app called 'Al-Ma'thurat: Daily Dhikr App'.[26] Raef remembers that his impression was that a lot of people in the USA used the Awakening version of *al-Ma'thurat* due to the quality of the print. And because of this, many were aware of this new company when they issued their first CD with Sami Yusuf.

The text of al-Banna's *al-Ma'thurat* is compiled from the Qur'an and the hadith (such excerpts are often referred to as *hizb*). The texts are meant to strengthen Muslims in their resolution to lead a Muslim life, the key element being remembrance of Allah and the relation between Allah, the creator, and humans, the created. As is well known, Hasan al-Banna had a Sufi past (he was inaugurated into the al-Husafiyya order) when founding the Muslim Brotherhood in 1928 and, in the early years, he stressed the importance of the Sufi inheritance.[27] This should not lead to the idea that the Muslim

---

[26] https://appadvice.com/app/al-mathurat/1184222126 (last accessed 5 July 2021).

[27] For example, in an oft quoted speech, at their fifth conference, al-Banna said that the Muslim Brotherhood rested on, among other things, a 'Sufi truth' (*haqiqa sufiyya*) because Sufis know that the key to doing good lies in the purity of the soul and heart (see Mitchell 1993: 14). Also, among so-called *al-wasatiyya* intellectuals, Sufism is accepted, if not in all its forms; see Kamali 2015: chapter XII.

Brotherhood is a Sufi order or similar conflations; rather, the point being made is that it is also important to acknowledge the spiritual side and spiritual techniques of Islamic political movements. The Muslim Brotherhood, as well as other politically oriented Islamic groups, uses spiritual techniques like *dhikr* (remembrance of Allah) consisting of *hizb* and poetry stemming from the rich historical tradition; on the other hand, *al-Ma'thurat* is widely circulated outside Muslim Brotherhood circles and has become a modern classic of Sunni Islamic piety regardless of the author's personal background.

Another publication by Awakening that emphasises the poetic spirituality of Islam is the audio CD, *Selections from the Burdah of Imam al-Busairi* (2006). It is a recording by the Tunisian *munshid* and *mu'adhdhin* (caller to prayer) Ahmed Jalmam, of parts of *al-Burda* (referring to the cloak of the Prophet Muhammad), a classical poem by al-Busiri (d. 1294). There is no doubt about its being written and still being used in a Sufi context. Further, the *munshid* Ahmed Jalmam features in Sufi connections and, as far as I can tell, is a Sufi himself. Still, *al-Burda* has status as high culture and is enjoyed outside Sufi contexts. In the early days of Awakening, the company experimented with publishing in a number of different Islamic directions. It was not a controversial act to publish an audio CD by a Sufi artist reciting Sufi poetry, as poetry praising Muhammad is acceptable to, if not embraced by, all Muslim interpretations. Excerpts from the poem have also been recorded by Mesut Kurtis in the song 'Burdah' on his debut album *Salawat* (2004), Maher Zain in 'Mawlaya' (My protector, i.e. Allah) on *Forgive Me* (2012) and Raef in the song 'Mawlaya' on his debut album *The Path* (2014).

Jasser Auda started his career in the UK and now has an international reputation, being especially noted for his thoughts on *maqasid al-shari'a*, the overall purposes of shari'a, Islamic jurisprudence (Auda 2008).[28] In his introduction to *A Journey to God: Reflections on the Hikam of Ibn Ata'illah* (2012), published by Awakening, the writer addresses Sufism. The book is a comment on a classic Sufi manual, *Hikam* by the Shadhiliyya Sufi and Maliki scholar Ibn 'Ata' Allah al-Sakandari (d. 1309). Because of his assumed audience, Auda addresses Sufism carefully. He points out that many Sufis have

---

[28] Jasser Auda is a member of the European Council for Fatwa and Research and the Fiqh Council of North America.

gone astray, but so have many scholars of *fiqh*; Sufism should not be blamed for this. Instead, Auda argues we should learn from those who have kept the balance, whom he specifies as those who are well-versed in *fiqh and* Sufism, which are both portrayed as essential parts of shari'a. Ultimately, Auda claims the book is about perfecting and 'reforming our manners with God' which 'will lead to reforming our manners with people' (Auda 2012: 107). He is thus promoting an ethical and spiritual Sufi praxis, not Sufism as a separate tendency. Manners and ethics are the centre of attention.

Shaykh Abd al-Fattah Abu Ghuddah (d. 1997) was a highly important hadith scholar of the Hanafi creed, once the supreme guide of the Syrian Muslim Brotherhood.[29] He spent the later part of his life as a teacher and researcher in Saudi Arabian academia. Awakening has published two of his books, one on manners and the other on time. While the latter book is an argument about how time should be used efficiently, employing classical scholars' reading and writing abilities as examples, its only relevance for the topic discussed here lies in the rejection of unproductive knowledge and time usage (laziness) stressed by the author. This ties into classic arguments against professional musicians who have to practice a lot and against being idle while listening to music, both activities which take up time better spent in devotion to Allah. This argument is not, however, made in Abu Ghuddah's book; his reasoning is merely similar (Abu Ghuddah 2011a). Rather, it is his book *Islamic Manners* (2011b) that is of interest; this has had four editions between 2001 and 2011, indicating that it is a fairly popular title. It is also one of the first titles Awakening published. Abu Ghuddah is keen on stressing the presentation of the self, neatness and politeness being overall themes. He advises Muslims to 'Dress neatly, even with friends and relatives' (2011b: 5), 'if you enter a room, greet everyone inside' (p. 22), and 'Observe full respect and reverence to your father and mother for they are the most worthy of your consideration' (p. 43). These examples are not randomly chosen. Rather, the quotations express a conservative, character-centred, Islamic understanding of the ethical self.

Below I discuss how an ethical Islamic masculinity is of great importance for the performers of Awakening, exemplified by their moderate, stylish dress code

---

[29] Awakening has also published a book (*The Islamic Civilization*, 2001) by the founder of the Muslim Brotherhood in Syria, Dr Mustafa Siba'i, translated by Sharif Banna.

(at least up until 2014, see below); the way they greet their audiences with the traditional, recommended Islamic greetings; and Maher Zain's popular song, 'Number One for Me' from *Forgive Me* (2012), about putting a smile on his mother's face every day. I have seen him on stage encouraging the audience to say that they love their mothers and asking everyone in the audience to hug their mothers if they are there with them or send her a SMS saying that they love her. Many in the audience lean over and hug parents (also fathers) and others start fiddling with their phones, possibly sending an SMS. It is a nice thing to do, and Maher Zain does it in a pop cultural setting, but the act is also in accordance with Islamic ethics. He is not the only Awakening artist who has written a song to his mother; Sami Yusuf, for example, has a song on his second album (2005) simply called 'Mother'.

As I toured with Awakening in 2014, sitting in the tour bus for long hours, we played a game of deceit called Mafia. In the midst of the joking, quibbling and arguing, one of the musicians said: 'It's not me, *wallahi*!' Immediately two people reproached him, one saying, 'You do not swear by Allah in a game of lies and deceit; anyone who does that will be out.' '*Wallahi*' is an expression frequently used in colloquial Arabic with the function of stressing what has been or what will be said: the equivalent to 'promise', 'I swear', 'really', 'it was really like that' and so on. This was how the musician used it, but it was not how it was received. Instead, it was fitted into an Islamic ethical discourse spelt out by Abu Ghuddah (2011b: 31): 'To confirm or emphasise a statement, many resort to swearing by the name of Allah or one of His attributes. This is a bad habit that should be resisted. The name of Allah should not be used so casually, and to swear by it is a very serious matter.' Regardless of the playfulness of the game, Awakening people take their religious ethics seriously.

The book *Preparing for the Day of Judgement*, by Ibn Hajar al-'Asqalani (d. 1449), consists of hadiths meant to give guidance to Muslims about what to avoid and what to celebrate and cherish in life. It also contains a hadith that discusses music. Umar, the second caliph, is the authority and he first names the nine sons of Satan and then specifies in which fields they operate to challenge humans. Among them: 'Murra commands licentious music' (al-'Asqalani 2004). The translation is made by Sharif Banna, whose Arabic is completely fluent and who has translated a number of the Awakening books from Arabic. Still, the translation is problematic. The Arabic text reads: 'and as for Murra he is the master of *al-mazamir* (al-'Asqalani, no date: 110). Sharif Banna's translation, however, moves from the Arabic text's *al-mazamir*, which translates as the wind instruments (written in the plural) – sometimes a specific, sometimes a generic name for them – to licentious music. In writings critical of musical instruments, the *mazamir* have symbolically stood for instruments that are understood as illicit compared to drums. As such the category has been enlarged, particularly in Islamic jurisprudence. What Sharif Banna has done is to change the target from instruments to morally blameworthy music. The first edition of the book was issued in the same year as the first music album was released on the Awakening label. Once again, an agenda of ethics can be detected. Instead of leaving the interpretation of 'the master of *al-mazamir*' open, Sharif Banna offers a clear reading: it is a certain type of music that is haram (forbidden). Yet, contextually and in Sharif Banna's defence, the phrase might imply that Murra is the master of the wind instruments with which he is making people dance and join the singing and music, thus instigating their sinning. Still, such a broad condemnation does not fit comfortably with Awakening discourse.

Awakening is today a highly successful, globally active media company, receiving awards, sponsorship and attention from a wide variety of companies, non-governmental organisations (NGOs), rulers and policymakers. Among temporary collaboration partners are Vodafone, Pepsi, McDonalds, Sony and Maroc Telecom. In its business contacts Awakening has no scruples about working with multinational giants, indeed, aspiring to be one of them. Further, Awakening has collaborated with several aid organisations, for example Human Appeal, UNHCR (the UN Refugee Agency), Save an Orphan, Islamic Relief and Penny Appeal and has signed a cooperation agreement with the Turkish Red Cross (in 2017). Awakening also founded its own charity organisation called One Family in 2017. In Chapters 5–7 I discuss Awakening's social engagement in greater detail.

4

SETTING THE STAGE:
IDEAS IN PROGRESS

If it wasn't for *Awakening*, it would be very difficult to legitimise music in the global Islamic market.

Sharif Banna in *the Awakening book*, p. 33

Sharif Banna allows himself this great claim in *the Awakening book*, admittedly with the purpose of promoting the company. But when does a trend really start? It is notoriously difficult to pin down the date or even the persons responsible; there is always someone who can be said to have paved the way, a now unknown artist, thinker, amateur or what have you. Following Foucault's ([1971] 1998) notion of Nietzsche's ([1887] 2017) work, a genealogical approach further complicates issues. Impulses might come from outside the presumed discourse, and most certainly have. In the case of pop-nashid and Islamic pop, all the above elements become particularly evident and problematic.

The aim of Chapter 4 is to paint a background to Awakening's particular way of doing pop-nashid and Islamic pop by drawing attention to the most significant developments and actors leading to the broader trend with which my study engages. First, I follow the development of the Islamic discourse that came to legitimate and promote the trend; second, I present and discuss the music of those who are generally considered to pioneer the field; finally, I examine non-Islamic inspiration.

46

I admit, dear reader, that you probably do not need to know all of this to understand my analysis of Awakening but, as the history of the genre turned out to be richer and more fascinating than anticipated, I felt I had to expand on it.

The Idea of Purposeful Art and Clean Pop

> Due to the global lack of clean art, the success story in the West quickly spread to the Middle East. Music is part of our everyday lives, and our vision is for it to be entertaining, inspiring and meaningful.
>
> Sharif Banna quoted in *the Awakening book*, p. 132

In the quotation above, Sharif Banna has chosen to use the concept 'clean art'. It was most likely a very conscious choice. At the time, he was pursuing a PhD in Islamic jurisprudence at al-Azhar in Cairo, in which he focused on minority jurisprudence, *fiqh al-aqaliyya*. One of the cases he discusses deals with art and culture. Clean art, or *al-fann al-nazif*, and *al-fann al-hadif*, purposeful art (alluded to by means of the last word of the quotation), have been topics of discussion for a couple of decades in Muslim circles. However, when discussing my interpretation with Sharif Banna, he stresses that he personally is ambivalent about the terms mentioned, not being entirely satisfied with their connotations. Wassim Malak explicitly does not like the term 'clean art', finding that the implication that other art is 'dirty' is insulting.[1] Still, the ideas of purposeful and clean art are important for the growth of the kind of music produced by Awakening.

Trying to use the art forms introduced during colonial domination for the purpose of promoting Islam was not unheard of before Islamic pop. Again, it is the development in Egypt that is particularly interesting. In the early, formative days of the Muslim Brotherhood in Egypt,[2] it attempted to engage Muslims through theatre and novels but eventually abandoned

[1] Conversation with Wassim Malak, 20 October 2014.
[2] The 1930s and a large part of the 1940s are seen as the formative decades by specialists: see Lia 1998; Poljarevic 2012.

this strategy in the early 1950s when being outmanoeuvred by the Egyptian military in the political power game (see van Nieuwkerk 2013: 191–2).[3]

An early attempt to revisit the discussion about art was made by the Egyptian Muslim Brotherhood thinker Muhammad Qutb, with his *Minhaj al-Fann al-Islami* (lit. a programme for Islamic art, [1960] 1983). Muhammad Qutb, like his brother Sayyid Qutb, was mainly concerned with literature, merely mentioning other art forms. As far as I have found, he does not use the concept of purposeful art; Islamic art is rather portrayed as art complying with Islamic norms, thus framing the discussion with a discourse of compliance rather than possibilities. Snir (2006: 24) points out that in 1965 Sayyid Qutb pushed for a 'committed Islamist literature' inspired by secular discussions on *iltizam* (commitment) as an ideal in literature, once again mainly stressing commitment to Islamic values.

Yet another early example is Yusuf al-Qaradawi's extremely well-circulated book, *al-Halal wa-l-Haram fi-l-Islam* (The allowed and the forbidden in Islam), originally issued in 1960. In a section on recreation (*al-lahw*) and play, there is a short passage on music and singing that has acquired the status of the final say on the matters to some, according to van Nieuwkerk (2013: 167). Apart from claiming that singing and music-making is not forbidden *per se* – rather, it is a neutral category – most of the text is preoccupied with noting, as five points, what is indeed forbidden. The first two concern the topic of songs and the manner of performance, which should not contradict Islamic ethics and teachings (*adab al-islam wa-ta'alimihu*). The third is about time and excess: if the entertainment takes time that ought to be set aside for religious obligations, it is wrong. The fourth concerns individual control: if music makes someone lose control, it is not good for that person. The fifth warns against mixing music and singing with activities like drinking wine or obscenity (al-Qaradawi [1960] 1997: 264).

Discussions about the positive use of art started to emerge again in the 1980s in both Sunni (first in Egypt; see Baker 2003; van Nieuwkerk 2013) and Shi'i circles (mainly in Iran and Lebanon: see Alagha 2016; Siamdoust 2017). The

---

[3] In a famous formulation in an address from February 1939 (*Risalat al-Mu'tamar al-Khamis*), the founder, Hasan al-Banna, called the brotherhood, among other things, 'a cultural-educational union' (quoted in Mitchell 1993: 14).

chief goal expressed in the discourse was to reconceptualise art and utilise its powerful expressions to spread the Islamic message. Up until then, in Muslim social settings, art in its new manifestations (theatre, films, paintings, novels and recorded music) was mainly associated with Westernisation and the national, secular culture of local elites (i.e. Arab, Iranian, Pakistani, etc.), or possibly with commercial mass culture (Armbrust 1996; van Nieuwkerk 2013; Siamdoust 2017). Typically, in a co-authored text from 1976, Muhammad Qutb places Islamic art in a defensive relationship with art built on a foreign 'intellectual invasion' aiming to ruin Islam (Snir 2006: 25).

Within the Sunni *al-wasatiyya*[4] (middle way) trend, associated with moderate thinkers especially in Egypt, increasing numbers started to promote *al-fann al-hadif* and *al-fann al-nazif*. The central idea behind *al-fann al-hadif* was to promote an Islamic lifestyle while using new popular forms of expression. In music, this meant that lyrics should be decent, preferably offering praise to Allah, Muhammad or an Islamic lifestyle; at the very least, they should avoid the indecent, hence the label 'clean art'. The discourse slowly had an impact among local activists and eventually inspired more commercialised forms, a development partially sponsored by Gulf financiers bringing sensitivities and demands from the Gulf into, for example, the Egyptian art scene (van Nieuwkerk 2013). Similar developments took place in Syria where television dramas were increasingly being sponsored by Gulf businessmen and therefore adjusted to Gulf tastes and norms (Salamandra 2016). The discourse also spread to Malaysia, as we will see below.

Egyptian journalist Husam Tammam, who wrote extensively on the Muslim Brotherhood, claims that the term *al-fann al-hadif* was used by al-Hasan al-Banna, possibly even coined by him; while I have not been able

---

[4] From the beginning, *al-wasatiyya* became associated with a trend among scholars vaguely connected to the Muslim Brotherhood but it was soon applied more broadly, including among intellectuals critical of the Muslim Brotherhood. The term was probably coined during the early twentieth century. It gained wider popularity through the writings of, not least, Yusuf al-Qaradawi and Muhammad 'Imara (Kamali 2015: 10). Today, it is a positive buzzword picked up by numerous thinkers from different strands including Sufis, Shi'is and Salafis worldwide.

to find a text in which he did so (Tammam and Haenni 2004),[5] al-Banna certainly saw art as useful in communicating the Brotherhood's message. As mentioned, however, after the Egyptian revolution in the 1950s enthusiasm for the arts lessened substantially and most Muslim brothers came to feel that art was associated with the secular.

Egyptian Muhammad al-Ghazali (d. 1996) was among the first prominent Sunni scholars to address this issue anew, this time systematically. He had a long-standing interest in the arts and had endorsed, for example, the modern Egyptian novel,[6] but also condemned what he claimed to be immoral elements in modern Egyptian art. He develops his ideas in parts of his work, like the book *Mustaqbal al-Islam Kharij Ardih: Kayfa Nufakkiru Fih* (The future of Islam beyond its main region: How do we think about it; 1984). When renowned novelist Naguib Mahfouz suffered a nearly fatal knife attack in October 1994 (Baker 2003), Al-Ghazali defended Mahfouz's writing and strongly condemned the use of violence.[7] Well aware of the harsh attitudes of reactionary Islamic scholars over the previous decades, he, and others of *al-wasatiyya*, claimed the deed to be an attack, not only on the novelist, but on art as such. Al-Ghazali took the opportunity to propose a more inclusive attitude to arts. The discourse had been developing over time and had found a form that can be read in, for example, Muhammad 'Imara's *al-Islam wa-al-Funun al-Jamila* (Islam and the Belle Arts, 1991)[8] and in Yusuf al-Qaradawi's rich production.

[5] This is repeated in different writings by Tammam in Arabic, English and French, but a reference is never given. Sadly H. Tammam passed away in 2011. I have checked with his co-author P. Haenni if he knew where Tammam got the idea from, but he did not. I have searched Arabic texts by al-Banna but as of now have not found the term. If you know where it may be found, please drop me a line.

[6] For example, al-Ghazali praised Naguib Mahfouz when he won the Nobel Prize for literature in 1989.

[7] Al-Ghazali's position on violence against the deviant and heretic is somewhat contradictory, or, as indicated by some, changed during the latter part of his life, with the Mahfouz incident as a turning point. When prominent social commentator and Islam critic professor Farag Fouda was murdered in 1992, al-Ghazali seemed to be supportive of violence against some opponents: see further in Winegar 2016; Mostyn 2002.

[8] About Muhammad 'Imara, see Høigilt 2010.

Two central ideas of this discourse are that neither art in itself nor artists as such are inherently blameworthy, and that art should be in an active relationship with Islam, being inspired by it and giving back inspiration. In their writing, pro-art Islamic scholars were more interested in discussing the content and structure of good art, including music, than engaging in explaining, yet again, why lyrics encouraging drinking and casual sex really cannot be called Islamically sound.

It should be noted that none of these authors, or others, for that matter, among *al-wasatiyya*, created space for women artists. It would take a number of female superstar artists who repented of their earlier lifestyles and re-entered the art scene as pious Muslims engaged in *da'wa* (the calling to Islam) to change that discourse (van Nieuwkerk 2013: 169).

One of the most influential voices in creating a more programmatic attitude to *al-fann al-hadif* was the Egyptian Internet and TV *da'iya* (someone promoting Islam), 'Amr Khaled. Khaled was not a trained theologian when he started his mission. He was a former accountant from an upper middle-class Egyptian family who initiated his religious career preaching in mosques in well-off areas of Cairo. Khaled has taken a similar stand as al-Qaradawi on music, promoting the production of music counter-discursive to the offensive songs. For example, during Ramadan (autumn) 2004, Khaled promoted Sami Yusuf, whose music had recently become popular in Egypt, on his Iqra TV show (*Sunna' al-Haya*, Life makers; see Armbrust 2005; Kubala 2005). What Khaled called for, both on his TV show and his webpages, was a modern *da'wa* using the artistic expressions of the present. 'What is needed are arts and culture that will propel youth toward work, development, and production', Khaled (2005) proclaims. Art should, according to him, be useful and moral; he objected to the sexualised trends within commercial music videos, seeing them as purposeless and morally offensive.

At first, the use of instruments was a sensitive issue even among pro-art scholars, causing musicians to develop a style using vocals and percussions only (see below); consequently, the concept of nashid became a perfect label as it signalled both 'song' and, in a narrower sense, songs that included religious praise while avoiding instruments (other than percussion). Still, the musical forms used diverged from the traditional performance and improvisation-oriented nashid and also the style of richly instrumented orchestral nashid that had developed regionally. Rather, the new nashids were composed and had set lyrics. The styles were many, as we shall see below, but a novelty was that nashid started to be composed in the style of contemporary Arab, Turkish or Malaysian pop, or using so-called 'Western' genres, making use of the aesthetics and technology developed in the commercial music industry with its global reach (see Malm and Wallis 1992: chapter 1). The military chants typical of early Hamas nashids, produced with a marked rhythm, were yet another form: male choirs singing repetitive, rather simple, undecorated melodies (for details, see below).

From the early twenty-first century, increasing numbers of musicians who engaged in pop-nashid and Islamic pop started to introduce musical instruments. At roughly the same time, a new openness to instruments developed in Islamic thought. For example, in 2007, Abdullah Al Judai' published a book called *al-Musiqa wa-l-Ghina'a fi Mizana l-Islam* (Music and song in the rulings [lit. balance] of Islam). As a scholar, he is not unknown among Muslims. A member of the European Council for Fatwa and Research – chairing it since 2018 – he is of Iraqi origin, has taught in Kuwait and other locations in the Gulf region, and is a prominent Muslim scholar in the UK, residing in Leeds. In the book, Al Judai' scrutinises the arguments about music and comes to the overall conclusion that due to the lack of unequivocal texts in the hadith collections and the Qur'an, and absence of scholarly consensus on the matter even among the most prominent of Islamic scholars, the matter of listening to music and playing must be understood through more overarching ethical principles of conduct. Music is a form of *lahw*, understood by Al Judai' as harmless entertainment rather than illicit activities as the term implies in Wahhabi discourse (Otterbeck 2012b).[9] It is only when music leads to vice that it should be restricted, according to the logic that what facilitates sinning is also forbidden. In themselves, music, musical instruments, listening to music and singing, a male listening to a female or the other way around is not forbidden, and thus permitted (about why these examples are chosen, see Chapter 9). Still, Al Judai' warns against overuse and being obsessed with music or music-making, once again a vice for the specific individual. Yet, as

---

[9] This is a fairly common understanding of the word found, for example, in al-Qaradawi ([1960] 1997), but it contrasts with Wahhabi discourse: see Chapter 9.

he writes, the fact that some people cannot control themselves does not make the phenomenon unlawful in itself (Al Judai' 2007: 597ff).

The book's tenets quickly entered the discussion, with some being upset by the conclusions of Al Judai', and others finding them refreshing and convincing. In an interesting thread on www.ahlalhdeeth.com, several conservative Muslims debated the issue of music, unable to get their heads around the position of Al Judai. He is obviously deeply respected but, in this instance, they did not like his opinions. The problem was that they had no means of refuting his book because it is far too comprehensive. One writer mentioned that he had it but had not yet found the time to read it, to which a reply reads: 'Do Not and I repeat do not read his book on music. It will mess you up. To be honest, he has some strong arguments that up until today I haven't heard a convincing response to.'[10] For some, the very conviction that music is forbidden is stronger than the arguments they manage to muster.

The book was also an inspiration for a fatwa by Saudi Sheikh Adel ibn Salam al-Kalbani who proclaimed that music was permitted in the summer of 2010. This caused a media storm in Saudi Arabia; his webpage was hacked and he was verbally attacked and character assassinated (Otterbeck 2012b). He also got the chance to defend himself, however, and in one TV studio, he held the book in his hand, claiming inspiration.[11] Further, Al Judai' has taught Islamic thought to Sharif Banna in the past, while, in Oxford in 2013, the first time I met Al Judai', we were both invited by Sharif Banna to a seminar on what is meant by the concept 'Islamic arts'.

For some, to me as yet unknown, reasons, the move from the almost universal condemnation of musical instruments by Islamic intellectuals to embracing musical instruments and so-called Western musical genres such as rock, hip-hop, R&B, by at least some (and not a few) happened around the same years during the first decade of the twenty-first century, and not only in Europe and in the Arab world. For example, Malaysia's Islamic movement PAS (Parti Islam Se-Malaysia) used to condemn all music and frivolous leisure activities but, since about 2005, has whole-heartedly embraced pop

---

[10] http://www.ahlalhdeeth.com/vbe/showthread.php?t=11810 (last accessed 11 November 2016).

[11] This was pointed out to me by Al Judai'. Interview, 31 March 2017.

music and pop stars as a means to spread Islam (Müller 2014, 2015). The movement's former spiritual leader, Nik Abdul Aziz Nik Mat (1931–2015), can be seen in press photos together with artists who were earlier condemned as scandalous but are now seen as having bettered their ways. In 2010 Nik Aziz declared that controlled art promoting Islam could be set apart from other art that was strictly forbidden according to Islamic law (van Dijk 2014). Thus, for example, the music of pop queen Siti Nurhaliza (who has dedicated a song to Nik Aziz) is acceptable, as is the music of rock artist Amy Search, who regularly performs at PAS meetings (Müller 2015).

Another person who has been in dialogue with the Awakening people over the years is the Oxford professor Tariq Ramadan, who addresses music in his *To be a European Muslim* (1999), published the same year in both English and French. In it, he lists four conditions for music to be acceptable.

1. The content of singing or the type of music must remain in agreement with Islamic ethics and not bring about an attitude which contradicts them.
2. Interpretation (its mode, moment and place) must also respect ethics.
3. This kind of entertainment must not lead people to forget their obligation toward God and fellow humans.
4. It is appropriate for the musician and the one who listens to him to measure, in full conscience, the impact and place that this art really takes in their lives. It is a question of establishing a balance of conscience which cannot be but personal and individual. (Ramadan 1999: 203)

In this passage, Ramadan spells out the importance of ethical discourse in relation to music and thus taps, early on, into the overall trend among intellectual, liberal interpreters to renegotiate the classical methodology of jurisprudence in favour of a more ethics driven, holistic hermeneutics searching for the *maqasid*, the overall purposes, of shari‘a.[12] The passage above is followed by an interesting sentence where Ramadan (1999: 204) states: 'Artistic

---

[12] Jasser Auda, an ally of Tariq Ramadan, also published by Awakening and mentioned above, has written extensively on the need for a holistic understanding of *maqasid al-shari‘a*; see, for example, Auda 2008.

expression in Islam is, in this sense, morally and humanly exacting.' Art, according to Ramadan, must be thought through and preferably original.

In later books, Ramadan addresses the shallowness and infantilism of many so-called Islamic activities offered to Muslim youth. He argues that people need relaxation and leisure activities but that these will have to be suitable and challenging if they are not to be set aside as boring in favour of much more interesting secular (popular) culture. Muslims should engage in creativity, participating in contemporary art's various channels, but taking care to meet the ethical challenge of being creative in new ways (Ramadan 2004, 2009). In his main manifesto, *Radical Reform: Islamic Ethics and Liberation* (2009), Ramadan makes himself particularly clear, from the short, three-word sentence, 'Faith needs art' (2009: 202) to the rather passionate call:

> Art should be reconciled with the true freedom of saying everything while inviting the heart and mind to transcend the worst degradation. We must certainly not produce a 'moral' art setting up an idyllic, untruthful image of reality and daily life: what is needed is 'truthful' art, which dares express the realities of life, in their specificity as well as their universality, and which invites us to look things in the face, to learn to tell ourselves sincerely while summoning us to transcend ourselves in respect, friendship, solidarity, and love. . . . It is urgent to invest time and thought in the now central area of culture and the arts, to devise an alternative that is altogether original, appealing, and faithful to the ethical outcomes. (Ramadan 2009: 205)

As a long-standing dialogue partner with Awakening, Ramadan encapsulates much of the development happening in Awakening's production and, of course, elsewhere. However, it would be a mistake to propose that Ramadan's writing is driving the process; rather, he gives voice to and legitimises people who agree with him.

Christopher Partridge (2013: 201) suggests three relevant areas of analysis of the relation between religion and popular music: religion against popular music; religion as the transformer of popular music; and religious popular music.[13] Certainly, Islam against popular music was and is still very important

---

[13] Partridge fails to mention popular music against religion(s), a very interesting field to study, but not one relevant to this study, see Otterbeck, Mattsson and Pastene 2018.

and powerful in Islamic discourse; books are produced, lectures held, articles published and discussions on the theme are present in social media. Furthermore, artists are attacked and boycotted, and threats are frequently issued of having molten lead poured into your ear in hell if you listen to music by scholars, parents, peers and radical self-proclaimed Muslims monitoring their local communities, as attested to by much scholarship (Ahmad 2010; Otterbeck 2008; for a fairly recent, anti-music book in English, see al-Athari 2013).

Of more interest here, are the second and third areas. *Al-fann al-hadif* discourse, like the Christian discourse on using rock and pop as means to Christian ends, takes its departure from the idea that music genres are not evil in themselves. By assuming that genre or style is neutral, and postulating that music has a universal appeal, the proponents suggest music should be bridled and domesticated to serve the Islamic cause: the Islamic content being the lyrics, the behaviour of the artists and the ethical marketing. However, there are several problems likely to be encountered if promoting such a view, especially the producers' inability to control audiences' relations to the music and the artists, and the problem of reaching out to people apart from the already convinced. Partridge (2013: 210) points out that Christian popular music has mainly stayed an insider affair, even when it has entered genres like extreme metal, whereas Muslim pop-nashid seems to have a wider reach, something discussed below along with the problem of control.

There are interesting lessons to be learnt from the context of Christian music. The Salvation Army launched its mission in the USA in 1880. When Evangeline Booth, the daughter of the movement's founder and a skilled musician and singer, became Commander of the United States in 1904 (a position she held until 1934) she soon became a poster star. She entered film, playing the redeeming sister, and largely due to this gained a platform and was listened to when preaching. Yet, eventually, it all got out of hand as demands for her as an entertainer became greater than for her evangelisation (Winston 2002). In this case, the music reached out, but the integrity of the message was felt to be compromised. To quote a favourite line from Michael Gilsenan's seminal *Recognizing Islam*, 'the control of the meaning of symbols is an uncertain operation' (1992: 60). In music studies, music is seldom seen as a mere vehicle for a message. Music does things to listeners but it is rather difficult to predict exactly what: less so at a political rally where a well-known beloved anthem is likely to create feelings of unity, or at least action signalling it (Berg 2017; Eyerman and Jamison 1998); more so when music is packaged and sold for consumption or put on stage at a concert venue (DeNora 2000). Music also does things to the performers, especially when packaged in the consumer culture form that makes singers into celebrities (I discuss the management of celebrity status in Chapter 6).

The last field mentioned by Partridge (2013: 217) is religious popular music, where his main example is roots reggae, a music style developed within the Rastafari community. Some aspects of pop-nashids are in fact to be regarded as developed within the community, especially the first pop-nashids that were vocals-only due to the most common understanding of Islamic rulings at the time. The vocals-only genre was developed production-wise and found expressions that became unique to it. As discussed below, even though some artists have chosen to introduce full instrumentation on recordings and stage, when they record their most devout songs they are prone to make them vocals-only productions like, for example, Malaysian Raihan (Otterbeck and Skjelbo 2020) and recently Mesut Kurtis' song 'Ilahi' (O Allah, but also a common name for devotional song in Turkish) released in connection with Ramadan 2018, where he is singing a poem ascribed to the fourth caliph, Ali ibn Abi Talib.

The *al-fann al-hadif* discourse of Islamic intellectuals has led to artists' taking an interest in both religion as the transformer of popular music and religious popular music. But music is a difficult beast to tame. One consistent message echoes all through Hellenistic Christian and Islamic discourses on music, regardless of whether authors are positive or negative about music: beware of music, it is powerful and affects the human body and soul/psyche (see further in Chapter 9).

We now turn to different musical expressions that, albeit in different ways, have all affected the growing trend of pop-nashids and Islamic pop and, in particular, Awakening's productions.

The New Political Nashid

I belong to a religious family who were involved in the Islamic field, so I was also exposed to *nasheed* as a genre from Syria, Jordan and Palestine. This is where the modern *nasheed* emerged from with themes like the struggle for freedom, the issue of hijab and so on.

Bara Kherigi, quoted in *the Awakening book*, p. 147

The music Bara Kherigi likely refers to here is the music of the social movements and social movement organisations loosely held together by a claim that political (Sunni) Islam provides the means to better the world, organisations like the Muslim Brotherhood, Jamaat-i Islami, Hamas and an-Nahda, for example. Nashids became popular in the mainstream of Islamic movements in the 1980s and 1990s (Said 2012). Shi'i Hizbullah also engaged in nashids early on (Berg 2017). To grasp topics and styles of early Sunni, political nashid lyrics, one may consult a unique four-volume collection of nashid lyrics of the Islamic movements, published between 1988 and 1990 by Husni Afham Jarar and Ahmad al-Jada, who compiled and commented on the lyrics. The title is *Anashid al-Da'wat al-Islamiyya* (Nashids of the Islamic call), published by Dar al-Diya' in Amman. The preface of volume one of the collections catches the sentiment of the time, the felt urgency of the nashid from the perspective of an aficionado:

> If we look at the present we need enthusiast poems and revolutionary nasheeds. Because Islam . . . needs nasheeds, remembering the glorious times of the past, documenting the ongoing Jihad and outline the way into the future. The youth of the da'wa needs nasheeds to arouse in them the sense for the cause which needs protections and the love to sacrifice and self-sacrifice. Our enemies have tried to take away from us this instrument [poems and nasheeds] in spreading national nasheeds and publishing filthy [*rakhisa*, literally cheap, low] songs, hoping that young Muslims would turn towards them. (Translated by Said 2012: 866, with minor changes by me.)

For example, the volumes feature poems by well-known theologian Yusuf al-Qaradawi, the Muslim brotherhood ideologist Sayyid Qutb (d. 1966), and his sister, the author and poet Amina Qutb (d. 2007), as well as those of poets like Palestinian Ibrahim Tuqan (d. 1941) and Egyptian Mustafa Sadiq al-Rafi'i (d. 1937) who had little to do with Islamic *da'wa* but whose nationalist poems expressed a resistance that appealed to the Islamic *da'wa* movement and were therefore appropriated.

Radwan 'Annan from Syria, more famous as Abu Mazen, was probably the first to profile himself by making political nashids drawing on Islamic sentiments. At least, he is given that role in informed accounts like that of music journalist Mazan al-Sayyid (2017). He recorded at least 119 songs[14] issued on cassettes during the 1970s that circulated among Sunni religio-political activists in Syria, many of them opposing the Hafez al-Assad regime. The cassettes also reached listeners of similar political preference outside Syria. Famous songs from Abu Mazen are, for example, the first he recorded, his musical rendering of a Sayyid Qutb poem, 'Akhi, Anta Hurrun (Wara' al-Sudud)' (Brother, you are free [Behind bars]) – about being free in a dictatorship due to one's faith – and his rendering of the Muhammad Iqbal poem 'al-Sinu lana wa-l-'Urabu lana (Watanuna l-Islami)' (China is ours, Arabia is ours [Our Islamic homeland]), about the world being meant for Islam. Al-Sayyid (2017) stresses that Abu Mazen especially favoured the Egyptian poet and preacher Ibrahim Ezzat (d. 1983), who was famous for his eloquence among Islamic political activists. Abu Mazen also wrote lyrics himself.

Inspired by the anti-instrument stance of scholars such as al-Albani (d. 1999), who was influential in Syria at the time, the recordings were made only using male voices but taking advantage of recording additives like reverb and an excessive use of echo.[15] His musical style is one of the foundations of the new political nashid, combining influences from the first wave of modern Arab composers, such as Egyptian Muhammad Abd al-Wahhab (d. 1991), with the militant hymns of the Arab leftist states and the sensitivities of the Islamic movements (see al-Sayyid 2017). Due to its being anti-establishment, low budget, disseminated via cassettes and avoiding excessive musical debauchery, Abu Mazen's music resembled – in the strangest way – the contemporaneous music of early DIY punk bands in Europe. Of course,

---

[14] In the book *Anashid Abi Mazan*, 119 lyrics are compiled. It can be found online at https://archive.org/stream/AnashedAboMazin/Anashed-AboMazin#page/n0/mode/1up (last accessed 27 June 2018).

[15] Al-Albani (2002: 132) would later lament that the singers introduced the *daff* and that their music came to be popular and used at, for example, weddings, contradicting the very purpose of the Islamic lyrics.

they are, at the same time, the very antithesis of each other. Abu Mazen left Syria for Egypt in the early 1980s.[16]

Abu Mazen was soon joined by other pioneers who started to compose nashids combining political activism and Islamic themes in the late 1970s, the most well known being three Syrian *munshidun*, Abu Dujana, Abu al-Joud and Abu Ratib (see Pieslak 2017: 68), whose first recordings were made in 1981 (Pieslak 2015: 259). They all had more musical training than Abu Mazen and brought melodic complexity to the recordings.

Muhammad Abu Ratib has an interesting story that is especially relevant to the genealogy of pop-nashid. After his pioneering years in Syria, he left for Jordan where he continued his singing career but also engaged in higher education. During this period, he toured extensively, mostly in the Arab world but also outside. Abu Ratib established, and became president of, *Rabitat al-Fann al-Islami al-'Alami* (the worldwide Islamic art association), also arranging festivals that became immensely popular and established him as one of the leading nashid singers of his generation.

In the early 1990s, Abu Ratib moved to the USA where he became one of the most sought after nashid singers at Islamic meetings during the decade, according to singer-songwriter Dawud Wharnsby.[17] Abu Ratib was arrested on 21 January 2010, accused of giving indirect support to Hamas through the Holy Land Foundation of which he claimed to have been the representative during 1997–8. He was set free eleven months later on condition that he left the USA, and he moved between Jordan and Bahrain in the following years,[18] even ending up in Sweden for a couple of them.[19] Where he lives now,

---

[16] An odd detail is that many recordings circulated as Abu Mazen's are in fact recordings made by an Egyptian musician living in Saudi Arabia, Abu Ziyad, who thought Abu Mazen's repertoire should get a wider audience. According to music journalist, Mazan al-Sayyid (2017), many of his generation mistook these recordings for actual Abu Mazen recordings as the line 'a collection of "anashid" by Abu Mazen' had been added to the covers.

[17] Interview with Dawud Wharnsby, 1 February 2018.

[18] http://arc2.alakhbar.info/17829-0-AB0-B--FCC--F-.html (last accessed 28 June 2018; no longer active).

[19] https://www.aljazeera.net/news/international/2010/12/15/كاأمير-بـاتب-ر-أبو-المنشد-عن-الإفراج (last accessed 5 July 2021). Conversations with Maher Zain, Bara Kherigi and Raef confirm that he lived in Sweden.

I do not know. Over the years, Abu Ratib has met and influenced most of the people discussed below as pioneers of the pop-nashid. For example, he features in the choir backing Yusuf Islam on one of the songs on his *The Life of The Last Prophet* (1995) and he certainly knows several of the Awakening people.

Although schooled as a violinist at a young age, Abu Ratib avoids instruments on recordings. The recordings I have heard are either strictly vocals-only, featuring lead vocals and choir, or include drumming and possibly a discreet synthesiser or pads. Much of his most popular nashid mixes romantic nationalism – most often Palestinian, if it is possible to pin it down – and Islamic themes. To avoid stirring up trouble in Jordan and later in the US, the Palestinian issue was the safest card to play for an Islamic activist. For example, the song 'al-Salam' is about the longing to return to the lost land, the home of prophets, and contains phrases like 'in it, the innocent die, here, a home is ruined, here, a child has to flee, here, the sky is weeping'. Another example is the song 'Awal al-Ghaith' (The first rain) containing phrases like, 'I will go to Jerusalem with determination and I will make Hittin come tomorrow', that is, crush the resistance like Saladin once defeated the crusaders at the Battle of Hittin. It continues: 'He cleansed it from the disgrace of the Jews, and we release the mosque from its imprisonment.' The lyrics are typical in their way of using 'Jews' as a category of the wrong-doing other. Other songs have more traditional topics, celebrating the glory of Allah or the qualities of Muhammad.

Hamas (and Hizbullah)

Hamas started to produce resistance nashids during the 1980s (Berg 2017; Berg and Schulz 2013; Oliver and Steinberg 2002), consciously choosing to create music that contrasted with the music of the Palestine Liberation Organisation/Fatah (McDonald 2013: 127–9). While the latter connected actively to Palestinian folk music, having produced their own music since the late 1960s (Sayigh 1997: 195), Hamas music typically had no instruments playing melodies, a male choir singing in unison to handclapping or a simple beat played on a *daff*. It was very much a continuation of the style initiated by Abu Mazen, mixing nationalist sentiments with Islamic morals and praise. Hamas' nashids were, at the start, not elaborated in the melody, and were repetitive and militant. Some productions did include instruments but always discreetly in the background (Funch 2000). Yet the music created was politically potent. Lyrics tended to demonise enemies, particularly Israel and Israelis (not seldom referred to as Jews), or to praise martyrs or leaders of the organisation. For example, Carin Berg (2012) has commented on a song called 'The Return of the Qassamist Falcons' where the lyrics included phrases like 'Hit the Qassam rocket. Shoot it into the liver of the oppressor.' As with Abu Mazen's and Abu Ratib's songs, some of the songs became popular in Islamic activist circles outside Hamas. The music has changed immensely over the years and, for at least a decade, Hamas has put much more effort and musical skill into its own production of nashid, operating studios and promoting and sponsoring bands that use a wide range of instruments (Berg 2017).

The second intifada, starting in September 2000, saw the emergence of an unlikely star. Only eleven years old when she first appeared on stage, and therefore called *al-tifl* (the child), but with a stunning voice, Palestinian-Jordanian Mais Shalash sang a mix of traditional nashid and new songs composed by her father about Islam and heroic Palestinian resistance and revolt. Soon she was nicknamed *sawt al-hurriyya* (the voice of freedom), also the title of one of her more popular albums. Her most well-known recordings were made between 2002 and 2006 (McDonald 2013), further helping to spread Hamas' nashid outside its narrow circles. There was a controversy around the female voice, and Mais Shalash singing to men as she grew older, causing Yusuf al-Qaradawi to speak in her defence with the claim that what she was doing was halal because its message was sound and politically vital.[20]

Hizbullah also engaged in nashids early on; initially they were more or less haphazardly composed, but eventually the music output was coordinated and controlled by *al-Risala*, the cultural division of Hizbullah (Alagha 2016; Berg 2017). Musicians tied to Hizbullah have managed to connect their protest music to the Shi'i ethos of the Iranian revolution, positioning the martyrology of Shi'i theology as an inspiration and thus being able to incorporate, for example, the *latmiyat* (laments) genre of the *ashura* (commemorations of the

---

[20] See, for example, http://muslim-peoples.blogspot.se/2010/09/biography-of-mais-shalash. html (last accessed 13 December 2015).

killing of Hussein, the grandson of the Prophet Muhammad) into the political message of resistance of Hizbullah (see Berg 2017). It has been difficult to pin down the precise influence of Hizbullah on Sunni pop music, but it seems like some Hizbullah nashids spread outside the Shi'i environment due to the ethos of the songs, celebrating resistance against, mainly, Israel. As far as I can tell, however, these are not part of the genealogy I am pursuing but a parallel development.

More radical Islamist networks like al-Qaida, and after them the different incarnations of the Islamic State (IS, ISIS), also took up the practice of nashid-listening and nashid-making. Lahoud (2017: 42) notes that in an internal al-Qaida document as early as the late 1980s, activists were being encouraged to listen to nashid. Again, however, this development is not directly part of the genealogy I am describing, but parallel to it.

The Influence of Political Nashids

Audio cassette tapes of resistance nashids had a wide circulation among activist Muslims, but barely reached non-Muslims (apart from some inquisitive researchers) and were seldom heard among Muslims outside activist circles and their radio broadcasts. The phenomenon might best be described as a globalised sub-culture: 'globalised' in the sense that the songs were listened to by activist Muslims in all corners of the world (particularly among those who understood Arabic), and 'sub-culture' in the sense that the music was played and listened to outside the central stages and markets of consumer cultural music.

Some might think that this political dimension compromises the entire genre of nashid, but this political background and development is only part of the genealogy; one also needs to understand the multiple functions of nashids. Listening to political music may also be a way to feel part of a social trend or even a social movement without having to do more than that or possibly attend a concert. I later develop an argument about an Islamic ethical empowerment discourse that is shared widely and that does not necessarily imply radicalism or a specific political standpoint. Then there is the aesthetic element. Some of the music is actually really good. A fellow researcher told me that her interest in nashids was born out of the sheer power of her first listening experience. Being driven in a car in an eastern Mediterranean country listening to some Hamas songs, she was very impressed by the best songs.

Thus, the political nashid was one of the sources of inspiration influencing Islamic environments globally to revive the nashid tradition and to merge it with an Islamic sense of justice and moral righteousness. This would eventually lead to cooperation between Islamic pop and pop-nashid artists and charity organisations, among the prime venues to host the new Islamic music.

Pioneering Pop-nashid and Islamic Pop

The Muslim 500 – a yearly list published since 2009 presenting the 500 most influential Muslims in the world – has gained considerable attention. It has a section for 'Arts & Culture' in which some music artists have featured every year: Yusuf Islam, Raihan, Dawud Wharnsby and Zain Bhikha. These are all pioneers of the new pop-nashid. Sami Yusuf has also been on all the lists, and Maher Zain has featured since 2010. A list like this is of course a very simple indication, but it does provide some proof of how familiar and famous these artists are.

A repeated claim by Awakening is that the company wanted to change the perception of nashid by bringing in quality production, something the nashids had not engaged in thus far. Still, when Awakening dreamt up a quality production Muslim pop star, there had already been a considerable drift in that direction. Below I present the key musicians in the pop-nashid genealogy leading to Awakening, centring on the above-mentioned artists. Of course, there were other early artists, like Mustaqiim Sahir from the USA, or Mehmet Emin Ay and Mustafa Demirci from Turkey (Stokes 2014), but they have not made an equal impression on the music from Awakening. Some of these artists are mentioned in the last part of this history of the pioneers of the new Islamic music genres, a section which also features a comment on the parallel development of music relating to Islam by African-American musicians, including hip-hop artists.

Yusuf Islam: a Greek Cypriot-Swedish Londoner Goes Muslim

Generally recognised as one of the finest voices in British pop music of his generation, Greek Cypriot-Swedish Londoner, Steven Demetre Georgiou had an impressive twelve-year music career as Cat Stevens, still remembered fondly by many. In 1979, he left the music industry, much to the surprise of his audience. He had converted to Islam in 1977, changed his named to

Yusuf Islam in 1978, and in 1979 symbolically auctioned off his instruments and gave the profit to charity. Yusuf Islam took a firm stance against music, later specified as the music industry, something he has reconsidered since (Islam 2017; Larsson 2011). He sorted his song catalogue into '*haram, makruh* (disliked) and *halal*',[21] making sure that all earnings from the *haram* and *makruh* songs were directed to charity (Islam 2017: 31).[22]

In late 1994, Yusuf Islam and Tayyeb Shah, a radio producer, set up a record label called Mountain of Light, a reference to the famous Meccan mountain where Muhammad had his first revelation. The company was created to issue Yusuf Islam's first recordings in 1995. It was the double CD *The Life of The Last Prophet* containing a pious rendering of Muhammad's life read by Yusuf Islam on CD1, and three 'Nasheeds (songs)' on CD2. Two of the tracks were traditional songs arranged by Yusuf Islam, and one was a new song which he wrote himself. The tracks featured male vocals, a children's choral group, and drumming – typical of the vocals-only expectations for nashids associated with Islamic movements at the time. These nashids are not pop songs; rather, the first two are popular, traditional songs in Muslim circles, especially 'Tala'a al-Badru 'Alayna', arguably the most popular of Islamic songs, but parts of the lyrics are sung in English, itself a novelty. Awakening artist Raef would later use parts of the English translation on his song 'The Bright Moon (Tala'al Badru)' on the album *The Path* (2014), preferring his own translations of other parts.

His return to recording caused a sensation, not least since Yusuf Islam's characteristic voice sounded the same as before. Soon, he was invited by the Malaysian nashid group Raihan (see below), to sing two songs with them, 'Seal of the Prophets' and 'God is the Light', for their second album, *Syukur* (1997). The success of the return also spawned another record label called

[21] The categories used by Yusuf Islam refer to Islamic jurisprudence. While haram and halal have entered English as common-usage terms, *makruh* – deeds and positions that are blameworthy or disliked but still allowed – is less known (see further in Chapter 9).

[22] It is a contested matter in Islamic jurisprudence whether that earned by unlawful means can be given to charity. Sheikh Mutawalli al-Darsh (d. 1997), who served as main imam of the Regent's Park mosque, was a main conversation partner of Yusuf Islam in his first years of conversion (Islam 2017). Even though I do not know his position on charity and haram money, al-Darsh generally held pragmatic views on economic matters for Muslim minorities in the United Kingdom and could very well have advised Yusuf Islam in this rather pragmatic solution (see Wiegers 2011).

Jamal Records, in 2015 remade into the Dubai-based company Let the Change Be, run by Yusuf Islam's daughter Hasanah Islam and her husband Majid Hussain.[23]

Edifying children's songs have been a cornerstone of Yusuf Islam's production. One of his albums, *A is for Allah* (2000), was a collection of children's songs that he had actually started to write in 1980 when his first child was born. Although Yusuf Islam occasionally performed some of these songs at Islamic meetings, and they were already bootlegged and distributed on cassettes in the 1980s, they were not officially released until 2000. The album was recorded with Zain Bhikha (see below) and Dawud Wharnsby (see below) on back-up vocals, together with the Islamia School Chorus (a Muslim private school in London founded by Yusuf Islam).

Another cornerstone in Yusuf Islam's musical endeavour has been his involvement with social justice and the disempowered. For example, he understood the value of motivational songs to keep hopes up and was fascinated by Bosnian nashids produced in connection with the Bosnian war starting in the early 1990s, something that caused him to re-evaluate his hard-line stance on music (Islam 2007). The person who introduced him to the Bosnian nashids, the then Bosnian Foreign Secretary Irfan Ljubijankić, was later killed in the war (1995). That made Yusuf Islam engage in the project 'I Have No Cannons That Roar', which resulted in an album with the same name in 2000, containing popular Bosnian music and two new Yusuf Islam songs. The title song was penned by Ljubijankić and given to Yusuf Islam with the expressed hope that he would do something for the Bosnian people.

Yusuf Islam has offered himself and his music to a number of charity events, and even created a charity of his own, Small Kindness, in 1999. Before that, he was instrumental in setting up the charity Muslim Aid in 1985, serving as its first chairman. Recently, in 2018, Yusuf Islam has taken the initiative to help

[23] Another interesting Muslim musician is Idris Phillips who issued his debut album *Star by Moon* in 2016 on the Let the Change Be label. Previously, he had cooperated with Zain Bhikha, Dawud Wharnsby, Yusuf Islam and others, adding solid musicianship to any recording or performance he has been involved in.

the Rohingya by cooperating with Penny Appeal. This work has led to multiple awards.

Yusuf Islam continued to record and perform nashids and children's songs in vocals-only style until early 2005. In response to the tsunami catastrophe in South-East Asia in December 2004, he wrote and recorded a song, 'Indian Ocean', using a guitar for the first time when recording as Yusuf Islam. His son had purchased a guitar in 2002 and brought it to their home, and on a quiet morning Yusuf Islam picked it up and new music came to him (Islam 2017: 65). Furthermore, on 21 April 2005, he performed with a guitar on stage in Abu Dhabi, a much talked-about event in Islamic activist circles. Since the Abu Dhabi performance, he has continued to add instruments to his recordings and performances (Otterbeck and Skjelbo 2020). Yusuf Islam has also reconnected with his previous genre of music on albums such as *An Other Cup* (2006), *Roadsinger* (2009) and the blues album *Tell 'Em I'm Gone* (2014). In 2016, he toured in the USA using both his new stage name (Yusuf) and his old (Cat Stevens) on posters, playing parts of his old catalogue again to a full band.

It is fair to claim that Yusuf Islam has, in many ways, been the inspiration, but also a very important networker, at the heart of the development of the new pop-nashid. It was he who brought Zain Bhikha and Dawud Wharnsby together, it was he who started the first nashid record label in UK, albeit on an unambitious level. He was also part of the first collaboration between the new European nashid and the vivid Malaysian scene by cooperating with Raihan.

Malaysian Raihan: the First Islamic Boy Band

Raihan's first album *Puji-Pujian* (Praises, 1996) became an instant hit record in Malaysia and, according to Barendregt (2012), is the most sold Malaysian pop music album ever; as far as I can tell, it remains so to this day. The group consisted of five handsome men singing *nasyid* with Islamic lyrics together in tight vocals-only arrangements with discreet percussion rhythms. The name is an oft-used term in connection with Islamic aesthetics meaning 'heavenly fragrance' (in Arabic, *rayhan*). Due to personal connections between Raihan's producer and Warner Music Malaysia, and of course due to the quality of the music, the group was given the benefit of being supported by the major company's distribution chain.

Before Raihan's fantastic success, the key members had another band, called The Zikr (1992–6), that also recorded vocals-only with some degree of success. The Malaysian vocals-only *nasyid* genre was inspired by the Arab nashids of the Islamic movements in the Middle East, and was connected to al-Arqam, an Islamic *dakwah* (call, mission and teaching; in Arabic *da'wa*) movement in Malaysia, outlawed in 1994. From the 1950s and onwards, before that inspiration affected Malaysian *nasyid*, a commercial *nasyid* market with recordings including a rich variety of instruments had developed in Malaysia, even though some *nasyid* was also vocals-only during this period (Matusky and Beng 2017).

Nada Murni (Noble Tone) – the pioneering group of the more politically oriented *nasyid* connected with *dakwah* – issued thirty-one albums over a period of ten years before splitting up in 1995, establishing what Bart Barendregt (2012) has nicknamed 'the Arqam sound'. Their albums were non-commercial in the sense that they were not produced and marketed, rather recorded and circulated (Tan 2007). However, it was Raihan that really popularised the genre, making both vocal and percussion arrangements more complex, a move that became an influence upon others.[24]

The lyrics on Raihan's debut album were not of the political kind; rather, they celebrated faith in fairly simple and straightforward terms. For example, part of the lyrics of the title song 'Puji Pujian' reads, in Barendregt's (2012) translation:

> There is no god but Allah
> Muhammad is the messenger of Allah
> When our successes are praised
> They are in fact not ours
> Therefore, always realise
> Everything comes from God
> Heartfelt happiness and joy
> That's a sign from God

---

[24] A similar *nasyed* scene emerged in Indonesia but never attained the same global success, although some groups, like Snada, became locally famous and collaborated with Muslim political social movement organisations (Rasmussen 2010: 203).

The humbleness expressed is an important ethical stance in Islamic discourse. As we shall see later, similar lyrics would also be typical of the Awakening artists.

The second album, *Syukur* (implicitly, [give] Thanks [to Allah], 1997), is in the same style but the rhythms are richer and more complex, introducing several pitched percussion instruments, often of local origin. This album also features songs in English and collaboration with Yusuf Islam (mentioned above), thereby increasing the group's popularity outside South-East Asia. In 1997, Raihan's first concert outside Malaysia was in Edinburgh, at the Commonwealth Heads of Government Meeting featuring a number of prominent political leaders, including Prince Charles.

With Raihan's fifth album, *Demi Masa* (By time, a reference to the first verse of Sura 103 of the Qur'an in Malay translation, 2001), other instruments were discreetly introduced even though the overall style did not change.[25] Since then, Raihan has continuously used musical instruments to an increasing degree, culminating with the fully orchestrated *Ameen* (2005). It is interesting, however, that the two songs on that album with the most elaborate Islamic theme, '99 names' and 'Ameen', are vocals-only songs. Possibly as a reaction to the group's increasing use of melodic instruments, they recorded a *nasyid* album in 2008, *The Spirit of Shalawat*, celebrating the values of prayer using nothing but their voices and some sparse drumming.

Early in their career, the members of Raihan claimed that they wanted their music to come across as moral, ethical and educational, specifying it as being suitable for the young and bringing people closer to Allah (Sarkissian 2005: 129). As with Yusuf Islam and Awakening artists, Raihan has been involved in a number of charity events, for instance, for the benefit of refugees; in 1999, together with eight other famous *nasyid* groups, they made a record with two songs for Kosovo, aiming to raise economic support (Sarkissian 2005: 130).

The commercial success of the Raihan concept encouraged similar acts and the Malaysian *nasyid* scene exploded. For example, two all-male *nasyid* groups, Rabbani[26] (lit. Our Lord) and Hijjaz, up and coming top acts, were

---

[25] A few instrumental melodies (probably made with a synthesiser) had already been introduced on the film soundtrack *Syukur 21* (2000).

[26] Rabbani has one song on *The Best of Islamic Music, Vol. 1* (2012) and one on *The Best of Islamic Music, Vol. 2* (2013), both compilations issued by Awakening.

given the chance to launch their respective careers at this time, while a number of all-female groups hit the market, notably Solehah (lit. Nice), four very young women (only thirteen years old when recording their first album) who produced four popular studio albums between 1997 and 2005 (Sarkissian 2005: 128f).

In July 2003, Raihan made its first full tour of the UK, and Sami Yusuf opened for them; this was before the first Sami Yusuf album was issued. Ever since, there has been a connection between Raihan and Awakening. For example, the Raihan songs 'Solatuwassalam' and 'Thank You Allah' appeared on the Awakening compilations *The Best of Islamic Music, Vol. 1* (2012) and *The Best of Islamic Music, Vol. 2* (2013).

Canadian Dawud Wharnsby: from Folk Music to Nashid

In 1993, at the age of twenty-one, Canadian musician David Wharnsby – a professional artist since his late teens playing in a variety of Celtic folk bands with quirky names like Crackenthorpe's Teapot – decided to convert to Islam. He took the name Dawud Wharnsby-Ali (at times known as Dawud Ali or, since 2003, Dawud Wharnsby) as a performer. After his conversion, he tried playing in bars and at festivals but found those arenas difficult to relate to. Instead, he started to perform in the streets in the hope of another type of audience and inspiration. Eventually he gave up performing live and decided to record a selection of the songs he had performed in recent years, which he thought of as closure to that period of his life, at least in retrospect.[27] The album, his first, *Blue Walls and the Big Sky* (1995), is a somewhat typical folk album with vocals, guitar picking and pleasant harmonies by a female singer, Heather Chappell.[28] Like many records of the time, it was released in a limited number, more or less for the benefit of friends and family. Then, for a while, he gave up music and engaged fully in the local Muslim environment until feeling cornered by what he felt to be unnecessary conservatism. Eventually, he turned his creativity back to music and the vehicle became his passion for a meaningful, positive children's culture.

---

[27] Interview with Dawud Wharnsby, 1 February 2018.

[28] Earlier, Heather Chappell and Dawud Wharnsby had played together in various bands. Wharnsby also wrote one of the tracks on Chappell's debut album, *The Moon, A Bullethole* (2007).

His next album, *A Whisper of Peace* (1996), was his first nashid album, featuring songs like 'Takbir (Days of Eid)', 'Al Khaliq' (The Creator), 'Animals Love Qur'an' and 'The Prophet'. It is probably the first officially distributed collection of recorded English nashids, and only features the voices of grown males and children and unobtrusive drumming.[29] The album implements several different traditional ritual tonal expressions used in Islam including *al-Fatiha*, the first Sura of the Qur'an that introduces the album, the call to prayer (on the second track 'Azan/Qad Qamatis Salah' [Call to prayer/ The prayer has started]) and the pilgrimage chant 'Labayka' (Here we come Allah), combining it with a tonal language found in Irish folk songs. The same pattern was repeated over the following years. Wharnsby's lyrics generally praise Allah, Muhammad, the creation and the ethics suggested by Islam. Some songs are directed to children, often with a humorous twist to them, like 'Animals Love Qur'an'. There are also songs that could be described as Muslim pride, for example 'The Veil', praising the integrity and modesty of Muslim *hijabis* (veil-wearers) challenged to remove the veil.

In his book *For Whom the Troubadour Sings: Collected Poetry and Songs* (2009), Dawud Wharnsby analyses his own lyrics and poems, creating five categories of topics: the first is the experience of the life journey, from birth to death; the second is lyrics 'to inspire . . . positive social action' (p. 133); the third gathers songs with the function 'to remind' everyone of the wisdom and experiences transmitted through history, particularly in the lives of prophets; the fourth category is 'for the faithful' (p. 95), assembling songs celebrating the spiritual aspects of faith; the fifth and final is described as 'for the King's court' (p. 117) and brings together songs 'sometimes satirical and sometimes scathing' (p. 134). Reading through his lyrics and poems and listening to his songs, I think his division provides a neat analysis. Further, it resonates with other artists' productions, including those of the Awakening artists.

Several of his albums between 1996 and 2003 were issued and distributed through a pioneering North American Islamic media house called Sound Vision. Through Sound Vision, Dawud Wharnsby was also involved in pioneering the Islamic children's TV show, *Adam's World*, a Sesame Street-styled

---

[29] The second track also features cricket and bird sounds. The use of sound effects and animal sounds are recurrent on Dawud Wharnsby's records.

show that started in the early 1990s.[30] In 1999, after some initial friendly correspondence with Yusuf Islam,[31] Dawud Wharnsby had the opportunity to work with him on his album *A is for Allah* (2000), when he also met and sang with Zain Bhikha (see below) for the first time, the start of a long-lasting friendship and collaboration between the two.

Beginning with the recording of *Vacuous Waxing* (2004), which commenced collaboration with childhood friend Bill Kocher, Dawud Wharnsby once again recorded with instruments other than percussion. Even though the artist himself does not consider these later records to be nashid albums, some tracks resemble his earlier nashid compositions: for example, 'The War/ La ilaha illallah' on *Out Seeing the Fields* (2007), with lyrics containing outspoken criticism of commercialism and shallowness. The turn to recording with instruments met with some disapproval but as, similar changes were taking place across the board, this soon died down. The Awakening artist Raef, who mentions Dawud Wharnsby as a great inspiration when growing up and later as a mentor when he toured with him, remembers the upset but also that listening to the actual music, which sounded really 'amazing', erased the criticism in his own circles of friends. Raef even specifically mentions *Out Seeing the Fields* as his favourite album on the Awakening webpage that presents him.[32]

Another of Dawud Wharnsby's projects is Abraham Jam, a primarily live act formed with a Christian and a Jewish musician, making a point about religious diversity. The first version of the band saw light in 2010 but it is still around in 2019 performing live in religious and community centres.[33]

In 2014, he released a particularly remarkable album, *Acoustic Simplicitea*, with his old vocals-only nashids now sung to guitar. In our conversation he mentioned that the songs were originally composed using a guitar, an instrument he claims he had never rejected despite choosing not to bring it on stage

---

[30] For more about *Adam's World*, see Moll 2009.

[31] Northern Spirit Radio (Quaker Community): http://northernspiritradio.org/episode/soul-food-kitchener-quran (last accessed 1 February 2018).

[32] https://awakening.org/artists/raef.htm (last accessed 29 December 2018; no longer active).

[33] https://abrahamjam.com/ (last accessed 1 February 2019).

or to record with it for almost ten years. Nowadays, he cannot really see any problems with the guitar and has performed with one since 2004/5. Dawud Wharnsby continually makes new music.

Dawud Wharnsby has an interesting, inclusive interpretation of Islam. For one thing, he prefers to write islam with a low case 'i', because he wants the word to transmit the act of 'entering into peace through surrender to the will of the Creator', not act as a noun for an institutional religion (Wharnsby 2009: 136). This inclusive understanding is something that has grown over the years. Typically, Dawud Wharnsby is Muslim but worships both in mosques and 'Unitarian churches',[34] as he does not like the exclusionary tendencies of religious labels.[35] He is, however, not a member of the Unitarians.[36]

One of the motivations and, indeed, necessities for Dawud Wharnsby has been to uphold his independence in relation to commercial actors and to hold at bay the cult of the artist that may develop in connection with recordings and concerts. He has crossed paths with Awakening numerous times. As early as 2001, he had noted Awakening and had discussions with someone representing the company. Early in Sami Yusuf's career, he asked Dawud Wharnsby if he would consider cooperating with him in making an album in solidarity with Palestinians, although nothing came of the conversation. It was after meeting Awakening staff and artists at numerous Islamic gatherings, and being good friends with two Awakening artists, that he finally ended up on an Awakening recording, the Raef duet 'All About Me' from 2019.

South African Zain Bhikha: the World-renowned Amateur

Zain Bhikha was raised in a Muslim home where poetry, listening to music and singing were important aspects of social life.[37] According to him, his family was more progressive than anyone he knew when growing up, in respect of

[34] Dawud Wharsby is referring to the Unitarian Universalist Association, a religiously inclusive, liberal association of diverse congregations that draw from a number of spiritual traditions. Once started as a Christian movement in 1961, it is now described as non-creedal (see Fiscella 2015).

[35] 'Global citizen: A glimpse into the life of Dawud Wharnsby', *Scouting* June/July 2010, p. 41, https://issuu.com/ukscouting/docs/mastercopy_junejuly (last accessed 5 July 2021).

[36] Interview with Dawud Wharnsby, 1 February 2018.

[37] This part is mainly built upon my interview with Zain Bhikha on 17 October 2017, https:// zainbhikha.com, and the documentary about him, *Songs of a Soul* (2014), directed by Amr Singh.

its relation to music. He started to write melodies and lyrics as a teen, mainly inspired by the tonal language of what he describes as 'mainstream music', specifying that he did not listen to Bollywood songs or qawwali music.

Zain Bhikha was nineteen years old, turning twenty, when the first free election after the dismantling of the Apartheid system was held in 1994. It was also the year when, according to him, he would find mature faith and direct his creative energy to music. Zain Bhikha's first album, *A Way of Life* (1994), was produced in some 2–300 copies on audio cassette which were not marketed but given away; it was later made available in other forms and can today be purchased on CD or found online. The album was not really produced, it was, rather, recorded straight off with Zain Bhikha simply singing into a microphone his own lyrics promoting Islamic beliefs. The songs were in English, something more or less unheard of at the time. According to Zain Bhikha, the only Islamic song in English he had heard was a bootleg version of Yusuf Islam's 'A is for Allah' recorded live from 'a mosque somewhere', he is not sure where. In fact, as far as I have been able to find out, and as far as Zain Bhikha knows, *A Way of Life* is the first album with a collection of Islamic songs in English.

At the time, Zain Bhikha did not define his music as nashid, rather he called it 'Islamic songs'; the label nashid was introduced later. To illustrate how unusual the idea of singing Islamic songs in English was, Zain Bhikha tells me that at one of his first public concerts, held in a South African mosque, someone offered him a *thawb* (an Islamic male robe) to perform in instead of his regular clothes and was asked politely if Muslims were even allowed to sing praise to Allah in English in a mosque. It was settled without difficulty but the uncertainty surrounding this type of new Islamic music genre has been mentioned to me many times in interviews with different artists.

At first Zain Bhikha's production was made as a modest side project, releasing albums without major distribution, simply trusting in word of mouth. Once, Zain Bhikha's father ran into Yusuf Islam at an Islamic conference and managed to give him an audio cassette of his son's music. A defining moment of Zain Bhikha's career was when he was given the chance to work with Yusuf Islam in London, in 1999, recording the latter's *A for Allah* (2000), an album of children's songs. While working with the album, he was introduced to Dawud Wharnsby, also working with Yusuf Islam for the first time. Zain Bhikha was signed to Jamal Records, a subdivision of Yusuf Islam's label, Mountain of Light.

Since then, he has established himself as one of the foremost exponents of the new pop-nashid. He has recorded or performed with all the above-mentioned artists and others like US act Native Deen, developing a close cooperation with Yusuf Islam – called 'his mentor' on Zain Bhikha's official homepage – and, especially, Dawud Wharnsby. In 2005, he founded Zain Bhikha Studios that today manages both his and other artists' projects, as well as the accounts; any profit goes directly to charity. Zain Bhikha has a full-time job; his music career is a side-line as his family owns a major company in which he works.

He has released several albums, never departing from the vocals-only idea; instead, he uses very advanced choral arrangements, drums and even beat-boxing. According to Zain Bhikha, when he started, he was convinced that music should only contain singing and drums; over the years, however, he has realised that other stances are possible but he has chosen not to change his artistic formula – yet. While he never introduces instruments other than percussion, he has, beginning with the album *A Way of Life* (2010, the second with that title), recorded some of his songs in two versions: a 'drum version' and a 'vocals-only', leaving out the percussion, presumably trying to cater to two different audiences (Otterbeck and Skjelbo 2020). When I asked him why he did not follow his peers and introduce instruments, Zain Bhikha replied that he respected different opinions on the matter but that he himself prefers the *a cappella* style. He is not trained in playing an instrument and further he is influenced by a strong South African tradition of *a cappella* and choir singing.

Zain Bhikha and Dawud Wharnsby share an interest in creating children's culture and the two have cooperated several times. Among other things, they have recorded the thirty-episode children's TV show, *Enjoying Islam with Zain and Dawud* (2009), containing a lot of singing, made for Peace TV, an Islamic TV channel broadcasting in English and Urdu. The songs are edi-fying, teaching children ethics based on 'the science of Islamic ethics', *'ilm al-akhlaq* encouraging them to reflect morally. Neither of the two singers are particularly proud of the result but as it was a pioneering project, recorded during a very short period of time, with good intentions, they see the value of it. Another project with Dawud Wharnsby that grew out of frequent contacts with children and youth and the experience of having children of their own were the 'The Art of Creative Expression' workshops in which the two artists work on self-esteem and creativity, trying to free the young participants from socially and mentally induced restrictions.

An interesting example of Zain Bhikha's engagement with children's songs is the humorous song 'Pizza in His Pocket' from *Allah Knows* (2006), which warns against overeating and promotes sharing and modest behaviour. After a rather funny description of a boy who eats food all over the world ('He ate dates in Damascus, which he thought were very nice. And hot samoosas in Sumatra, seasoned with a special spice.') Zain Bhikha turns the narrative around:

> Then one day he saw a little girl, who held her tummy tight,
> And he walked over and asked her if everything was alright.
> She said she was so hungry and had been hungry for so long,
> Then he realised the way he ate was very, very wrong.
> He looked down at his own tummy and he started feeling pain.
> Pain from eating too much food, but he knew not to complain.
> So he brought the girl some food, shared it with her family,
> Then they thanked Allah for what they had, and then he let them be.
> So let's try to learn a lesson and let's try to do what's right.
> Eat the food your parents give you without a fuss or fight.
> Always be thankful to Allah for all your yummy food,
> Share what you have with others, because not sharing is rude.
> Being thankful is what's really great.
> Eat the veggies on your plate.
> And don't be like the boy who always ate and ate and ate!

The explicit moral at the end hammers in the message. Further, the ethics is based on Muhammad's sunna, his way, that warns against overeating and stresses the right of people not to starve when others have food, which should be shared freely without making claims, not even demanding thanks because all praise is due to Allah. One should also respect one's parents and be thankful for what is provided, as everything ultimately stems from Allah, even bad times. This and a number of other songs are being turned into children's books by the company ZeeBeeKids, a division of Zain Bhikha Studios in cooperation with The Islamic Foundation, UK.[38] The Islamic Foundation has a history of pioneering Islamic children's books (Janson 2003).

Over time, Zain Bhikha has increasingly addressed social issues and ills, trying to raise social awareness among his listeners (for example, 'Can't U See' [2006] about drugs, 'Freedom will Come' [2009] about Palestine and 'Better Day' [2011] about domestic violence against women and children); this development has run in tandem with his increased engagement in creativity workshops. This is not a step away from faith-based art, rather the opposite according to Zain Bhikha; considering one's faith in relation to society and religious communities is a necessary way forward. Still, the lyrics are meant to be optimistic and bring hope.

In my interview with him, he stressed the importance of internalising Islamic ethics as there is no room for hypocrisy among nashid artists. There would be

> more honesty in what they [lonely rock stars on tour] are doing because they might be singing about rock 'n' roll and women and they are living their dream, whereas us, we are singing about God and his messenger and we're singing about everything that's wholesome. And if we don't love that life off the stage then we are lying to ourselves, and myself and Dawud we take that very seriously in a sense that the Qur'an doesn't speak about many professions but it speaks about the poets, the poets who speak one thing but they don't act upon what they say. And that, I think, is the biggest worry as human beings as artists – because we are mixing our faith with our art. We should always try to live it because we shouldn't let our egos and everything else take over.

Of course, I do not know if Zain Bhikha can live up to his high ideals, but I have no reason not to believe that he is trying his utmost to do so.

Zain Bhikha has a connection to Awakening. In 2005, after the release of *Mountains of Makkah* (2005), he was approached by Awakening who wanted

---

[38] At the time of writing, only one volume has appeared, Zain Bhikha, *Allah Made Everything: The Song Book* (2018) illustrated by Azra Momin. 'Pizza in His Pocket' has inspired a children's book before, published by Goodwordkidz in 2010.

to sign him, but Zain was hesitant, afraid of losing creative control, and since he has never had the ambition to be involved in music full time, the possible monetary benefits of a contract with a commercial company was not an issue. No contract was signed but his and Awakening's paths have crossed several times since, and he personally knows most of the artists who are or have been connected to Awakening. Additionally, one of his songs, 'Mountains of Makkah' appears on *The Best of Islamic Music, Vol. 1* (2012), a CD compilation put together by Awakening.

Other Nashid Artists of the Time

The artists mentioned here are, of course, not the only Muslim artists driving the new Islamic music towards pop. For example, from 1998, the media company Beyza Yapım has been very successful in Turkey in producing and distributing records (Stokes 2014). Its biggest star is Mehmet Emin Ay who started his career in 1989 when his first cassette album, *Dolunay* (Full moon), was released, cleverly introduced by his take on 'Taleal Bedru Aleyna' in which Muhammad is compared to the full moon. Throughout his career, Mehmet Emin Ay has recorded with instruments, often in a style reminiscent of the iconic Egyptian artists of the twentieth century, like Umm Kulthum and Abd al-Halim Hafiz. It appears that the vocals-only ideal has not been an issue in Turkey. Mehmet Emin Ay has recorded many albums together with singer Mustafa Demirci. In an interview with Martin Stokes (2014), Mustafa Demirci specified that in his involvement in production and recordings he ensures that musicians do not cross 'the red line' he has in his mind. Certain types of performances, intonations and styles were not welcome; still, Mustafa Demirci was open to change and taking risks. Beyza Yapım has been Awakening's distributor in Turkey and Awakening has collaborated with both Mehmet Emin Ay and Mustafa Demirci.

Various types of Sufi music have been part of several Awakening people's lives. Bara Kherigi told me he listened to a lot of Tunisian Sufi *hadra* music when growing up, and avoiding qawwali while growing up in the UK in the 1990s with an interest in music would probably have been a major feat. Consequently, Awakening's first record, Sami Yusuf's *al-Mu'allim*, contains two qawwali covers with English lyrics by Bara Kherigi and musical arrangement by Sami Yusuf: 'Allahu', which is an adaption of Nusrat Fatih Ali Khan's

'Allah hoo, Allah hoo', and 'Ya Mustafa' by the Sabri Brothers. The original songs celebrate Allah and Mohammad respectively, both from a Sufi perspective, but, as mentioned before, that love is part of general Islamic discourse. Qawwali also became immensely popular outside Muslim circles and anyone who took an interest in the development of so-called world music in the 1990s will already be acquainted with these qawwali stars. In fact, the word processor I am using to write this book neither autocorrects qawwali nor marks it as misspelt.

A pioneering enterprise in the UK was Meem music. It was started in 1997 by Tayyib Shah who used to work with Yusuf Islam and the company set up to distribute his new music, but as Yusuf Islam was not really interested in expanding and going into the music business commercially again, Tayyib Shah left. Meem signed Shaam (meaning Syria) in 1997, and Aashiq Al Rasul (Lover of the Prophet, clearly signalling the group's Sufi connection) in 1998; both groups are from Birmingham, and Meem tried to market the music as boyband pop music according to the Raihan formula. Both groups, starting as and remaining vocals-only, have done well and survived over the years. Just like Awakening's artists, they have been deeply involved in charity and community work but, apart from appearing on the same stage as Awakening, I have not found any formal cooperation. Sharif Banna tells me he was well-aware of Meem and its bands. During his university days, for example, Shaam was hired for cultural events and Eid parties, but there was no direct influence. Rather, the low budget and local ambitions of Meem music were exactly what Awakening wished to avoid.

All through the twentieth century and to this day, American (not least African American) musicians and singers have referred to Islam in a variety of ways and from diverse positions (Ackfeldt 2019); the more deliberately Islam-oriented music has exploded through hip-hop. A good way to explore this is through Muslimhiphop.com. Awakening artists have not collaborated with hip-hop artists other than being in the same line-ups at Islamic conferences, and Awakening has not, to my knowledge, tried to sign any hip-hop artists; when I have discussed music with the Awakening people no one has mentioned hip-hop acts as a major influence. Still, hip-hop acts that have the ambition to come across as Islamic were already recording in the 1990s, primarily in the USA and the UK. Mecca2Medina is the obvious example.

Formed in the UK, the group made its debut with the EP *Life after Death* in 1996 on Dawa Records. The group has survived over the years and has produced both hip-hop and nashid music and recorded with Raihan, although there seems to be no direct connection to Awakening. Another obvious example is UK hip-hop duo, Poetic Pilgrimage, which has appeared on the same stage as Awakening, and US hip-hop group, Native Deen.[39]

The Role of Other Music

When Bara Kherigi grew up in Tunisia and later in the UK, music was part of his life. He loved music and had an ear for it like others in the family, although he never learned to play an instrument. I have already mentioned influences on his output from Arab and Islamic music genres but, growing up in the 1990s, he listened to a wide range of other music as well, mentioning Blur as one band he particularly liked. His Walkman and later iPod held an eclectic collection of songs and, from our discussions, I can tell he knows a lot about American and British popular music. Raef grew up listening to American rock music and Maher Zain knows the lyrics to an amazing number of pop songs. Putting the three of them together in a tour bus together with the two non-Muslim singers doing choir parts behind Maher Zain, the repertoire of Islamic songs and other popular music was a never-ending stream.

Sami Yusuf was schooled in music, first by his father who is an accomplished musician and composer, and then in formal education including a stint at London's The Royal Academy of Music (although not completing his studies) and Salford University (Brown 2007). He is trained both in Iranian and Azeri music as well as the so-called Western classical tradition.

Raef is the Awakening artist who has made the most covers of non-Muslim popular music. He has posted several videos of himself playing covers with slightly rearranged lyrics. An important part of his years playing with a music collective, was to play covers with audiences who were provided with lyric sheets. During the tour I followed in October 2017, Raef opened for Maher Zain. The first song he played was John Lennon's 'Imagine' with slight

---

[39] Native Deen has a song 'M-U-S-L-I-M' on *The Best of Islamic Music, Vol. 2* (2013), issued by Awakening.

changes in the lyrics, like 'imagine we're in heaven' instead of 'imagine there's no heaven', as well as 'and no divisions too' rather than 'and no religions too'. Raef pointed out to me that the Prophet Muhammad often asked believers to imagine being in heaven. The 'no divisions too' was a smart reference to the religious divisions in this world, both within Islam and beyond. Furthermore, as heaven is a recurrent topic of the song, 'division' also refers to the end of days when the division of Islam into seventy-two sects (plus one rightful one) finally ceases according to standard Sunni eschatology. At a few shows, he opened with his take on Rebecca Black's 'Friday' called 'It's Jumuah [Friday]' (2011) with humorous lyrics about getting to the mosque to pray on Friday. The song has become one of Raef's trademarks – many in the audiences recognised it at once – even though originally recorded as a joke.

Raef loves Christmas music and has made his own version of 'Deck the Halls', launched on the Awakening YouTube channel as 'the Muslim Christmas song'. Dressed in a woollen sweater in front of a blazing fire in an open fireplace with a generous mantelpiece, all signalling a well-to-do Bing Crosbyish Christmas, he rips off the song with a big smile. Online comments go in two directions. One group simply does not understand it and condemns it, the other loves it and defends Raef, thereby illustrating the different relations to non-Muslim popular music. The first group draws a distinction between 'our' and 'their' culture. My argument is that Raef simply does not experience such a division: as Street (2012: 104) points out, being American is also a relation to music, not least a generational relation; that is, certain music becomes embodied reference points for people, regardless of if they like it or not. Raef as an Egyptian American, Maher Zain as Lebanese-Swedish and Bara Kherigi as Tunisian-British make multifaceted soundtracks to their lives and the possible division between 'our' music and 'their' music is simply not relevant; 'both' categories are theirs. When they think music – chords, sounds, scales, melodies – there is no division, or at least, not one that causes a separation likely to motivate compartmentalisation.

From this we may deduce that key persons in Awakening grew up listening to a wide variety of music. We may also note that their stance against the so-called hedonistic popular culture lifestyles promoted in mainstream culture, particularly in popular music, is grounded in consumption experience. Still, they have recorded a great deal of music in styles developed in the very same popular music genres of the USA and UK (soul, R&B, rock, boyband pop, ballads) but also with influences from reggae, qawwali, Sufi poetry and much more. As has been pointed out before, the recorded music complies with the dominant form of popular music regarding the length of songs, soundscapes, production ideals and marketing.

5

THE MESSAGE AND ITS MEDIA

Music is at the forefront of a cultural conduit which reaches and impacts millions. It is everywhere. Faith-conscious Muslim artists are now producing 'Islamic music' as an attempt to provide an alternative to mainstream pop-culture.

Sharif Banna, CEO Awakening, *the Awakening book*, p. 15

In her seminal work *Music in Everyday Life* (2000), Tia DeNora elaborates on the possibility of intrinsic values of music. When listening, does music make us do things or compel a certain mind-set, or do we to a large extent project our own emotions and deeds onto music? DeNora shows how music theorists have argued for both extremes, but suggests a position in-between. Music affords relations to it – for example some music calms, other invites dancing – but in our interaction with music, a complex web of personal experiences, culturally specific genre expectations and moral and ethical discourses contribute to its interpretation and use (DeNora 2000).

When Awakening started to produce music, it had a clear idea about its music's affordance, how the music would affect people. The music was made within a context of *al-fann al-hadif* (art with a purpose) and should nurture Islam in the listener. Thus, it is of particular interest to see how, over time, Awakening communicated its message in a consumer culture world, while taking the realities of running a company into account.

In what follows, I begin by discussing the lyrics of Awakening songs, then move onto sound and instrumentation. In the next chapter, the focus moves to the performance of ethical masculinity on stage and in videos, before reconnecting to lyrics, sounds and instrumentation. In Chapter 7, I discuss the political implications of the positions taken by Awakening.

Words from a Wonderful World

Manchester's O2 stadium, 26 October 2014. At a charity concert arranged by Human Appeal and Awakening, Maher Zain is in the middle of his set and the gig is going fine. The crowd is active, waving glowsticks, and seems to be having a good time. It is a really impressive venue where many of the greatest bands have played, judging from the numerous framed photos backstage. Unexpectedly, Maher Zain announces that he is going to play a favourite song of his. A cover. I did not know he did covers, apart from some well-known nashids.[1] He declares that he really loves the lyrics and the band starts to play, 'What a Wonderful World', the old Louis Armstrong song. The audience responds positively. Maher Zain sings it well; the band is steady as a rock, as always. I remember listening to the lyrics, thinking, is this, in any meaningful sense, at this very moment, an Islamic song?

Afterwards, I ran into Maher Zain backstage and commended him for his choice and chanced the observation that it was his newly acquired vocal coach who had assigned it to him (a typical choice). Maher Zain gave me a big smile and asked how I knew. He then told me he had found this impressive version of the song by a young girl on the Internet that he had taken inspiration from in order to hit some high notes. The performance is part of Maher Zain's ambitions as a singer, and the song's lyrics are fine, in the tradition of clean pop, although not necessarily purposeful as such. Yet the situation beckons the question: What kind of lyrics can the new pop-nashid and Islamic pop make use of and still be described as 'faith-based and value-driven'?

Anyone who has written lyrics to a song knows that it is actually quite difficult. At times sentences are too simple or too complex. There has to be a rhythm to the prose, the syllables have to be adjusted to key tones and the sound of

---

[1] It turned out that Maher Zain actually does a number of covers. For example, on the UK tour in Autumn 2017 he covered Michael Jackson's 'Heal the World' (1991).

different vowels and consonants (and the combination of them) will have to be considered. Words carry meaning and the stresses need to be right, but they are also part of the musical texture and will hopefully contribute to it or, at least, fit. Some lyric writers are simply very good at this, and some need more help. On top of that, Awakening's artists have to get the message right too.

The lyrics often narrate the Islamic convictions and ethics of the artists and the company. At times when writing lyrics, however, words are added that convey ideas not in complete harmony with the understanding of Islam. When discussing this with Raef, he tells me that he runs his lyrics by Bara Kherigi, who is very knowledgeable, but mostly Bara Kherigi does not interfere too much as Raef knows his religion well. He mentions one instance when Bara Kherigi asked him to change 'he's [Allah] on your side' to 'he's by your side' as 'on' would be too direct, implying that you know that you have Allah's support instead of hoping for it. At other times, lyric writers have not had the necessary sensitivity, as when someone (a new, external lyrics writer) suggested the line, 'I wanna shower you with my blessings' in a song about the Prophet Muhammad. The problem is that you can pray for Allah to bless Muhammad, you cannot bless him yourself. Not everyone participating in writing lyrics is a Muslim and some may need some extra help finding the right nuances. In an interview I had with Maher Zain in 2014, he also claimed that all the lyrics that he has recorded with Awakening are checked or co-written by Bara Kherigi who, apart from being trained in Islam, has a good ear for both English and Arabic.

During the UK tour in October 2017, I had a good demonstration of how lyrics may be penned. Bara Kherigi and Raef were sitting opposite me in the tour bus, one earplug each connected to Raef's phone which was playing a demo without vocals. Raef scribbled an idea that he had conjured up before, prompting Bara Kherigi to discuss the overall topic. They quickly agreed that it was about being true to yourself and accepting diversity, then started to try out new phrases. Soon a rough sketch was developed and then they worked side by side, trying out lines, singing together, weighing the words for content and sound value. In this way, after a while it becomes impossible to tell who has written what, as lyrics become a joint venture.

It needs to be stressed that lyrics are not only narrative – even though typical Awakening lyrics do have some kind of narrative – they also aim to be affective and often are, both for singer and listener or audience. For example, 'For the Rest of My Life' (2009), sung by Maher Zain, has a part in one verse that culminates in the words 'I pray we're together in *janna* [paradise]' (1:51). *Janna* is picked up by the choir, which makes the word resonate in the mix for a couple of seconds, producing a warm texture that is taken over by a synthesiser in the same register. Live, it has proven difficult to emphasise those words, as another phrase follows quickly after; instead, the audience and Maher Zain himself tend to stress a phrase that is the last line of two verses 'and there's a couple of words I wanna say', words much more banal and less pregnant as to meaning, but affectively efficient as they open up to the beloved chorus.

I begin by examining some Maher Zain lyrics as I find that they present a default position for Awakening songs. His songs are recorded in a number of languages – English, Arabic, Malay, Urdu, Turkish, French – sometimes meaning that the same song has different angles in different languages. Here I concentrate on the versions on the original album release, whatever that means today.

The first examples are from the debut album *Thank You Allah* (2009), which sets the tone for Maher Zain's artistry. When discussing the lyrics with Maher Zain in 2014, he made the point that lyrics to the first album were, in a way, simple and straightforward. He used Islamic phrases that are part of everyday language, like *al-hamdu lillah*. He claims that topics were such that people took them to their hearts. When making the second album, which was more advanced production-wise, they tried to repeat the straightforwardness of the first album but an audience analysis by Awakening has indicated that the first album was a bit more embraced.

Thank You, Allah has four main topics: praise for Allah; homage to Muhammad; a spiritual awakening after being lost; love. Lyrics are mostly in English but sometimes in Arabic, Turkish or Urdu. One single song may have passages sung in different languages. The English lyrics are often characterised by 'Islamic English', English interlaced with Arabic-Islamic words and phrases, for example, 'Oh, Rasul [messenger, referring to Muhammad], peace be upon you' (from 'Ya Nabi Salam Alayka').

Praising Allah

Some songs such as 'Subahana Allah' (Praise Allah), 'Allahi Allah Kiya Karo' (Keep saying Allah's name) and 'Always Be There' are essentially tributes to

Allah. The refrain to 'Subahana Allah' praises Allah and declares that nothing can be compared to the greatness of Allah (*ma a'zama sha'nak*) and that 'we invoke you [i.e. Allah] and ask for your forgiveness' (*nad'uka wa-narju ghufranaka*). Neither the lyrics nor the melody of the refrain are Maher Zain's own; they are taken from a popular nashid that, for example, one of Egypt's most renown nashid singers of the twentieth century, Sheikh Sayyid al-Naqshabadi (d. 1976), recorded and made popular. With the borrowing, Awakening and Maher Zain mark the continuity between pop-nashid and the classic form of Islamic nashid. The same goes for the refrain in 'Allahi Allah Kiya Karo' which is a song that the already mentioned Pakistani qawwali group, The Sabri Brothers, has made famous.

According to the lyrics of Maher Zain songs, Allah is a god who is present, a perception clearly expressed in 'Always Be There':

> As he promised he will always be there
> To bless us with his love and his mercy
> (Be)cause, as he promised he will always be there
> He's always watching us, guiding us
> And he knows what's deep in my heart

The idea of such an active relationship could be mistaken for a Sufi influence, but it is also an ingredient in Sunni piety in general (Hirschkind 2006b: 122). For example, in an essay from 2012 posted on the CILE website,[2] Sharif Banna calls for a spirituality beyond Sufism and civil society engagement beyond Islamism.[3]

It is worth noting that on Maher Zain's debut album, '*allahu akbar*' (Allah is the greatest) are the first words heard, the last being '*al-hamdu lillah*' (praise Allah): that is, if ignoring the two bonus songs at the end. In this way, two of the most famous of Islamic phrases frame the album. Further, *al-hamdu lillah* expresses gratitude and can be exclaimed after someone has finished a task.

---

[2] CILE, Research Centre for Islamic Legislation and Ethics, is the brainchild of Tariq Ramadan, created in 2012; see www.cilecenter.org/en/ (last accessed 11 February 2019).

[3] Banna's article can be read at https://www.cilecenter.org/en/articles-essays/spirituality-and-civic-engagement-the-prophetic-model/ (last accessed 21 January 2019).

There is no doubt that Maher Zain and Awakening wanted the album to be perceived as deeply devout. This is further stressed in interviews. 'My music is a message of Islam. But I want people to understand what Islam is about. It's a message of peace, brotherhood, humanity, respect and love', Maher Zain pointed out to journalist Omar Shahid in 2011.[4]

The theme of praising Allah runs through the Awakening songs. For example, another Maher Zain song 'The Power', from the album *One* (2016), celebrates the power of *dhikr*, remembrance of Allah performed by repeating phrases. Just like in *dhikr*, the song features familiar phrases like *al-hamdu lillah* (praise be to Allah). Maher Zain tells me in 2017 that the song is of particular importance to him. It is 'a very spiritual song' and he likes performing it as it emphasises the message of his music. A further example is Maher Zain's 'Radhitu Billahi Rabba' (I've accepted – or am pleased with – Allah as my Lord) from *Forgive Me* (2012) where the lyrics praise Allah, but also Muhammad. The Arabic words of the refrain are from a well-known hadith, claiming that whoever recites these words sincerely can be assured of paradise.[5] The words are '*radiytu billahi rabba(n) wa-bi-l-islami dina(n) wa-bi-muhammad(in) salla allahi 'alayhu wa-sallam nabiyya(n) wa-rasul(an)*[6] (I've accepted Allah as my lord and Islam as creed and Muhammad – Allah's peace and blessings upon him – as prophet and messenger).

Muhammad

The love of Muhammad is clearly expressed in songs like 'The Chosen One' and 'Ya Nabi Salam Alayka' (Oh Prophet, peace be upon you). Classically, but also at, for example, Sufi *hadras*, these hymns celebrating Muhammad have often been called *madih*. In 'The Chosen One', Muhammad is described as the teacher, a light, the best among people, the crown of creation, devoted, honest, uninterested in material things or, in short, Allah's chosen one.

---

[4] Omar Shahid is a journalist working in Muslim environments in the UK.
[5] The hadith can be found in Abu Dawud's *Sunan* and al-Nasa'i's *Al-sunan al-Kubra*.
[6] Letters within parenthesis are not pronounced.

Your face was brighter than the sun
Your beauty equalled by none
You are Allah's chosen one
Muhammad *khaira khalq illah* [the best of Allah's creation]
Sallu 'ala rasul illah [blessings upon the messenger of Allah]
Habib al-mustafa [Beloved al-Mustafa: the name means 'the chosen one'
and is used for Muhammad, especially in devotional lyrics and poems]
Peace be upon the messenger
The chosen one (excerpt from 'The Chosen One')

The idea that Muhammad was exceptionally beautiful is well-rooted in the *shama'il* (appearance) literature and the *hilya* tradition,[7] in itself based on the hadiths and sunna (Janson and Otterbeck 2014: 82; Schimmel 1985). In fact, the nashid tradition, both the pop version and the classic, takes inspiration from these traditional sources and their poetry. Another well-established, important trope is that Muhammad is light ('brighter than the sun' and earlier in the lyrics 'your soul was full of light'). In Sufi poetry this is often tied to a cosmological understanding of Muhammad as Allah's light, an interpretation from which the Awakening artists refrain (see, for example, Hoffman 1995: chapter 3); instead, the light is associated with Muhammad as the example for mankind.[8] Towards the end of the same song, Maher Zain sings about imitating 'the chosen one'.

I will try to follow your way
And do my best to live my life
As you taught me
I pray to be close to you
On that day and see you smile (excerpt from 'The Chosen One')

The lyrics relate to classical theology and the importance of following Muhammad's sunna, and the possibility of being brought forward by him on the Day of Judgement ('that day'), to be among the righteous supported

---

[7] The Arabic *shama'il* literature is well spread in history praising the (physical) qualities of the Prophet Muhammad. The *hilya* tradition is an Ottoman genre using both images and texts to do the same.

[8] See also, for example, Sami Yusuf's 'al-Mu'allim'.

by Muhammad.[9] At the same time, the text is personal: the song's 'I' will do his or her best, and addresses Muhammad in the second person. Instead of focusing on the seriousness of the ultimate judgment, the text focuses on Muhammad's smile and the joy of meeting him. The smile connects to Islamic tradition as it is well attested that Muhammad often smiled. Later, Mesut Kurtis would record a song about the smiling prophet called 'Tabassam' (He smiled, 2014).

The other song, 'Ya Nabi Salam Alayka', is sung in two versions: one in Arabic all through, while the other is called the 'international version' and is a bonus track sung in Turkish, English, Arabic and Urdu. The lyrics of the refrain are widely popular as a prayer to Muhammad and included in several praise song genres such as *na'at, sholawat* (Indonesian)/*shalawat* (Malay): '*ya nabi, salam 'alayka, ya rasul, salam 'alayka, ya habib, salam 'alayka, salawatullah 'alayka*', (Oh Prophet, peace be upon you, Oh Messenger, peace be upon you, Oh Beloved, peace be upon you, Allah's blessings be upon you). The verses are not identical in the two versions but they share a classic, metaphorical, poetic language. The Urdu verse may serve as a typical example:

> *Teri muhabbat ki mehak say*
> *Yeh zameen o asman abaad hai*
> *Rehmat ki barsaat aati hai*
> *Dil o jaan ya rasul allah*

In translation:

> From the fragrance of your love
> The earth and the skies have prospered
> And the rain of mercy has poured upon us
> [with my] heart and soul [an intimate, standardised greeting], oh
> Messenger of Allah

As the Norwegian theologian Robert Kvalvaag (2015) has pointed out, this text contains a typical Sufi metaphor describing Muhammad as life-giving rain. Awakening's lyricists often borrow from these well-established metaphors and

---

[9] The same idea can be found in Hamza Robertson's 'Your Beauty' with its lines: 'Will I be from those you welcome with a smile as you call your nation: "Come to my side!"'

stylistic figures, seemingly without having pretensions to be perceived as Sufi. The exuberant love of Muhammad is common to most Muslim poetic and artistic expressions, and has very old roots. For example, the famous *qasidas* (odes) of the poet Ibn al-Farid (d. 1234) often address the love for Muhammad and his beauty (Waugh 1989: 104). Other already mentioned examples of direct connections to Sufism are the use of Imam al-Busiri's famous poem *al-Burda* in songs by Mesut Kurtis, Maher Zain and Raef.

In a conversation with Stefanie Kolbusa, a scholar of Tanzanian music and tradition, I realised that the Awakening lyrics are generally not rich in metaphors, apart from when borrowing from the Sufi tradition as above. Rather, lyrics address topics straightforwardly. When Raef sings, 'won't you be my partner after this world', in 'You Are the One' (2014), he is not referring to anything besides the Islamic notion of married couples being reunited in heaven. The exception is when lyrics are commissioned in other languages and poets are contracted, then at times poetic metaphors enter the lyrics, as described above.

A Spiritual Awakening After Being Lost and Personal Dignity

In many broadcast and published interviews with Maher Zain, as well as in our conversations, Maher Zain brings up the story of his early music career, which led him to New York as an aspiring songwriter. It ends with Maher Zain giving up the dream, returning to Stockholm and finding peace in Islam. Eventually, he finds a way to combine his music skill with his Islamic worldview. A similar topic recurs on Maher Zain's debut album. The tracks 'Insha Allah', 'Awaken', 'Open Your Eyes' – possibly also 'Hold My Hand' and 'Allahi Allah Kiya Karo' – all include this narrative. 'Insha Allah' addresses this directly:

> Every time you commit one more mistake
> You feel you can't repent
> And that it's way too late
> You're so confused, wrong decisions you have made
> Haunt your mind and your heart is full of shame
> Don't despair and never lose hope
> (Be)cause Allah is always by your side

And, if you take shelter with Allah, he will show you 'the way'. 'Insha Allah' is one of Maher Zain's most popular songs. It addresses the self-doubt I have encountered among a number of young Muslims in Europe (Otterbeck 2010, 2015), but it also illustrates the need to return to Allah through the continual repentance, or *tawba*, which is central to Islamic piety.

Another way is to point out all the miracles of Allah around us, as in 'Open Your Eyes'. We should open our eyes and 'see the signs' because the universe is in 'such perfect harmony', and because our biology conceals 'such a perfect order', and because babies grow from being 'helpless and weak'. The song ends by stating, 'Allah, you created everything, we belong to You, *ya rabb* [oh Lord], we raise our hands, forever we thank you'. Drawing attention to personal weaknesses that have been overcome, and viewing nature as Allah's ever-present miracle have long been common themes of apologetic Sunni theology (Hedin 1988: 83; Otterbeck 2000: 209).

Overcoming personal weakness is the way to personal dignity and integrity. To reflect on and regret shortcomings and sins has long been a part of Islam; the renown Islamic scholar al-Ghazali (d. 1111) allowed for lamentation provoking such sadness (MacDonald 1901–2: 223). John Street (2012: 168) argues, with the help of, among others, Martha Nussbaum and Simon Reynolds, that music has the potential to evoke emotions and empathy and, further, to enable people to envision other worlds, 'both utopian future ones and real, alternative past ones'. The Awakening lyrics repeatedly appeal exactly to that; the lyrics create alternative narratives, other possibilities. Imagine your own shortcomings or others' suffering, and think of the change you will make if you commit to Islam. To those who already feel they have taken that step, the lyrics give support and confirmation.

Regret and forgiveness are difficult topics. On the tour bus, on our way back to the hotel in Glasgow after the soundcheck (2017), the following discussion took place. I had just arrived and reconnected with artists, musicians and met Bara Kherigi for the first time. It was to be the first gig of the tour, but the atmosphere was relaxed. Raef started to tell stories from his Indonesian travels made as part of an Indonesian Ramadan television series he has recorded over the last three years.[10] He mentioned that he interviewed

---

[10] The idea of the programme is that Raef, an Egyptian-American Muslim, narrates Indonesian history from his perspective. Raef is touring the many islands of Indonesia on a motorbike, meeting and interviewing interesting people. The programme is made by Indonesian media company DNA, and has been quite successful.

a super-rich, reformed criminal and murderer, now an Islamic intellectual. Maher Zain asked if Allah really can forgive such crimes. Raef pointed out that Allah is the most merciful. But Maher Zain persisted: what about the victims? Should they not be compensated? Then Bara Kherigi entered the discussion and pointed out that by being given free will, we have the ability to make grave mistakes. Eventually the discussion became framed through the theodicy problem. The discussion continued; I bit my tongue not to intervene by throwing in an argument about *al-kaba'ir* (the major sins). These are truly difficult questions to make pop music about. Behind lyrics are ongoing discussions like this, backstage, on the bus, when writing and exchanging ideas.

Love

'I sing about love all the time. Love for Allah, love for the Prophet, love for my wife, love for my daughter,' Maher Zain said when I interviewed him in 2014. I have discussed the love for Allah and Muhammad above. What about other ways of addressing love?

'Baraka Allahu Lakuma' (Blessings of Allah upon you) and 'For the Rest of My Life' both celebrate marriage. The first song has an up-tempo Arab pop beat and lyrics with phrases like 'Let's raise our hands and make *du'a* [prayer], like the Prophet taught us' and a refrain proclaiming '*Baraka allah lakuma, wa-baraka 'alaykuma, wa-jama' baynakuma fi khayr*' (Blessings of Allah upon you, and blessings upon you both, and gather together in [what's] good). When Maher Zain performs the song live, he occasionally asks whether there are newlyweds in the audience; as there generally are, a sense of the celebration of love fills the venue when the singer addresses the couples personally, dedicates the song to them and praises marriage.

In several interviews and at concerts, Maher Zain has explained that the second song is a love song to his wife but, as is often the case with popular music, the song is a collaborative effort and the lyrics are by Maher Zain, Charbel Amso, Abou-Danniel and Bara Kherigi. It is likely that the very core of the lyrics is by Maher Zain and the rest have advised him. This song could also be seen as a general love song, but certain things should be noted. Unlike many love songs, the persona of the song does not sing about his love's beauty. Rather, in a particularly passionately sung vocal part, she is described as 'my wife and my friend and my strength'. The still-influential

Islamic thinker al-Ghazali (d. 1111) wrote that a man should not sing about the grace or looks of his wife (or lover) to other men (al-Ghazali 2002). By not praising his wife's looks, Maher Zain cleverly avoids a taboo in Islamically informed pop, and gets a love song on the repertoire.

Another topic is friendship. 'So Soon' from *Forgive Me* (2012) is about a beloved friend who has passed away. Even though the lyrics are marked by the tragic death, there are some optimistic elements to the song expressed as, 'I remember you in every prayer I make', 'keep my faith and be strong', and 'to God we all belong and to him we'll return'. As Maher Zain said when discussing these lyrics with me in 2014, 'We always remind the listener of the positive in our lyrics.'

The topics above are repeated in different ways by Awakening artists, but of course other topics are also addressed and some artists do not fit the pattern, especially Hamza Namira's production.

Other Topics

Awakening artists also try to create soundtracks to Muslim lives by recording songs about celebrations and important events. Thus, I know for sure that Raef's 'You Are the One' and Maher Zain's 'Baraka Allahu Lakuma' are both used at weddings. Most artists also have a Ramadan single, Raef's 'Ramadan is Here' (2018) and Maher Zain's 'Ramadan' (2013). Songs are consciously marketed in relation to the fasting month. The Mesut Kurtis song 'Asma Allah Alhusna' (The beautiful names of Allah) is called his 'new Ramadan 2020 song' on Awakening's official YouTube channel. The many songs about Muhammad fit well with *mawlid* celebrations.[11] Just as Christmas equals certain music for many celebrating it, I argue that Awakening's music is working its way into Muslim tastes and sentiments, especially in rituals and celebrations engaging the family. My proof as of now is merely anecdotal, but it is an educated guess.

An engagement with the betterment of the world is easily detected in Awakening promotional material and the company's recurrent cooperation

---

[11] In his study of nashid musicians in the UK, several musicians point out to Carl Morris (2013: 136) that it is useful to have a 'wedding nasheed' on the repertoire if you want to be booked at such events. I never discussed this explicitly with anyone connected to Awakening but I would expect, judging from other discussions, similar answers.

with charity organisations and UNHCR. Sharif Banna argues that Islam contains a prophetic model for engagement:

> Civic engagement is not . . . limited to political participation only. The prophetic model is one that calls for engaging with all spheres of civic life. Our challenge as Muslims and citizens – wherever we may live – is to articulate a vision transcending identity-politics and move towards what may be termed – 'Islamic humanism'. Our Prophet was sent as a mercy to all of mankind. His was a message rooted in ethics and human dignity. In our quest to impart the radiance of this prophetic mercy on a societal level, particular focus needs to be paid to areas such as good governance, environmental issues, social justice and combating materialism, poverty and illiteracy. (al-Banna 2012)

The importance of civil engagement can be heard in the songs of several Awakening artists, including Hamza Namira, Sami Yusuf, Raef and Maher Zain. I return to this below but here I look more closely into Hamza Namira's production.

In an email to me, Hamza Namira opposes the label 'Islamic artist' and writes that he cannot be labelled as such, instead insisting he is an 'artist that respects his belief'. I re-read the email I had sent to him but found I had not used the concept; rather, this was probably something he had expected from my explaining I was writing about Awakening and its artists. The response does, however, give a key to Hamza Namira's artistry. His lyrics differ quite substantially from those I have mentioned above; still, they share the element of pride and righteousness, while also adding anger and at times hopelessness, particularly on the album *Esmaani* (Listen to me, 2014). The title track effectively illustrates Hamza Namira's style, with the first verse and the chorus reading like this (the original in colloquial Egyptian):

> My life has never been according to my preference
> Against my will, you're forcing me taking my decisions
> you treat me as if I am a mere shadow
> and that our generation, all of it, are some children
> No! We are tired of the silence
> No! Enough, say it with a loud voice
> (Chorus)

Listen to me!
You made me get lost, to the past, you dragged me, and want me confined
in it.
My dreams! You are the one who ruined them, when you controlled them,
what is left for me?[12]

The combination of lament and a way forward is rather typical of Hamza Namira's lyrics on the *Esmaani* album. At times they are humorous, like 'Dallemet Keda Leh' (Why did it become so dark) about being caught up in the Cairo traffic regardless of whether you are obedient to rules or creative, but even this is clearly an unsmiling allegory of the hopelessness of Egyptian (oppositional) politics. At other times, they are quite disillusioned and emotional, like 'Tesmahy' (Can you spare me)[13] and 'Ma'assalama' (Goodbye), both songs about powerlessness and despair.

Earlier albums by Hamza Namira were more hopeful and addressed Egyptian identity with a particular pride, like in 'Balady ya Balady' (My country, oh, my country) or 'El-Midan' (The square) from *Insan* (Human, 2011). Because of Awakening's preference for non-political engagement, and Hamza Namira's increasing engagement in what was happening in Egypt, eventually collaboration was amicably discontinued.

Another artist, Humood, stresses a positive attitude. He fits neatly with the idea of *al-fann al-nazif*. His most popular song to date is 'Kun Anta' (Be yourself, 2016), a song about not capitulating to the pressure of others just to please them if that means betraying yourself. It has the catchy final phrase of the chorus '*kun anta tazdad jamalan*' (be yourself and you will become more beautiful). He also has a song about the importance of education called 'Kun Fiduliyan' (Be curious, 2018). One of the key parts encourages the listener to ask many questions, 'observe, search and ponder' because a generation which seeks knowledge is better off. Whether this is a critique of closed minds or just a song that is positive about education is hard to tell.[14]

[12] Thanks to Walid Ghali for helping me out with some nuances of the translation.

[13] The translation of the title makes more sense when listening to the first sentence of the song 'Oh mother, can you spare me a moment?'

[14] I have not been able to put this question to Humood in person.

Lyrics generally do not put the artists in roles other than their own persona. At times, an inclusive 'we' is used but without abandoning the persona. An alternate possibility would, of course, be to let the singer give voice to a character within the song as Cat Stevens does in 'Father and Son' (1970), where two perspectives are present. There are very few exceptions, one of which is Maher Zain's 'Palestine Will Be Free' (2009) in which the singer expresses the grief of a Palestinian child in the first person. The song is discussed at length in Chapter 7.

Some topics that dominate much pop music are more or less absent, like sexual desire, falling in love, drunkenness and self-pity. Instead, one largely finds artists displaying a deep commitment to an Islamic faith, making them grateful for life and its possibilities. While a few songs, especially in Hamza Namira's song catalogue, differ somewhat (especially in *Esmaani* where self-pity is at times a theme), this does not change the overall impression of Awakening's productions as being primarily 'faith-driven', sensitive to Islamic norms and theology, and particularly attentive and positive towards Islamic ethics.

Music as a Message: the Instrumentation of Pop-nashids

Islamic legal discourse is not only centred on the lyrics, but also on instrumentation, musical genre and performance. As pointed out above, instrumentation was sparse at the beginning of pop-nashid.[15] All attention was on the male voice. It was common to have several voices singing in unison and, at times, rather sophisticated choir arrangements. The most common accompaniment was different types of hand drums.

These restrictions have had three interesting effects: first, the development of tricks for producing albums with only vocals and percussion; second, the appearance of the market strategy of recording songs and albums in two versions, one with full instrumentation and one vocals-only (that might include percussion); third, the mixed signal that full instrumentation is brave, modern and progressive or the opposite: depraved, corrupt and unauthentic.

As has been stressed earlier, Awakening's music complies with music industry norms of how to produce music – for example, cutting songs that are a few

[15] This section is partly built on research and discussions with musicologist Johannes Frandsen Skjelbo that resulted in an article, Otterbeck and Skjelbo 2020.

minutes long with a centrally placed, repeated chorus – and how to market and stage it. Still, Awakening takes on the expectations of consumer society in a slightly different way compared to many global record companies. When it comes to music arrangement and instrumentation, Awakening has been progressive, allowing for musical creativity from the start; yet the company has also been respectful of conservative Islamic interpretations of instrumentation. Awakening's music productions are manifestations of complex relations between commercial interests, cultural creativity and religious normative principles.

In the production of Sami Yusuf's *al-Mu'allim* (2004), a wide variety of percussion instruments were used, but also digitally processed male voices and choir parts singing in harmonies, creating a rich texture. At the time, few artists making nashids had introduced other tonal/pitched instruments besides percussion, one exception being Raihan. Raihan was known to Sami Yusuf who, as previously mentioned, opened for Raihan when the group toured the UK in 2003 before the release of Sami Yusuf's debut album. Then again, Raihan's most famous songs were vocals-only. Mesut Kurtis' *Salawat* (2004) was produced in a similar fashion but included what appears to be bass lines played on an electric bass on some songs, such as 'No One but Allah'; however, if listened to using advanced studio equipment, it is possible to discern that all musical phrases are actually generated by (male) voices.[16]

It was with Sami Yusuf's *My Ummah* (2005) that new ground was broken. A schooled violinist and pianist, Sami Yusuf played instruments both on the album and in music videos for all to see. The criticism was immediate. Some Muslim venues did not allow the instruments on stage, others did. As shown above, over the following years the tolerance for instruments would increase, even if the criticism has not in any way disappeared.

The same year, *My Ummah* was also issued in a so-called 'percussion version', turning the original release into a 'music version'. Eventually, Awakening even invented icons to put on covers that, for example, can be seen on later editions of this record: the music version icon included part of a stylised keyboard, the percussion version icon a stylised drum. Over time, these were only sparsely used; rather, phrases like 'vocals only' were printed on the covers.

---

[16] Thanks to Johannes Frandsen Skjelbo who took on that laborious task.

Not all albums have been recorded in two versions, there has to be a demand. *Thank You Allah* (2009), Maher Zain's debut, was recorded with full instrumentation and re-recorded as a vocals-only album in 2012 to cater for those who liked the songs but did not want to listen to instruments. The albums are remarkably similar. Musicologist Johannes Frandsen Skjelbo and I have examined one song from the album, 'Always be There' particularly closely. The vocals-only version is clearly built around the same lead vocal track as the original.[17] The guitar and bass tracks have been transcribed and are faithfully reproduced by a male voice, even regarding the sound. The bass voice is compressed and sung with an attack on the consonant 'd', producing a bass guitar-like sound.

As digital recording technology has become more advanced and the experience in vocals-only productions has grown, some vocals-only recordings have become difficult to separate from those including instruments. The title song on Mesut Kurtis' album *Tabassam* (He smiled, 2015) is illustrative and I have also explored this track with Johannes Frandsen Skjelbo. It clearly sounds different in the two versions even though the vocals-only version, as far as we can detect, has been created using exactly the same lead vocal track as the original version. There are no instruments on the vocals-only version, apart from the minimal use of chimes. The vocals-generated chords resemble the synthesiser-generated textures of the original. The use of reverb and delay produces percussive effects that replace the percussion instruments and rhythm guitars.[18] The bass notes are so heavily compressed and filtered that it is close to impossible to discern the source of the sounds being made. They sound very much like a bass guitar or a bass synthesiser, with the attack from the consonant 'd' being the sole indicator that the notes originate in the human voice, which is the claim. The playing style of the bass parts is closely reproduced by the male voice (Otterbeck and Skjelbo 2020).

Taking the vocals-only claim seriously (as one should), the Mesut Kurtis album is an example of what can be seen as quite extensive pragmatism. It does not matter that the album sounds as if instruments are being used;

---

[17] The two tracks can be played simultaneously without ever getting out of sync. The vocals-only version fades a bit more quickly.
[18] This effect is clearly audible at 3:10 to 3:25.

what is important is that musical instruments are not included. The claim that the CD is vocals-only is, more than anything else, substantiated by the listeners trusting the artists and producers. The issue has been addressed in Muslim discussions on-line, exposing a wide variety of attitudes. As might be expected, the most restrictive of these argues that if music sounds like it contains an instrument it is forbidden, while the more lenient claims that as long as only the voice is used, and used for the right ends, the music is allowable. Of course, an increasingly prevalent and more liberal attitude is to allow instruments.

The issue about instruments, not least guitars, affects live performances. Over time the tolerance for instruments on stage at Islamic conferences has increased. It leads to strange situations, however. It is not uncommon that artists are contracted to sing playback to a track containing musical instruments; that is, the audience can hear the instruments but they are not played on stage. Obviously, such requests are compromises directed at trying to navigate a changing world rather than clear theological positions. In autumn 2014, Wassim Malak and Mesut Kurtis told me about an incident earlier that year when Mesut Kurtis had been contracted to sing at an Islamic conference in Canada. Once there, he was asked to sing without music, not even playback. After he protested about this, the arrangers had Mesut Kurtis sit down with a sheikh who, it was hoped, would convince him of the necessity of not including the music. As Mesut Kurtis is really well read on the issue it ended with his convincing the sheikh to compromise: the audience should be informed that the concert would include recorded musical instruments and then be given a choice to stay or leave. According to Mesut Kurtis only three left.

In 2014 Raef told me that, a number of years earlier, he had been asked to perform at an Islamic gathering, but without guitar. He insisted that the guitar was essential for his performance, and the arranger suggested that the guitar could be covered by a screen. Raef refused to play and offered a recording of the music instead. We laughed a lot about it so I guess the discussion stuck in Raef's mind. Late in November 2018, I received an email from Raef saying that these situations were not entirely of the past in the US, quoting a recent email he had received about a concert request: 'as a reminder we do not want you holding the guitar while singing as agreed in the contract. Music playing as a background track is fine.'

Those who are responsible sometimes worry about doing the right thing and about reactions to staging musical acts, but audiences are generally immersed in contemporary culture and could not care less. I have discussed these issues with several people who work as volunteers at concerts. A minority has expressed doubts about the form the music has taken lately (with full-blown concerts) but still attend, legitimating their presence by referring to the concerts being for a good cause. The vast majority, however, tend to claim that music is a debated topic and, as there are a variety of opinions, they have the right to prefer an interpretation that allows music and musical instruments.

Attitudes are also very different in different regions and it must be remembered that Awakening musicians tour globally. Raef mentioned (in 2014) that the audience in Malaysia generally dance uninhibitedly, and Wassim Malak (also in 2014) described partying and dancing audiences in West Africa, saying I should join them for a 'real' concert. I have had to settle for watching them on social media but I understand what they are talking about. At these places there are no guards trying to control the crowd or asking people to sit down, which I experienced on tour in 2014, although not in 2017. Many in the audience stand up, dance and sway, and generally enjoy the music, men as well as women.

There was also a marked shift in the attitudes to instrumental performance on stage between the tours with Awakening artists in 2014 and 2017. In 2014, the whole focus was on performing the song, very little on the musicians, but during the 2017 tour, Maher Zain gave space to the guitarist and the violinist, letting them show off. I do not want to push the interpretation that this was due to a change in perceptions; it might as well be that the musicians were better rehearsed and more comfortable on stage during the second tour, but I would like to point out that my experience was that audiences were also more relaxed and spontaneous during the second tour. As pop-nashid and Islamic pop become more integrated and concerts become more common, an unwritten contract between artists and crowd develops; however, this contract is still under negotiation, as we shall see later.

The Modern Sounds of Pop-nashids and Islamic Pop

The new Islamic music genres differ significantly from the older nashid genre through their costly production and commercial marketing, with records, concerts, music videos and promotional material. While classical nashid usually consists of a man singing very ornately according to classical Arab (or other local) modes, pop-nashid and Islamic pop often borrow from contemporary Arab or Turkish pop and various globally spread versions of pop music such as soul, reggae and R&B, not least in terms of arrangements. Maher Zain points out that he often spontaneously composes in *maqam bayyati* (TRTWorld 2016). The *maqam bayyati* is immensely popular in Turkish and Arabic pop. Yet, just as often, Maher Zain composes without the Arab modes, conjuring up melodies similar to contemporary US or European pop and R&B.

Frequently, production cleverly combines conventions from different genres. For example, Maher Zain's 'Medina' (2016) starts with a child's voice singing a simple melody, then adds a Red Hot Chilli Peppers-inspired guitar figure, in both production style and melody. Maher Zain's voice is added, slightly affected by autotune, followed by a pop-reggae melody for the refrain. At 2:11, the famous traditional nashid 'Tala'a al-Badru 'Alayna' is interfolded for fifty seconds in the production, blending in an Arab pop soundscape. The production is rich and includes instruments making short phrases only to immediately disappear again. It sounds very contemporary.

Music signals time. When Neil Young made *Trans* (1982), the production made use of the latest in synthesisers and other new electronic equipment and it probably sounded very advanced at the time (even though it received bad reviews). Now it is more out-dated production-wise than any of his earlier albums due to the dated technologies used. On more than one occasion, the Awakening founders have stressed that they wish to contemporise and professionalise Islamic media production, slighting earlier products for being low quality. The ambition has been to provide modern Muslims with appealing soundtracks to their lives. It is clear from Awakening's own production that even though the goal has been the same since the start, with experience and means, a higher quality has ensued.

Many production fads affecting the general recording industry are used in the arrangements and productions of Awakening's music. This is in no way strange. It is not only the Awakening artists that act as musicians, technicians, mixers, producers and arrangers on the recordings, even though both Maher Zain and Hamza Namira, in particular, are skilled at arranging and producing. The music is not made in a cultural vacuum, but rather the opposite – as an ongoing development in the global recording industry. For example, American Tom Coyne, who has won a number of awards including seven Grammys, mastered Maher Zain's *One* (2016). The same year as he worked with *One*, he also mastered music by Bruno Mars, De La Soul, Ariana Grande, Lady Gaga and Tokio Hotel, among others. Over time he has worked with New Kids on the Block, Adele, Taylor Swift, One Direction, Mary J. Blige, Beyoncé, Britney Spears, George Michael, Amy Winehouse and, going back in time to the late 1970s and early 1980s, with James Brown, Kool & the Gang and A Flock of Seagulls, among others.

The mixing of the *One* album was done by Swede Niklas Flykt, also a very experienced studio technician, who is credited on numerous records, among them songs by Robyn and Britney Spears. The recording and the engineering of the *One* songs involved fourteen different studios: Maher Zain's private studio, Mohito Studios, Atlantis Studios, Rixmix Studio, Soundtrade Studio (all in Stockholm), Jazzworx Studios in Johannesburg, Studio EmREC, RMS Marsandiz Studio and MC Studios in Istanbul, Music Airlines Studio in Casablanca, Wah Wah Studios in Mumbai, S.U. Studios in Lahore, G Studio in Cairo and Livingston Studios in London. In all of them, studio engineers, technicians, studio musicians and others were creatively involved in the tracks, giving them their final form before presenting them to the market. This can be compared to the first record by Sami Yusuf, which was recorded in one studio and engineered in a number of unnamed studios, with very few people involved. It is interesting that so many Awakening recordings have, in one form or another, connections with Sweden, being recorded, mastered, mixed or in other ways affected by environments that also have a part in numerous mainstream music hits – sometimes referred to as the Swedish music wonder or the Swedish hit factory.

The electric guitar presents a special case in recordings. According to Sharif Banna, there are different opinions within Awakening about the distorted electric guitar. Some artists have strong opinions about not wanting to record with distorted guitars. Neither Mesut Kurtis nor Maher Zain record, to date, with distorted guitars. On the other hand, Hamza Namira quite regularly used distorted guitar sounds, and Raef at times uses a somewhat distorted rhythm guitar sound: on a couple of songs on his debut album from 2014, for example, both arranged by Swedish musician and studio technician Oliver Börnfelt:[19] 'The Path', 'Mawlaya' and 'Call on Him'. Raef's latest album, *Mercy* (2019), which is recorded in Nashville, features a lot of distorted guitar sounds. The last Awakening release in 2018 was a live album with Harris J called *Live in Concert*. It features a lot of distorted electric guitar and a band that at times sounds like a rock band. It appears to be the association with rock music that makes singers like Mesut Kurtis and Maher Zain refrain from the distorted electric guitar, while guitarists like Hamza Namira and Raef simply have a different relationship to the sound.

Can Music Sound Islamic?

What does this question even mean? I have been struggling with it. Most people who listen to Christian pop, like Hill Song, or Christian rock from the 1970s and 1980s would probably say that the music has, and had, a specific sound to it. But there is Christian pop and rock that sounds just like any other music; it is only discernible as such due to the lyrics. Listen, for example, to Krystal Meyers, who was a Christian pop punk singer in the USA.

Islamic sounds are possible to describe if concentrating on the prototypical sounds, those that stand as typical representative sounds, metonyms if you wish, of the plethora of possible Islamic sounds, such as the call to prayer. Certain melodies and lyrics are associated with beloved, well-established nashids and might, especially to Muslims, carry a quality of Islam, but what else? The musical styles used by the artists tap into all kinds of pop music, local styles as well as global, shared with non-Islamic expressions. Because this study does not examine how the music is received by audiences, as of now I cannot answer this question, but I can speculate. As pop-nashids and Islamic pop become part of listeners' experience and intertwined with their lives, they will acquire an aura of Islamicness. As already pointed out, some songs by Raef and Maher Zain are now played at weddings; other songs are about Ramadan or dreaming of going to Medina. Religious emotions will be tied, by individuals,

---

[19] For some reason his surname is frequently misspelt on Awakening records (Björnfelt). Börnfelt has work with several different Awakening records since he first got in contact with the company when playing a part in Asha Khan's 2008 record for Awakening (online conversation with Börnfelt, 25 April 2020).

to songs and these will be consecrated as Islamic in the process (see Riis and Woodhead 2010). Not all songs with the pretention to become special will be embraced, but some will, and those will sound Islamic to a generation of listeners. Johannes Frandsen Skjelbo and I have speculated that, in the future, artists who have some songs in their repertoire that are more outspokenly connecting to Islam will record them vocals-only while other songs will be fully orchestrated, making the vocals-only stick out production-wise and thus sound-wise, thereby signalling the Islamic dimension; we do not have any proof of this, naturally, I am merely sharing a thought (Otterbeck and Skjelbo 2020).

When discussing the nature of 'Islamic music' on his webpage, Sami Yusuf takes a stand against those who approve of 'any sort of music as long as it is branded "Halal", as if Islamic phrases can simply be copy-pasted over the music of the day, whatever its form'.[20] Instead he assumes a rather conservative position, claiming that to be considered 'Islamic music', the sounds and expressions will have to relate to the numerous different heritages that have grown organically through history in Muslim contexts and be 'fully conscious of its Origin, Truth, the One and only Reality, Allah'. In a particularly harsh paragraph, he states:

Young Muslims of today need to have humility when entering this field if they are truly eager to call their music 'Islamic'. They must understand that the sincere apprenticeship to our traditions and the assimilation of their spirit must come before innovation and da'wah (proselytising), no matter how good the intentions may be. Truth must never be mixed with error, for all this will do is create the tribulations of fitnah [chaos] and confusion. Being a 'Halal' 'alternative' to the latest pop sensation does not qualify music as being Islamic. This trend of distorting our traditions to suit the passing fancies of the times can only lead to a loss of not only what has been passed down to us but also our sense of who we really are.

---

[20] https://samiyusufofficial.com/what-is-islamic-music-by-sami-yusuf/, written in 2015 (last accessed 2 December 2018).

Although Sami Yusuf only stresses music as sound three times in the article, it is obviously the sound and form of 'halal' pop – rather than its instrumentation, for example – that disturbs him. The sound does not connect to tradition, and this discontinuity confuses rather than elevates. Heritage – implying identity and spiritual continuity – is disrupted, according to him. As we shall learn below, the CEO of Awakening, Sharif Banna, more or less shares Sami Yusuf's critique, but not his solution.

As consumer culture ideas about music become more and more intertwined due to technical developments and the blending of musical taste cultures, the discernible sound ideals once established through political nashid recordings (see Chapter 4) are no longer dominant; rather, the sound that makes music Islamic will have to be more specifically tied to the aura of specific songs. Sami Yusuf stresses the importance of heritage and continuity, Awakening of contemporaneity – at times involving Muslim heritage, at times not.

6

PERFORMING AN ETHICAL ISLAMIC MASCULINITY

Much of the mainstream's celebrity-obsession also seems to be evident in the Islamic cultural industry – apart from the 'Islamic' lyrics. Art continues to operate in the spiritually bankrupt and commercialised environment of modern hedonistic lifestyles. Art, in the Islamic ethos, is a spiritual experience, not one of self-gratification or mere entertainment. Lyrics changed to reflect direct Islamic teachings may be a halal endeavour but can remaining subservient to a dominant culture which is driven by an obsession with fame, materialism and consumerism, be considered Islamic? *Awakening* endeavours to tackle this head-on, creating a new cultural paradigm.

Sharif Banna in *the Awakening book*, p. 45

In the quotation above, included in *the Awakening book* over which Sharif Banna had complete control, he sounds like one of the religious scholars who are sceptical of the arts in general, or like Sami Yusuf earlier, apart from in the last sentence. To create 'a new cultural paradigm' is, however, a responsibility not to be undertaken lightly. In another context, Sharif Banna writes:

I would contend that the term 'Islamic' has both legal and ethical dimensions. If it is *permissible* in law, then it is 'halal' or 'mubah' [permitted] and *if it is validated by the ethical standards of Islam, only then does it become 'Islamic'.* Legislation and ethics are two sides of the same coin and should depend on each other as an integrated whole. Traditionally, this distinction did not exist and thus the master jurist Imam Abu Hanifa defined *fiqh* [Islamic jurisprudence] itself as 'knowledge of the responsibilities and liabilities of one's self.' This definition encompasses both the legal and ethical facets. (al-Banna 2016)

Sharif Banna proposes that understanding ethics is a way forward for Islamic thinking. By suggesting that ethics and *fiqh* are dependent on each other, thereby not giving *fiqh* primacy, an important component is added to Islamic thinking, but also a key provided to how to understand what Awakening means by 'faith-driven' and 'inspired by faith'.

This chapter aims to discuss the difficulties of being a media company wanting to come across as faith-driven in a consumer-culture market. How to gain credibility and be perceived as authentic and ethically sound? This steers the discussion towards masculinity, because gender is at the heart of the matter. Awakening artists and founders appear to be very conscious of the problem of fame and appearance and repeatedly return to it in conversations and texts. A telling quotation from Bara Kherigi goes, 'We give them [the artists] training, work on performance, on their speech, on their image' (*the Awakening book*, p. 56). The very idea that the artists need to be schooled echoes two things: Islamic notions of nurturing the ethical self and the method used by Motown founder Berry Gordy Jr to train his skilled artists to 'act as royalty', although many of them came from the poor projects of industrial Detroit. By educating them in how to dress and behave, Motown initiated a changed view of African-American artists. While I can only speculate about the influence of the latter (having publishing the hunch about the parallel to Motown in *the Awakening book* (Otterbeck 2014a) and thus possibly affecting my informants' understanding), the first aspect, the ethical self, is something crucial to this study.

It is important to stress the complex relationship between purposeful art and mass-mediated consumer culture. To be able to package and market music as halal, nashids, Islamic, faith-driven or the like, artists cannot simply avoid sensitive subjects like sexuality and drugs in lyrics, or only take into consideration the instrumentation of music, its sound or its relation to heritage and contemporary soundscape trends; they must also set good examples and, for example, take part in charity events and perform at Islamic gatherings. In short, they need to cultivate and signal an Islamic ethical self (Hirschkind 2006a, 2006b; Mahmood 2005), while making a profit.

When Michel Foucault (1990a: 26) comments on morality and the self, he highlights 'the manner in which one ought to form oneself as an ethical subject acting in reference to the prescriptive elements that make up the code'. Codes of conduct are always related to subjectivation. In relation to pop-nashid and Islamic pop, the art performed by the artists has to be an enunciation of 'the truth' in one form or another, while the artists themselves must abide by the importance of the ethical code (i.e. Islam, although, of course, narrowed down to the particular interpretation of Islam in question), and provide confirmation of their adherence to 'the code' (Foucault 1990b). Artists engaged in different new forms of popular Islamic music seem to build their trustworthiness by cultivating an ethical self, a persona which is consumed by their audience. Judging from their commentaries (in social media, in conversations with me), fans claim that they take inspiration from the Awakening artists to strive after 'an ever more complete mastery of the self', to use Foucault's words (1990a: 38), increasing the pressure on the artists to behave in a morally irreproachable manner because of their being possible role models. Thus, the ethical selves are not only shaped in relation to a narrow understanding of individual morals, behaviour and character, but also in terms of what can be considered the public good. At the same time, overall aesthetic trends in films, music videos and marketing frame the aesthetics of the songs, promotional material and music videos provided to market artists. Artists take on this challenge in different ways. While Maher Zain is very comfortable with the responsibility of being a role model, Raef does not immediately define himself as such, even though aware of the need to be conscious about how he presents himself and with what he engages (cf. Jouili 2015: 18).

Criticising Saba Mahmood's theorisation and research of ethical selves, Samuli Schielke (2009, 2015) stresses the importance of not only looking at attempts to cultivate an ethical self, but also at ambivalences in the process, at outright failures or the compartmentalisation in time and space of the cultivation of piety. When marketing and staging ethical artistic personas, the situation is somewhat different from honing personal piety. One of the reasons for going on tour with Awakening artists was to see if the rather homogeneous image in the medialised products was also lived practice.

The restrictions put on female bodies (in performance or not) are well researched in the social sciences and human arts, and also in relation to Islam (Mahmood 2005; Weintraub 2008; van Wichelen 2012), but consumer culture discourses together with religious agendas for the performing male body are not as well scrutinised. In relation to Islamic political movement organisations, some academics, notably Asef Bayat (2007) and Karin van Nieuwkerk (2011), have observed that such groups support cultural politics that are restrictive and negative about 'fun' and relaxed leisure activities, if not downright condemnatory. Both note that this includes an ordering of bodily movements and the idea that dancing is highly problematic and should be avoided; the spontaneous is particularly problematic as this is not controlled, while some controlled pleasures are allowed. However, the proponents of *al-wasatiyya* are much more inclined to allow fun, albeit warning against nihilism and always counselling moderation. Fun, accordingly, should be channelled through the aesthetics of ethical Islam and can be – and should be – contemporary. As pointed out above, some argue about the role of heritage in regard to music.

As a specialist in the anthropology of dance, van Nieuwkerk points out that the performing body on stage tends to be sexualised, which is perceived as a problem, 'and for that reason the body must be neutralized or desexualized' (2011: 20f).[1] In regard to male performers in Egypt within the Islamic entertainment business, she points out that not only female but also 'male singers must perform the "art of no seduction"'. Male bodies, she suggests, should refrain from moving too much while singing and avoid imitating 'feminine' movements, adding, 'Abundant swaying on stage can tip the balance from religion to pop' (2011: 21). Thus, male artists must engage in 'ethical self-making in accordance with religious ideologies' (van Nieuwkerk 2011: 18). The spontaneous must be curbed and limits on the ethical presentation of the artist's persona must be taught and displayed. Thus, the performance of masculinity, and the accompanying, inescapably intertwined male body (Connell 1995) are of great interest if we are to understand the male artistry of a religiously motivated ethical self.

Further, the halal consumption ethos (or, as it is sometimes referred to, market Islam) is an idea far wider than music, the content and performance of songs and the individual conduct and general persona of the artists. It has the

---

[1] Just like music, the legality of dance is a topic of discussion in Islamic doctrinal history (Alagha 2014; Michot 1991; Shehadi 1995).

potential to include moral and ethical issues involving the economic structure and marketing strategies of Awakening: where, with whom and in what context is the company seen? In fact, moral and ethical discussions originally stemming from discussions outside Islamic discourse, like fair trade, human rights and environmental issues, are now part of Islamic ethical discourses taken seriously by Muslim consumers (Janmohamed 2016; *State of Global Islamic Economy Report 2019/20*). The Awakening founders are well aware of their company being a high-profile, highly public entity and have the ambition to internalise such values in their business. In fact, Sharif Banna's PhD thesis includes a case study on Islamic minority jurisprudence and ecology.

Normative Masculinity

It would be tremendously naive (and entirely erroneous) to assume the existence of a single Islamic masculinity running through 1,400 years of Islamic interpretations, anchored in the minds of Muslims, at any given place. Masculinity is constructed in time and space as an ongoing, never ending, plural project, although certain features do appear with a high frequency due to, for example, a common discursive tradition, economic conditions and patriarchal contexts (Bourdieu 2001). However, in normative literature certain advice about manliness cut across centuries. In Sunni twentieth century *'ilm al-akhlaq* (the knowledge of the character) literature, clear character models are promoted, giving Muslim men (and women) unambiguous advice on all matters from personal hygiene to how to relate to other people. A man is heterosexual, preferably married, a father, has means and shares with the needy. He is mild-mannered, just, honest, polite, tidy and clean, and active and serious in his religiosity. Further, he is ready to take a stance on behalf of his community – morally, economically and, if necessary, by force. A man is not greedy, selfish, smallminded or prone to gossip and, of course, he is not the opposite of the already mentioned qualities. But to a growing extent, the ideology of personality celebrated in societies marked by both individualisation and individuation is prompting active Muslims to live and accept a diversity of lifestyles as valid and possible. In a pluralist and individualist world, how does a man dress then? How does he relate to other genders, adherents of other religions, to political powers, to music?

In literature published by Awakening, one clearly finds a preference for the mild-mannered and tidy man who is serious about his religion, for example in Abu Ghuddah's ([2001] 2011b) *Islamic Manners*. Is this masculinity also enacted in Awakening media? In *the Awakening book*, one can read the following:

> Then we brainstormed different characters with Bara and Maher. They chose the idea of having Maher in the United States, conveying a modern and trendy individual who is spreading love and happiness to the different characters in the video. (Director Hamzah Jamjoom in *the Awakening book*, p. 112)

Here the director is discussing the widely viewed music video 'Ya Nabi Salam Alayka' (Oh Prophet, peace be upon you, 2011), shot at different locations in Chicago, in which Maher Zain walks around offering people handwritten letters containing the Arabic words '*salla 'ala l-habib*' (blessings upon the beloved, i.e. the Prophet Muhammad). As with a number of other Awakening songs, it is composed in relation to a celebration, in this case *mawlid al-nabi*, the celebration of the birth of Muhammad. In the music video, Maher Zain is casually dressed, wears a *tasbih*, an Islamic rosary, as a necklace, and has the broadest of smiles. Hamzah Jamjoom had insisted that he wanted to show Maher Zain as happy and untroubled, according to an interview I had with Maher Zain in 2014. Maher Zain hugs male recipients, or shakes their hands, but not female ones, he ruffles the hair of a child. He seeks out Muslims from all over Chicago, of different ethnicities, engaged in various professions, and gives them this reminder of Muhammad, and as each one opens the envelope a spark takes to the sky. Eventually, an astronaut looking down at Earth sees all the sparks and smiles. The pace of the video is rather slow, giving room for the different characters to express their happiness.

The song 'Salam Alaikum' (2015) by Harris J has a similar music video. Again, the pace is slow, people are of different ethnicities. Harris J, in his mid-teens at the time, is casually dressed in a bluish knit cap, red jacket, beige trousers, a blue shirt and red sneakers. He smiles throughout, shaking hands with male but not female friends. In the children's book version of the song (yes, there is one), *Salam Alaikum: A Message of Peace* (2017) by Harris J and US-based illustrator Ward Jenkins, that kind of cross-gender contact is not avoided. Why this is so, I simply do not know.

In many ways, these two music videos are typical in terms of topic and positive message, the pace, the relations between people, the ethnic composition of characters and the beauty of the scenery. They are also typical in that they feature a planned ethical masculinity, not merely a lived one, engaged in a 'discursive intervention' (Asad 1993: 164), thus endeavouring to challenge powerful discourses (both Muslim and non-Muslim) about Muslim masculinity.

In order to develop the argument about masculinity, I first discuss Awakening's many music videos and hundreds of live clips (on YouTube) which I have studied, featuring artists signed to the company. Up until around 2014, there is a discernible pattern that then changes. My analysis is that this has to do with the break-through of Instagram and Twitter which allow and enable – in fact, demand – a different way of presenting the artists. I tried out this division on Sharif Banna in our final interview, and even though we could not pin-point the exact time, he agreed that the change I am positing had taken place.

The Serious, Loving Man: 2003–14

From 2003 until 2014, it is possible to discern a somewhat shared aesthetic.[2] It is possible to read the Awakening artists' ethical selves, songs and performances as anti-texts to such consumer-culture pop that sells itself by means of sexuality, provocation, profanities, party lifestyles and so on, but also as a new, modern, male Muslimness. What follows contains descriptions and discussions of how the artists come across in music videos, live performances, promotional material and, to a degree, through televised interviews. Music videos are a special format in terms of how the artists are presented. While the persona generally stays the same in the lyrics, the artists play roles in the narratives of the music videos. As many people today 'listen to music by looking' at the music videos (Arnold *et al.* 2017: 5), these images become part and parcel of experiencing the song.

---

[2] The one exception being Hussein Zahawy who presents himself as a Kurdish artist, at times dressed in traditional Kurdish clothing. Hussein Zahawy was not part of the pop-nashid or Islamic pop scene, and was never contracted to Awakening, and is henceforth left out of the description.

Dress

The male Awakening performers were rarely shown wearing typical Islamic garb, although there were a few occasions when the artists flirted with traditional clothing, as in the music video to 'Burdah' (2007) by Mesut Kurtis, and when Maher Zain wore a prayer cap in the music video to 'For the Rest of My Life' (at 1:23). Rather, dress was, to paraphrase Najmabadi (1991: 49) when discussing Iranian females in modernity, 'modern, yet modest'. In music videos, but also live, the preferred outfits were sweaters, scarves, hats and caps, trousers, shirts, jackets, at times suits. Favoured colours were black, white, brown, green, grey, blue and orange – preferably colours in earth tones. The artists were most often not clean-shaven, but rather had a trendy stubble. Performers displayed a casual, fashionable modernity.

Clothes were also motivated by the various roles the artists played in different music videos. For example, in 'Hasbi Rabbi' (My lord is sufficient for me, 2005), Sami Yusuf starts in a dark suit, pinkish tie, white, discreetly checked shirt and black leather shoes in central London on his way to the office where he has a meeting; then suddenly he appears in central Istanbul in a reddish knitted sweater, greyish trousers and brown leather shoes with a violin case over his shoulder on his way to a rehearsal, only to be found in Agra teaching children and then playing games with them in the vicinity of the Taj Mahal. Here he either wears all white, or a blue shirt with white trousers and grey suede shoes, all in a modern north-Indian style with his Nehru-collar shirt hanging loosely, not tucked in at the waist. Finally, he ends up in Cairo taking the bus from Tahrir Square to Khan al-Khalili where he is seen engaging in the traditional craft of woodcarving dressed in beige trousers and a yellowish, checked, short-sleeve shirt with a green and red pattern to it, wearing sandals. He never wears a hat or cap. Regardless of the clothing, he comes across as comfortable and modern.

A similar music video, but with another twist, is made to Mesut Kurtis' 'Rouhi Fidak' (My soul, I would sacrifice for you, 2014). It starts with Mesut Kurtis heading a meeting in dark suit, black tie and a white shirt. Throughout the encounter he looks troubled, finally simply walking out, to the astonishment of the others. Towards the end of his troubled day, he seeks the peace and quiet of solidary prayer at night in the beautiful, modernist Yeşil Vadi mosque in Istanbul. Finally, he steps out transformed, now barefoot and dressed in white clothes, greeting the dawn on a sandy beach. All through, the lyrics praise Muhammad as the guide and the balm of the soul, and the singer expresses his longing for his beloved prophet.

Dress styles changed somewhat over time at live performances. In the beginning of Maher Zain's career, when he was singing playback, alone on stage at Islamic conferences, he would often be dressed in a dark suit and white shirt, after a while adding a cap. As he grew more famous and recognised from his music videos, he shifted to a more casual dress code in line with the music videos. When I discussed this with Maher Zain in 2017, he pointed out that there was also another pattern and that was the degree of formality at the concert. If it was a special occasion with dignitaries he dressed more formally, and at more everyday concerts he had dressed quite casually from early on. Looking into live clips from Sami Yusuf concerts this could very well be a pattern but it is difficult to substantiate further.

Clothes were, at times, also negotiated in the green room, backstage. During one of the tours in which I took part, a thin jacket with rather large roses on it caused polite discussion, although it was never clear to me whether the bottom line was that it was 'too girlie' or if there was another objection. One rather new artist was advised not to wear it but he persisted and I was drawn into the discussion. I could not help but comment that the rose is a symbol of Muhammad, not least under the Ottoman Empire (Gruber 2014), which immediately drew Mesut Kurtis into the conversation as he has a great interest in the Ottoman era. Eventually the artist took to the stage wearing the jacket and nothing more was said on the matter, at least not in my presence.

The presentation of the self through dress is important. In the field of nashid artistry, traditional or modernised Islamic dress, signalling the Islamic belonging of the artist, is very common. Likewise, the pioneers of pop-nashid all chose to signal an Islamic belonging through their dress, albeit in different ways. For example, Zain Bhikha often only used a kufi or prayer cap as an identifier while Dawud Wharnsby often wore clothes in accordance with Pakistani traditional male garb; he has a close affinity with Pakistan through his wife. As pointed out above, this was not the case at all among the Awakening artists who rarely used Islamic dress in music videos although cultural dress styles following local Muslim customs might feature, worn by the music videos' actors.

The veil often features in the style initiated by the so-called Turkish *tesettür* (covered) fashion industry, but not all female characters are veiled. If inspiration is taken from Muslim lifestyle magazines such as *Emel, Muslim Girl, Sisters, Azizah*, I cannot tell, but these magazines started to flourish at the same time as the new Islamic music genres started to produce music videos and the magazines were aware of what was going on (Lewis 2015). For example, British *Emel* has had cover images of Native Deen (January/February 2004), Yusuf Islam (January/February 2005), Kareem Salama (July 2009), Zain Bhikha (June 2010) and Maher Zain (July 2011), all mentioned in this book. The magazines are in a captivating way both descriptive and proscriptive. For example, Ausma Khan, editor of Canadian *Muslim Girl*, consciously tries to 'represent as many different girls as possible and all their different approaches to faith' in the magazine, picking up on, but also spreading, knowledge about ongoing trends (Khan quoted in Lewis 2015: 125). Reina Lewis notes that ethics are an aspect of the magazines, at times formulated as 'ethical consumerism' and 'ethical perspectives' (Lewis 2015: 132). In the case of both fashion and music, Islam can be seen as the transformer of the given consumer-culture genres. When arguing for the authenticity of this transformation and when marketing the products, ethics are important.

The Body in Motion

In directed music videos, the artists often moved slowly. They walked slowly and they made gestures slowly. They changed their body posture slowly when singing a particularly passionate part of the lyrics, raising their face slightly upwards and closing their eyelids slightly. The directors are careful not to cut up the music videos by changing angles all the time as is so popular in general music videos, although there are a few exceptions like Sami Yusuf's 'Hasbi Rabbi' (2005). Moving in time with the music was rare and it was quite common for artists to sing sitting on a chair or in an armchair, making movement unnecessary. Awakening also released official music videos featuring a nice photograph of the artist with the lyrics running as subtitles throughout the song, in a way accentuating the motionlessness of the artists, despite its being primarily a cheap way to offer a music video to those who listen to music through social media sites.

Dance was out of the question. No one danced in music videos, regardless of how rhythmical the music was, not the artists, nor any actors. There were not even any dancelike moves. As mentioned in the beginning, Awakening emerged around the time that a public dispute about music videos was raging in Egypt, a row that motivated Yusuf al-Qaradawi to author a book on the jurisprudence of entertainment and recreation (*Fiqh al-Lahw wa-l-Tarawih*, 2005). In it, al-Qaradawi approves of gender-segregated folk dancing but takes a clear stance against, in particular, female (semi) nudity, 'Oriental (belly) dancing' and the erotic dancing in music videos (Kubala 2010: 193). Even though Awakening artists are not likely to aspire to anything of the sort, dancing in itself in music videos was problematic for anyone wanting to come across as authentically Islamic. In fact, in the Egyptian controversy on music videos, Sami Yusuf's debut video 'al-Mu'allim' was hailed as resistance to those 'insulting art', according to Patricia Kubala (2010: 210); that video in particular started a new trend.

In clips from live performances during this period, a similar pattern emerges. Even though artists did encourage the audience to clap in time, they seldom performed other bodily movements in time with the music apart from facial expressions (of passion) and the frequent, slow, lifting of hands or the touching of the artist's heart to stress phrases. Legs, feet and pelvis seldom marked the beat of the songs, not even when songs were rhythmical; occasionally Maher Zain might discreetly tap his foot, as did Mesut Kurtis, while Raef, when playing the guitar, swayed a bit in time with the music.

When following Awakening on tour in 2014, I noticed that Maher Zain in particular had adopted some tricks to fill the stage with his presence without resorting to dancing. For example, he would throw the microphone between his hands, thereby creating unexpected movement. Further, he would twitch his shoulders and at times use his arms to mark the rhythm indirectly, but the prime purpose, in my interpretation, was to fill out the stage. Another device of his was to have a high chair on stage. It allowed him a varied scene presence and made it natural not to move about too much.

The musicians were another issue though. Playing the bass rhythmically almost demands that you move in time and my experience is that a good drummer 'dances' the drums, not only bangs them. When discussing movements on stage with tour manager Wassim Malak in 2014, our conversation was overheard by the bass player. 'Aren't we allowed to move on stage?' he said, quite concerned. Wassim Malak immediately turned to him and affirmed that he was allowed to move. More people joined in and I could tell I had unintentionally put Wassim Malak in a tight spot. Not all live musicians were Muslims; they were contracted because they were good. The issue had obviously been noted by the non-Muslims, but not aired before. Eventually discussions died down, but a consensus had been reached that moving about was of course allowed but explicit dancing would be inappropriate. These guidelines were never made explicit to non-Muslim musicians and when I discussed this with another musician performing live with Awakening, he mentioned he had discovered them for himself pretty quickly, without anyone having to tell him.

Male Handsomeness

The performers have always been allowed to look handsome and be suave in front of the audience. Or has this been required of them? Male handsomeness was something that was developed particularly in music videos in which singers, while enacting Islamic ethics (being loving sons and kind to others), look handsome, if not boy-bandish cute. The last expression alludes to a quotation from Lena Khan, independent filmmaker from the USA who directed the music video to Maher Zain's 'For the Rest of My Life'. In it, Maher Zain is moving about in 'his' well-to-do home, tidying, doing the laundry, cooking and, yes, praying. Finally, when the work is done, he sits in an armchair, with a broad smile, all dressed for a wedding. When asking Lena Khan how she dealt with the fact that Maher Zain looked very handsome in front of the camera, she provided an elaborate answer:

> Whether out loud or just inferred, that topic came up often. There is a balance we had to strike: Maher isn't dressed 'handsomely' in order to appeal to women. He is dressed as he would like to be. At the end of the day, he is a pop artist and has his own style. He is also a younger man, and is dressed modern and 'cool'. As long as Maher maintained his modesty and we helped him do this, I believe Awakening was okay with this. That said, we had to be

more careful in a video like 'For the Rest of My Life'. Some shots were considered 'too much', and might elicit too much of a reaction from the female audience, so we cut them. If some shots felt too much like a boy band video, we cut them.[3]

The practice of 'the art of no seduction', as van Nieuwkerk nicknamed it, is counter-intuitive to modern celebrity culture where exposure and teasing have been keys in a game played ever since modern consumer culture emerged with the launching of mass media. For example, Cashmore (2014: 3) argues that as long as a celebrity evokes strong emotions, 'she remains in business' even if hated or despised. Celebrities only need to fear and avoid indifference.[4] In a religious setting, this general rule of celebrity culture does not hold true. Of course, religious celebrities need to arouse strong emotions and avoid indifference, but not by any possible means. A scandal involving an Awakening artist would not be taken lightly and would most likely be devastating, as the persona of an Awakening artist is dependent on Islamic ethics. The 'imagined intimacy' (Morgan 2011: 99) that fans are allowed to develop with Awakening artists relies on an ethical contract that is only binding to the artists, as the fans consumption and fantasies are a more private matter, not yet researched (I point this out, trying to entice MA and PhD students to do just this and then share their results with me). Fans may allow themselves to flirt and scream out loud when part of an audience, and send gifts and letters, but it would be highly inappropriate and unexpected if any of the artists were to relate to one of the fans in a comparable way.

In a thought-provoking article about Zionist leaders in the US, Berkowitz (2002) focuses on their male handsomeness and masculinity, presenting the thesis that this was of importance to both male and female spectators and followers. The handsomeness and masculinity of the leaders refuted and contrasted the stereotypical image of the ugly, less-than-manly Jew. I propose that Awakening's artists fill a similar position. Their mild-mannered appearance, handsome faces and downplayed bodily presence provide a model for

---

[3] Lena Khan, email interview, 19 October 2012.

[4] To be fair to Cashmore, difficult to control and destructive scandals are mentioned in her chapter 11.

the modern male Muslim, one to be promoted in contrast to the stereotypical male Islamist who has been invading the public consciousness in Muslim as well as non-Muslim environments in the past decades, with his specific 'anti-Western' dress, long, unkempt beard and angry visage. Parenthetically, the negative stereotype has further led to a reaction among both jihadist and pietist Salafis who, in their own separate ways, seek out a more stylish masculinity (Aidi 2014; Ostovar 2017). The importance of the marketing of masculinity to enforce particular religious interpretations is grossly understudied.

The music videos of Awakening also serve as anti-texts to the music video sexuality so common worldwide and also specifically in the Arab world, Turkey and South East Asia. Yet even if Awakening music videos abide by different rules than normal, the Awakening artists are also handsome men. Being able to engage 'poster boys' like Sami Yusuf or Maher Zain makes the Islamic conference or charity that books their acts and supports them as preferred role models more appealing and attractive as an alternative in the market place of ideas and leisure time activities. Going to an Islamic meeting might actually be fun and up-to-date. Since gender segregation is upheld in many Islamic ritual gatherings, but seldom at Islamic conferences and charity events, these might also function as public places for men and women to meet and socialise across gender borders. With the staged acts come the spectators.

The Female Gaze

In the wake of the success of the Awakening artists, a discussion emerged about the behaviour of female audiences in their appreciation of the artists, their excitement over them and the concert environment. How should the male performers react to a possibly sexualising female gaze? In an interview with three Awakening artists (Maher Zain, Irfan Makki, Mesut Kurtis) on 'Thursday Night Live with Sajid Varda' (spring 2012) on Islam Channel Live, the host posed the question, 'How do you intend to control the screaming sisters?'[5] Maher Zain first responded that it is a marginal phenomenon but then continued to give examples of female fans screaming when they see him or at concerts, and taking pictures of him and themselves. He then concluded

---

[5] www.youtube.com/watch?v=fls_RyWq_uY (last accessed 27 May 2014).

that it makes him uncomfortable. He has even asked audiences (or particularly the female part of it) not to scream, but in a kind, joking manner. I experienced similar occasions myself on tour in 2014: for example, when Maher Zain encouraged the audience in Slough to 'let that energy loose, we are going to enjoy ourselves, in a halal way!' This issue of audience behaviour has been addressed in the media before; in 2006, Yvonne Ridley, journalist and convert to Islam, wrote a confrontational piece on Sami Yusuf's music and performance:

> The reason I am expressing concern is that just a few days ago at a venue in Central London, sisters went wild in the aisles as some form of pop-mania swept through the concert venue. And I'm not just talking about silly, little girls who don't know any better; I am talking about sisters in their 20's, 30's and 40's, who squealed, shouted, swayed and danced. Even the security guys who looked more like pipe cleaners than bulldozers were left looking dazed and confused as they tried to stop hijabi sisters from standing on their chairs. Of course the stage groupies did not help at all as they waved and encouraged the largely female Muslim crowd to 'get up and sing along'. (Ridley 2006a)

Sami Yusuf wrote an eloquent response (2006) marginalising the phenomenon and pointing out that he consults with scholars about music to stay informed of the Islamic perspective so important to him. Ridley replied by pointing to a *Time Magazine* article entitled 'Meet Islam's Biggest Rock Star' (Wise 2006), published with the consent of Sami Yusuf, in which he is portrayed as a rock star that causes a 'Beatle-sized frenzy', and concluded that she really cannot see that she erred in her reasoning (Ridley 2006b).

Regardless of their diverging opinions, something crucial is touched upon here. Both agreed on the nature of inappropriate behaviour (Maher Zain and the TV host also agree). They filled the sisters' behaviour with meaning when contrasting their screams and dancing in public with an ideal of modest, Allah-fearing behaviour. Asef Bayat (2007: 139) claims that Islamist movements have waged a 'battle against fun, playfulness, and diversion', an observation that does not only apply to the Islamist movements but also to many Islamic organisations that have found it difficult to incorporate playfulness and musical performances. This discourse on the appropriate is clearly visible as a reference in the discussions related above.

Yet to the artists and the audience, other references are also close at hand: for example, the representations of how to behave at concerts disseminated through advertisements, movies, YouTube clips, music videos and so on form expectations. When at a concert, it becomes possible to take on the role of screaming fan to enhance one's own experience, to physically enter the narrative of the fan-star relation, not necessarily in a reflective way, but certainly through praxis. Again, the Awakening concerts and their stars offer an arena – maybe a projection surface – where all behaviour is not set.

At all concerts I have attended, I have moved about in the largely female audience, looking at the ways the concerts are enacted from the side of the audience. One of the most important gadgets for a concert is the mobile phone, obviously. It provides the flashlight replacing the previously obligatory lighter to be waved during ballads. It records the concert experience by filming snippets or several songs in a row. Some turn the camera to themselves making selfies with the stage as background. Yet others are bored by some of the artists and sit patiently waiting for their favourite while flipping through social media sites. When the artists perform one of their most popular songs, they are filmed by hundreds of mobile phones. It makes me wonder if the experience of the concerts only acquires full reality when seen through the camera of the phone or whether the latter provides proof of the experience, documentation to show others.

When I discussed similar issues with Raef in 2014, he mentioned that he has experienced a spreading shallowness when it comes to pictures and social media. People come up to him and ask if they can take a picture and then immediately post it on social media, without engaging with him. The image becomes social currency, a trophy, more important than the meeting as such. 'I met Raef', but Raef deplored that the meeting was superficial.

A New Playfulness: 2014 and Onwards

As I mentioned above, during the years immediately preceding 2014, something started to change. As social media became increasingly important, it was not merely enough for the artists to be promoted in official presentations – such as promotion photos, music videos, shows – in a one-way communication. Instead, Twitter, Instagram, Facebook and other social media platforms created a demand for immediacy over which it became much more difficult to have overall control. As a consequence, the artists gained greater agency in constructing their personas. Celebrity is a narrative connecting to real persons through their personas, which celebrities try to manage but whose consumption, of course, cannot be controlled. One of the appeals of a celebrity narrative is that, as yet, 'it has no final chapter' (Cashmore 2014: 314). Rather, it evolves organically as mass media; the artists themselves and their fans provide clues to the overall narrative, allowing fans to 'get to know' the artists. The texts and photos an artist posts in social media act, through the very process of composing and posting them, upon the one who initiated the sharing, to paraphrase Foucault (2000: 214). The messages and images must fit the overall narrative of the personas of the artists; thus, the artists discipline their output and are then disciplined by it in return. This has affected the presentation of the personas of the artists, including in terms of their masculinity. Yet social media have also created opportunities for the artists. Presentations become more multifaceted as the artists are also portrayed in other roles than those for which they are famed: for example, appearing in everyday situations as normal people – eating, training, travelling. As a result, a new, playful and relaxed masculinity emerges, although, in a participatory culture, fans, and possibly others less positive-minded, also post about artists in a number of different media channels, leaving little room for 'a bad hair day'.

When discussing social media with Sharif Banna, he is very clear about the need to keep up with the audience, but in a responsible way. Today, social media is part of any business venture, and also the music industry, and when artists are on tour they are asked to communicate with fans. The Awakening artists display a variety of attitudes to social media. While everyone accepts its importance, Raef, Harris J and Humood participate eagerly on Twitter and on Instagram, with Raef posting twice as much as Maher Zain or Mesut Kurtis who are less prone to use these media when not on tour.

Most posts are just ordinary and predictable, but the immediacy that takes away the middle men also allows the passage of images that are not entirely thought through and perhaps of poorer quality, putting the artists in situations less easy to control. Harris J's Instagram account is interesting, both because of the posts and the comments. In a video clip posted 22 December 2018, Harris J freestyle raps to prove he can, and gets a lot of feedback in words and emojis explicitly suggesting that he is hot, sexy and that he should 'take me' – as a girlfriend, wife or whatever else might be implied. He also receives criticism for not being Islamic enough and a few note that he is swearing in the short clip. This mix of overt romance, even eroticism, and critical commentary was found in every post I examined, regardless of its content (Harris J in the pool, with friends, on stage, at a dinner, etc.). At times, discussions become really heated. A post by Harris J from 22 August 2017 showing Harris J leaning his head towards a woman cousin of his with the heading, 'Have a weak spot for my baby sister', caused fans to argue endlessly about whether this photo showed something haram or was just a normal shot of two cousins who are friends. The poses in photos Harris J posts are often somewhat ironic – for example, Harris J posing on a desert four-wheel bike in a self-consciously 'bad-ass' manner (13 May 2018) – but his Instagram account also shows him praying, at mosques or by the Ka'ba, stressing his serious religiosity. There is simply a richness to the imagery and the reactions allowing for a degree of playfulness, debate and ambiguity that is quite a distance from the discussion about more or less appropriate patterns on clothes on stage that took place in 2014. This richness, if not including the same extremes, can be found in the social media of the other artists as well.

The playfulness can also be found live as something special may happen at gigs. Anticipation builds up around certain songs and some songs are beloved by almost all of an audience. They hope they will be played and when they are, something is released in the crowd. A skilled artist like Maher Zain knows how to use this something. In Manchester 22 October 2017, he challenges the crowd to guess which song the guitarist will start to play next. The guitarist gently plays variations of the verse to a song and then the violin steps in and Maher says, 'Do you recognise it now?' The melody becomes more like it is on the recording and Maher starts singing, 'For the Rest of My Life'. There is a roar in the stadium and many start singing or looking on with beaming smiles. The atmosphere is difficult to describe. Can one really write there is love in the air without being too corny? A fairly young couple – he with a beard that many would say signals conservatism and she in a hijab – sits smiling, both filming Maher Zain onstage, bending towards each other saying things. It looks intimate and sweet; it seems to be their song. All this is yet another example of the much more relaxed relations that have developed between Awakening artists and audiences of late, compared to before. It comes with success, confidence and routine, yes, but it also is a sign of the times. Consumer culture with pretentions to come across as Islamic and therefore appealing to Muslim audiences has gained a more diverse social repertoire. The trial and error of companies like Awakening, in fact prominently Awakening, have pushed the limits of the possible.

Audiences have changed over time and are less concerned with keeping to old forms. Take, for example, how appreciation is shown. In the tour bus in 2014, I asked about the way the audiences had applauded: clapping as musicians were ending the songs and stopping short only seconds after the musicians, resulting in silence before the singers started to address the audience or the band started a new song. According to a consensus reached on the basis of experiences of touring the world, audiences were very different. At charity gigs in Britain, where there were a lot of families, audiences were often a bit reserved. As a spin off, a Muslim journalist following the tour raised the issue of applauding in the first place. He was of the opinion that clapping was not the Muslim way of giving thanks; rather, someone in the audience should show appreciation by taking the initiative to shout '*takbir!*' and others should answer '*allahu akbar*', which is the traditional way. His concerns were not really shared by the others. Maher Zain and Raef did not mind and, indeed, rather appreciated the applause. Raef added that ten years earlier at concerts in Muslim venues in the US, it was rare for an audience to applaud, but it has changed over time. When on tour in 2017, the British charity audiences applauded for longer, not creating the odd silences any more.

Still, certain things are unlikely. Like dancing on stage. Up until September 2016, I had not observed one single dancelike step. Then it happened. On stage in Beirut, 12 September, Maher Zain brought singer Mohammad Omari on stage to perform a Lebanese folksong, and in the middle of the song a troupe of *dabke*[6] dancers entered the stage with a drummer. For a short while, 3:50 into the song, Maher Zain joined the dancers – for just fifteen seconds. The song is rhythmical and there is a party atmosphere. His movements are careful and not extravagant, but this is still very unusual for Awakening artists;[7] on the

---

[6] *Dabke* is a 'form of collective dancing' popular in most societies along the Eastern coast of the Mediterranean (see van Aken 2007).

[7] https://www.youtube.com/watch?v=XVyfMsZQZX4 (last accessed 10 January 2019).

tour I followed in 2017, there was no dancing, at least not on stage. However, while the pattern from the 2014 tour was repeated by the 2017 audiences (sitting in the chairs and swaying, women more active than men), there were far more who stood up and danced during a song or two, and no one disciplined them. The young volunteers in particular behaved in a more carefree manner than in 2014, dancing, singing and shouting out to Maher Zain that they loved him, almost fainting when he occasionally waved back and shot a smile in their general direction.

A further step was taken with the music video to Maher Zain's 'Medina' issued in 2017, produced by Lena Khan, in which the singer uses moves developed on stage, creating a sense of flowing movement and rhythm – if not dancing, at least using all his body, especially the arms. Yet another step was taken in the spring of 2018, at the very start of Ramadan, when Raef issued a new single and music video called 'Ramadan is Here'. In it Raef is playing his Taylor mini guitar, swaying in a dancing manner and jumping up and down to the beat of the catchy tune. When I asked Raef about the moves he simply replied that it was not planned; it just happened because he was 'super happy' at the shoot.[8] Once again, movements are spontaneous, allowing for a playfulness and a less controlled masculinity than before; nonetheless, neither of the above permits explicit dancing.

Yet another example of playfulness is the already mentioned Raef cover of 'Deck the Halls' launched as 'The Muslim Christmas Song' in December 2016. Raef told me the song sparked some controversy. In the many comments about the music video on Awakening's official YouTube channel, people either defend the song and their love of Jesus or proclaim music haram, denounce the song as an imitation of the West or simply try to address Raef respectfully while schooling him on Islam. When discussing the music video, what struck me was that Raef and others at Awakening were not too concerned about the negative attitudes; rather, they saw it as part of the trade. The video was obviously meant to be fun – not everyone is prepared for that, however.

This increased variety can also be seen in clothing styles: from Harris J's torn jeans on Instagram (in many photos in 2018) to Maher Zain in *ihram*[9]

---

[8] Email conversation with Raef, 18 May 2018.

[9] *Ihram* is the prescribed clothing when performing hajj or *umra* (the two main pilgrimage types) to Mecca.

in Mecca (Instagram 4 November 2017 and 14 June 2018). Today, music videos also allow for a multiplicity of forms, and the rather homogenous way of presenting the Awakening artists has been replaced by something more unpredictable. In 2020, some initiatives are likely to push the limits even further. Still, the Islamic ethical dimension continues to be nurtured and many of the tropes of earlier music videos persist in later ones.

Nature, Pride and Heritage

There are other aspects to Awakening music videos, three of which I briefly explore below: representations of nature; Islamic pride; and Islamic heritage.

In an email interview with director Lena Khan about the music video 'I Believe', with Irfan Makki (featuring Maher Zain), I asked her why it was set in nature.

> Lena Khan: Much belief for many Muslims comes from a faith based on reflection – reflecting upon life, about creation, and . . . the utter perfection of nature and the world around us. 'I Believe' is set in nature to mirror that aspect of faith. Also, open fields convey a sense of freedom, which is also meant to reflect faith. Faith to one who does not believe seems oppressive, but to one with faith, it opens them up to a world of possibilities.
>
> Jonas: Thank you for the fine answer. I saw that connection but wasn't sure if I, as a researcher, was over-interpreting the 'nature as signs of God' connection. Was this discussed with the artists? Or was it just self-evident?
>
> Lena Khan: It was discussed with the artists, and immediately accepted because the idea of seeing God and faith in the majesty of God's creation is such a known and felt concept in our faith. It was set in Malibu, California.

This aspect of Awakening's production, also present in lyrics, follows a very broad trend in Islamic apologetics which is repeated in other music videos; Harris J's 'Save Me from Myself' (2017), for example, contrasts indoor environments that restrain the singer and outdoor images representing freedom, vastness and ultimately Allah's creation. Another typical example is the music video to Maher Zain's 'Close to You' (2016), which is utterly explicit in the connection it makes between nature and Allah, both in the lyrics and the video, the latter shot in South Africa by director Amr Singh who has worked on many occasions with Zain Bhikha. Yet another example is the lyrics and 'official Lyric Video' to Raef's 'Subhan Allah' (Glory to Allah, 2019). The lyrics praise Allah and promote the idea that, 'our story starts with clay, it's in our DNA, we say Subhan Allah, so many genes we share, all the signs are there, we say Subhan Allah'. Images show humans, animals, cells and views of nature to support the interconnectedness of the world, thus stressing that it and all beings on it are created by Allah.

Islamic pride is made visible in different ways, with perhaps the most common mode being through the ethics of those appearing in the music videos (including the artists of course). From the first music video, Sami Yusuf's 'al-Mu'allim' (2005), to more recent ones such as Maher Zain's and Mustafa Ceceli's 'The Way of Love' (2016), the characters who appear are often helping each other, caring for children, embracing each other, and sharing a smile. For example, in 'The Way of Love', a German Muslim woman police officer in Berlin, with a headscarf, spots a homeless child (my interpretation is that he represents homeless Moroccan youth), invites him to a coffee house and hears him out, gains his trust and helps him get in contact with the right authorities. The music video is full of sub-narratives not present in the lyrics. It also portrays Maher Zain and the Turkish singer-songwriter and producer, Mustafa Ceceli as devout and bonded in friendship, creating a foundation of general Islamic ethics for the more specific narrative of the child and the police woman.

Islamic pride is expressed through the simple means of showing Muslims as professionals (the police officer, for example) and as well-to-do, in other words, as contributing. In this way music videos clearly offer a contrast to the notions held, especially by European populists, of Muslims as welfare-dependent, unproductive or possibly the owners of small family businesses. It also frames the Awakening artists. The aspect of contributing is a key element of Awakening's production. Early on in their careers, the founders were invited to speak at a conference on entrepreneurship and Islam and, as Sharif Banna remembers it, they were all surprised; they had not framed what they were doing in those words but, thinking it through, they embraced the idea of entrepreneurship as important to the Islamic faith.[10] The very idea of making a cultural contribution and because of it being able to help others with donations, work with charities and creating employment opportunities is central to Sharif Banna's philosophy and that of the other Awakening founders. To work and to be able to contribute to the well-being of others is at the heart of classic Islamic ethics.

The Islamic heritage is stressed in many ways. In music videos it is common to show impressive historical Islamic buildings and monuments like the Blue Mosque and the Taj Mahal, while some video clips appeal to traditional Islamic art as an expression of Islamic authenticity and aesthetics. At times, as in Maher Zain's 'Mawlaya' (2012), it is obviously a low budget solution to let calligraphic writing rotate on the screen, but the music video to his song 'Allah Ya Moulana' (Allah, oh our Lord, 2016) instead connects to the use of geometric patterns in classical Islamic art and is sophisticated in design and production.

Another way of celebrating cultural heritage can be seen in the music video to Mesut Kurtis' 'Burdah' (2007), shot on the coastline of Turkey, directed by Hani Osama, in which Mesut Kurtis works side by side with other men all dressed in traditional clothing and practicing Islam together.

Female Artists?

When I was walking back to the hotel with Sharif Banna in Oxford in the spring of 2013 after a long day's seminar, I asked him if he had considered launching a female artist. Sharif Banna replied that they wanted to but still had not figured out how. They were discussing it with scholars. A particular problem was the risk of sexualisation of a young female artist. I did not raise the obvious objection that the young handsome men they market are also sexualised. Then again, I know Sharif Banna is well aware of that. In a sexist world, with different measures for men and women, his concerns are reasonable, and not ideological but entrepreneurial.

---

[10] Interview with Sharif Banna, 11 December 2018. *The Awakening book*, pp. 86–7, offers a short reflection on entrepreneurship according to Awakening. In 2017, Claritas Books issued Muhammed Faris' *The Productive Muslim: Where Faith Meets Productivity*. As the title suggests, Faris celebrates creative entrepreneurship.

However, Awakening had actually already issued a CD by a female artist in 2013, Egyptian Mariam Elhiny. The CD *Ghanni ma'a l-asdiqa'*, or *Sing Along With Friends* as it is also called, is directed at young children, and its twelve songs are short, catchy and sung in an easy-to-follow Arabic. The folder contains the lyrics in Arabic with English translation. Songs are about topics like the joy of friendship and going to the zoo. At times, Islamic ideas are brought into the record, but discreetly. For example, in a song about planting, the singer sings that she prays the plant will grow and that Allah has created the flowers. Mariam Elhiny has a distinctive voice and, as the music contains instruments like the guitar, violin and saxophone, earlier concerns about instrumentation are clearly not taken into consideration. However, Mariam Elhiny was not marketed as a woman artist. She is not portrayed on the cover, nor does she feature in the official, animated music videos of the songs such as 'Qubba'a' or 'the Hat'. In fact, her name is not even written on the outside of the gatefold CD sleeve, only on the inside (and then not specified as the singer) and in the folder, where she is given due credit.

At times, Awakening artists have performed with women: for example, they have been contracted to sing at the yearly Mošus Pejgamberov (the Musk of the Prophet) event in Sarajevo. Behind the event is a women's education organisation called Kewser, known for its Shi'i affiliation. The Musk of the Prophet is a celebration of the birthday of Fatima, daughter of the Prophet Muhammad.[11] In 2011, Both Maher Zain and Mesut Kurtis sang at the event, backed by a full orchestra with a female darbuka player and a large choir comprising twenty-eight women and an equal number of men. In 2012, Nazeel Azami and Mesut Kurtis represented Awakening and once again played with the same band and choir.[12]

At another concert, Maher Zain performed 'Ya Nabi Salam Alayka' as a duet with a teenage girl in Grozny, Chechnya in 2014. It was a special occasion as the girl, Aishat, is the oldest daughter of the President of Chechnya, Ramzan Kadyrov. Dressed in a white headscarf and a floor-length dress, she stayed still throughout the song, merely moving her hands to mark the words.

---

[11] Alibašić 2014: 450.

[12] Both occasions were televised by the privately owned, Sarajevo-based Hayat TV.

In the audience, one easily recognised the proud father. In 2017, Aishat made her debut as a fashion designer.[13] There are a few more similar occasions, but generally these incidents were exceptions.

Nonetheless, during the October 2017 tour, Bara Kherigi told me that Awakening had contracted the company's first woman singer, Eman, a Moroccan-German woman studying at university at the time. Maher Zain mentioned that he had met her at a concert in Germany. She was working as a volunteer, and had been for two nights in a row. Her sister found the courage to ask Maher Zain for five minutes so that her sister could sing for him; according to Maher Zain, it happens to him now and then. This time, however, the performance blew Maher Zain's mind and he invited her to sing with him later. She even performed a song by herself. Since then, Awakening has contracted her and Maher Zain has helped her record. January 2020, Sharif Banna tells me that her first set of songs will be launched during spring 2020 but due to the Covid-19 pandemic it has been postponed. In fact, Eman was not the first female solo artist Awakening tried to contract but it is the first time both the company and the artist have agreed and signed a contract, according to Sharif Banna.

Eman's official debut on stage was at a London concert on 30 October 2017. She was introduced by comedian Omar Regan, who asked rhetorically, 'Who is going to inspire the Muslim sisters?' He then said that Awakening records had now signed the first Muslim female singer. Well, it should have been 'its' as there were already quite a number out there. Omar Regan went on to introduce her, pointing out that it was her London debut, and then left the stage to her with a prolonged 'Emaaaaaaan!' The stage was set for Maher Zain, but a high stool and a microphone were produced for Eman. The pianist Ruben Drenthe had already taken the stage, all dressed in white. Eman came on dressed in tight black trousers, a black blouse reaching almost to her knees and a brown-green hijab. She looked casually stylish. She greeted the audience and then sang three songs with piano. It went down well. The audience gave her love, just as Omar Regan had asked us to, but she was really nervous, making her stage debut in front of 1,500 people after just being

---

[13] http://www.reuters.com/article/us-russia-chechnya-fashion/chechnyas-first-daughter-shows-off-fashion-collection-idUSKBN16P07E (last accessed 16 January 2019).

presented as the new inspiration for all the sisters in the audience, who made up the majority by far. In fact, Eman sneaked off stage before the pianist had completely finished the last song, but it was to wild cheers from the audience. When talking to Eman backstage, I could see she was quite happy with the gig, and I was too. Before ending my fieldwork, I had received a glimpse of a possible future.[14]

[14] In April 2021, Sharif Banna informed me that Awakening had discontinued its collaboration with Eman, despite already finished recordings and investments. For a number of reasons, this possible future never happened.

7

THE POLITICS OF ENTERTAINMENT

The messages in the *Awakening* songs of hope, self-improvement and serving the community resonate with their audiences who identify with this vision. It is aspirational.

the Awakening book, p. 34

It is tempting to describe Awakening as a non-political and chiefly commercial enterprise, but that would be reductive. To start with, as has been mentioned, Awakening's self-description includes phrases like 'faith-based' and 'value driven'; the importance of social awareness, civil engagement and of promoting the Muslim community and its image among non-Muslims and Muslims alike have also been stressed. In other words, there is a potentially political side to Awakening if we include in 'politics' the engagement in the social, the distribution of resources and the insistence on making space for an Islamic, ethical discourse in the 'publicness'[1] of societies.

John Street's book *Music and Politics* (2012) makes the plausible claim that music – not only the lyrics of songs, but the tonal and rhythmic language

[1] Armando Salvatore (2007) has convincingly argued for a change in the English translation of Habermas' concept 'Öffentlichkeit'. 'Publicness' is preferred to the common translation 'public sphere', seeking to preserve the grammatical construct of the German concept and creating associations to a discursive, powerful sphere of ideas.

of music itself – has the ability to emphasise, or even convey, political ideas efficiently through its emotive power and its ability to constitute and consolidate groups and group belonging. Street (2012: 7) refers to Colin Hay as he describes the political in four features.

> To count as 'political', a situation must present people with a *choice*, and one which they can act upon; they must have *agency*. And in exercising agency, people must be able to *deliberate publicly* and with others and for the outcome to have an impact on others; it must be *social, not personal* [my emphasis].

With this definition in mind, I next discuss three aspects of Awakening's operations: involvement with charity, the message of the output and some specific performances for political leaders.

Charity

A large number of Awakening concerts are charity events; during the two tours in which I participated (2014, 2017), it cooperated with Human Appeal and then Penny Appeal. Other cooperation partners over the years have included Islamic Relief, Swedish State Television (a charity event) and UNHCR. Islamic aid organisations are often described in terms of claimed links to Islamic political organisations – even in the research literature – which has much to do with US political trends since the so-called war on terror (Juul Petersen 2012). In Britain, on the other hand, where Islamic Relief and Penny Appeal, among others, originate, politicians have been much more prone to collaborate and acknowledge the work of Islamic charities (Juul Petersen 2015: 119).

As Juul Petersen (2015: 119) proves, many Islamic charities, especially long-standing ones like Islamic Relief, have histories that are intertwined with Islamic political organisations such as the Muslim Brotherhood or Saudi Arabian transnational organisations. Some trustees, board members, staff and donors come from the so-called (Sunni) Islamic revival movement that has played a key role in organising Islamic organisations, NGOs, printing houses, student organisations and the like, all over the world (Otterbeck 2000). However, even though some of the founders and first trustees may still be around, an organisation like Islamic Relief, which in 2010/11 was the second largest transnational Muslim NGO, has diversified, been professionalised and is now a highly heterogeneous movement (Juul Petersen 2015: 120). Thus, even if there are still links and cooperation, a description that concentrates on relations with, for example, the Muslim Brotherhood, seriously misrepresents the complexity, networks and diversity in the charity work of the organisations.

Naeem Raza – a professional presenter and communication specialist who has often collaborated with Awakening over the years – acted as host on both the tours I attended. He pointed out to me that charity concerts work in two ways: they provide the organising charities with support and attention, while the artists get the finance to tour by cooperating with the charities. His intention was not to question the engagement of the artists but, rather, to point out the complexity of involvement; the charities give both artists and audience an opportunity and a choice to do a good deed. Naeem Raza also stressed the potential for agency and the chance to help and do good with little effort. In 2017, for example, support was provided for girls' education in poor communities in Asia and Africa. Maher Zain, the main act, took the time during his set to address the importance of charity and education for girls. He had been travelling with Penny Appeal in sub-Saharan Africa and, before his performance, a skilfully arranged video was screened showing Maher Zain meeting children in a dump – not figuratively speaking, but in an actual dump, collecting rubbish to be recycled – and discussing their dreams, but also featuring him in a school with happy pupils and articulate teachers. Both Naeem Raza and Maher Zain emphasise the role of Islam for charity, as a personal choice and as a self-evident part of Islam.

As in most major religious traditions, Islamic thinking promotes charity, both through an obligation to give (*zakat*) and through encouragement to give optionally (*sadaqa*). The donation form handed out by Penny Appeal during Maher Zain's UK tour in October 2017 contained four options: donations could be labelled '*Zaqat*', '*Sadaqah*', '*Lillah*'[2] or 'General'. Contemporary Islamic discourse also stresses the importance of not only individual but also

---

[2] This means 'for Allah' and implies any kind of voluntary charity. In Islamic theory, *sadaqa* is broken down into several categories and *lillah* is a part of *sadaqa nafila*, or optional charity.

corporate social responsibility. By working with charities and starting one of its own, Awakening tries to fulfil that responsibility.[3]

To states, this 'welfare element' of Islam may be seen as inherently political. Some, but surprisingly few, have incorporated the *zakat* idea into the taxation system; other states calculate and depend on Islamic charity to keep up welfare work; while yet others are challenged by Islamic charities, which, by performing welfare work, make the shortcomings of some governments visible. The competition in the publicness provokes some governments to try to limit, coerce or crush such initiatives (Alazrak and Saleh 2016: 222; Olsson 2015). As Awakening has collaborated (and still does) with partners operating in several states with extreme economic inequality where there is little solidarity between the ruling elite and the dispossessed, charity work may also become challenging in Muslim majority contexts.

Street (2012: 41) suggests that to be listened to politically requires more than being able to be heard: you need legitimacy. 'To speak *for* a people or cause' (emphasis in the original) is to represent someone. To have the legitimacy to represent people or a cause, one needs to be acknowledged as righteous. In the case of charity events, Awakening has a long reputation. From the initial charity concerts and the company's first major charity event on 21 October 2007 at Wembley Arena and onwards, Awakening has built up a solid reputation as a company taking social responsibility, and through its activities it has accumulated moral capital for the company and its artists, some of whom, particularly Sami Yusuf in the past and Maher Zain now, have been given, and taken on, the responsibility of being the voice. Both artists combine civil engagement with creative activism, allowing values and responsibility-taking to have impact on their respective art. For example, Maher Zain has actively supported and cooperated with UNHCR since the organisation of World Refugee Day 2013, especially in connection with the aid provided to Syrian refugees by UNHCR in Lebanon.[4] He is a so-called high-profile supporter. During the Nansen Award gala in Geneva 2014, he performed, for the first time, his song 'One Day' written in support of and in

---

[3] For an interesting, normative article on corporate social responsibility, see Dusuki and Abdullah 2007.

[4] See www.unhcr.org/maher-zain.html (last accessed 14 January 2019).

solidarity with the world's refugees. It would later end up on his third album. By performing an ethical Islamic masculinity in public and by signalling that there is no difference between the public artist's persona and the private person, it seems that both the artists discussed here and others have gained the trust of a large number of fans and ordinary members of the public. At least, they and Awakening act from this belief.

The performances at live charity events rest on the reputation of the artists, Awakening and the organisation behind the charities, but the concerts still need to convey more than the message; the performances need to motivate action, and well-received music has the ability to generate emotions, to '"energize" our moral sentiments' (Street 2012: 73) – in this case built on moral indignation – and to appeal to collective identities (2012: 92). When artists participate in charity events, they also bind themselves to the ethical codes they pursue, affecting expectations of their present and future artistry. At the end of the day, their respective artistic personas, as well as Awakening itself, become intertwined with discourses on politico-ethical authenticity.[5]

Awakening artists are also active in awareness campaigns. I met Rina Novita in Bradford in October 2017. Ebu Rina (as she is known as) is Executive Director of the Indonesian media company DNA. In cooperation with Awakening, she launched an anti-bullying campaign (especially cyber-bullying) in an Indonesian soap opera called 'Salam', using Harris J as figurehead. Harris J plays himself arriving in Indonesia as an exchange student interested in learning about Indonesian ways of celebrating Ramadan. The campaign was also supported by IndoSat – Indonesia's leading telecom company – and further buttressed by a tour of schools. Ebu Rina also engages Raef in campaigns for the acceptance of social diversity. Again, Awakening is involved in campaigns driven by ethics, but in political settings where diversity is not self-evident, and when pop-artists are introduced as more highly principled than politicians, such actions potentially pose challenges and become political in context.

---

[5] As pointed out by Jouili (2015: 18), the Aristotelian concept *phronesis* covers this aspect of ethics. It is not only in relation to the person but to the common good. However, I will not introduce it in the text as there are other ways of expressing this that come across clearer.

Message

The politico-ethical authenticity sought by the artists and Awakening is at times made clear and explicit. Let me dwell on the many layers of a single song. Maher Zain's first album *Thank You Allah* (2009) has lyrics that generally celebrate an Islamic lifestyle, praise Allah and Muhammad, or are simply about friendship and the importance of being kind and generous. One song, 'Palestine Will Be Free', breaks the pattern in that it directly addresses a clearly political issue.[6] The music is written by Maher Zain and Hamza Namira with lyrics by Maher Zain and Bara Kherigi. Here I examine the lyrics and images from the song and its accompanying music video (also from 2009) and then trace the genealogical layers of these.

Every day we tell each other
That this day will be, will be the last
And tomorrow we all can go home free
And all this will finally end
Palestine tomorrow will be free [x2]

No mother no father to wipe away my tears
That's why I won't cry
I feel scared but I won't show my fears
I keep my head high
Deep in my heart I never have any doubt that
Palestine tomorrow will be free [x2]

I saw those rockets and bombs shining in the sky
Like drops of rain in the sun's light
Taking away everyone dear to my heart
Destroying my dreams in a blink of an eye
What happened to our human rights?
What happened to the sanctity of life?
And all those other lies?

---

[6] Other Awakening songs address political issues head on, like 'Zaman al-Hurriyya' (Time of liberty) by Moroccan-German singer, Saad Chemmari, who only issued one video through Awakening in 2010. The video and song explicitly take a politically pro-Palestinian stance.

> I know that I'm only a child
> But is your conscience still alive
> Oh . . . Yeah
> I will caress with my bare hands
> Every precious grain of sand
> Every stone and every tree
> (Be)cause no matter what they do
> They can never hurt you
> (Be)cause your soul will always be free
> Palestine tomorrow will be free [x2]

The lyrics do not call for military resistance, just for people to rise up in dignity and refuse to be suppressed and refuse to countenance the repression of others. Rather than making explicit references to religion (well, yes, there is the 'your soul will always be free' phrase towards the end) it queries, 'What happened to our human rights? What happened to the sanctity of life?' appealing to the global community to take responsibility, referring both to human rights and to moral positions. Still, the song shares with political nashids the stress on suffering, nationalist nostalgia, resistance, dignity and the refusal to bow down (Lahoud 2017: 55f).

Listening to the song, we get a further impression not available just by reading the lyrics. The passionate tone in Maher Zain's voice, enhanced by the melodic drama and the reed flute's tonal colours, signals honest engagement with the serious subject addressed. The drum intro is a couple of bars in 8/8. It has a military sound to it, but not as in European marching drums; rather, my thoughts go to military nashid and Palestinian wedding music (*'arada*), but I have not been able to pin-point the inspiration. I perceive it as belonging to the Palestinian side, ushering in the resistance.

Putting the lyrics and the song in the context of the album, a layer of deep devout engagement in Islam is added even if the lyrics of this particular song avoid or do not contain direct references to this. As mentioned above, the first song is proceeded by the phrase '*allahu akbar*' and the last song is followed by '*al-hamdu lillah*' (praise Allah), framing the album as a pious act.

Adding the layer of the music video enriches the impression yet again. The video is animated, designed and directed by British artist Andrew Morgan and produced by Darren Wall, another British artist, both working at Chase Animation at the time. The heart-breaking imbalance between Israeli tanks and stone-throwing children and youth is emphasised, and the destruction of civil society is signalled by the rubble the tanks drive through and the ruined buildings surrounding the scene. The music video consists of a visual, rather apparent political statement about the dignified physical resistance of Palestinian youth and the (partly) morally corrupt military. The music video uses the iconic image of a lone person (in this case a small girl) facing a tank, causing the fighting to pause, for a while. The video is the only one I can remember in which Maher Zain is without headgear. The background is still animated when he is in the shot; he is not smiling his characteristic warm smile and it adds to the drama that he is not as fashionably dressed as in other videos.

While references to Islam are absent from the lyrics, the video contains a scene when a tank-driving soldier purposely blows a minaret to pieces. Towards the end of it (5:04), the ruined minaret can be seen in the top left corner when the tank driver stands down and drives off and the camera focuses on the face of the girl who won this small victory.

The song is presented differently in the animated music video. The sounds of war are amplified, including the roar of jets attacking, strafing civilians and firing rockets at a school building with children inside, among them our girl hero. After this, the song proceeds as on the record, apart from the occasional bomb blast following the images of the music video.

When the video was launched, both Bara Kherigi and Maher Zain high-lighted the message of peace and the importance of ending violence and bloodshed.[7] In official press releases Awakening has stated that Maher Zain contextualises the song, saying:

It was during the bombing and attack on Gaza in January 2009 when I was moved to make a song about Palestine. But my first aim for making the track

---

[7] See, for example, http://www.emel.com/article?id=&a_id=1464 (last accessed 11 February 2019).

'Palestine Will Be Free' was to remind myself and everybody else that it is still going on, and that we should always give at least one thought every day to these human beings, who are just like us, their only crime is that they were born in Palestine, and who has any control over where he or she are born? Palestine is a symbol for struggling against injustice, so when I sing about Palestine, I am also singing about all other countries around the world in which my fellow brothers and sisters in humanity are suffering from injustice, irrespective of their faith or ethnicity.

Further, in the same promotion material, Bara Kherigi states:

We at Awakening Records have tried to use art and music to highlight the injustices being visited upon the Palestinians and to show our solidarity with them. This animated music video for our new star artist Maher Zain is just another step in that direction and certainly not the last insha-Allah. The aim or message of the music video is to highlight the plight of the Palestinians and show reality as it is but at the same time send out a message that we hope bloodshed and violence ends and peace prevails.

As can be noted, the words are carefully chosen. The song is about injustice done to humanity as a whole, not necessarily Muslims, and the motives for helping them are moral, not necessarily Islamic.

To summarise, looked at in isolation, the song and its lyrics combine to produce what is primarily an anti-war song about human dignity but, adding layers to this, it is positioned in an Islamic tradition of protest intermingled with Palestinian pride, homeland nostalgia, heroic descriptions of its fighters and the clear signal that the oppressor is destroying not only infrastructure and lives but also Islamic buildings, equally insensitive to all. Due to these signals, it is clear that the song and its different layers are interrelated with a genre of political nashids. This genre in itself signals an affinity to a certain global discourse – call it meaning-making worldview if you prefer – about politics, suffering and justice shared widely in Muslim environments. In fact, the discourse of the wickedness of Israel can gather the Muslim *umma* in an 'imagined solidarity' (Bayat 2005: 904), maybe one of the few political evaluations to find almost unanimous agreement.

Movement Artists?

To have a political function, lyrics do not have to contain political statements. In fact, a song by an acclaimed artist might work as well. At times, lyrics that are too explicit will only be censored or cause arrests, thus some caution is often called for (Kirkegaard *et al.* (eds) 2017). At any rate, ambiguity does not lessen the potential value of a song.

If we distinguish between social movements and social movement organisations, we gain a tool enabling greater precision. While the latter have a form, an organisation and are operational units with a cause – at times being incorporated into national politics as a political party – a social movement is rather more loosely construed. According to della Porta and Diani (2006: 7), social movements are essentially 'informal networks' based on 'shared beliefs'. They have participants, not members. Individuals act from similar cognitive maps and a shared sense of justice that 'taken together reinforce the feeling of belonging and of identity' (2006: 26).[8] Yet social movements harbour many different positions, among them what Eyerman and Jamison (1998) call 'movement intellectuals' and 'movement artists'. Movement artists are those who manage to capture the core spirit and message of a movement in their art, at times making songs that are appropriated as anthems by participants in the movement. Such songs can have immense importance; they may draw people to the movement and function ritually when sung by participants, conjuring up emotions of belonging, meaning and righteousness.

Why mention this? Via the Maher Zain song discussed above, Awakening signals a clear affinity with the sentiments and sense of justice that mobilise support for the Palestinians. Awakening is obviously not a social movement organisation; it is a commercial company. But could it be said to provide movement artists for a social movement? What social movement would that be?

Sean Foley (2013) makes the plausible assumption that the songs of Hamza Namira and Maher Zain managed to capture a sentiment during the period prior to the Arab Spring in 2011 and then became important soundtracks to the Egyptian revolution without the artists themselves causing

[8] I would like to acknowledge my debt to Emin Poljarevic and his unpublished PhD thesis 'Exploring Individual Motivation for Social Change' (Florence, July 2012) for bringing della Porta's and Diani's definition to my attention.

or organising demonstrations. 'Their work reflected a wide-spread feeling of discontent, a desire for a different future, and collective vision for how Arabs could reach that future' (Foley 2013: 340). This is, of course, very difficult to substantiate, but music has a documented ability to enable people to gather, engage and feel empowered (Street 2012).

Even though the intention of the original artists and production teams might not have been to write political songs – protest songs or songs to promote mobilisation – songs may be used that way by social movements and social movement organisations (see Cloonan 2017; Street 2012). Some songs may be taken to heart because of the lyrics, but the way that the lyrics are musically performed is often of vital importance. Repeatable, singable, pregnant, emotionally loaded phrases are preferred to complex wordy lyrics. Maher Zain's and Hamza Namira's songs, calling for dignity through non-violent, personal resistance and revival (in Maher Zain's case more clearly formulated as an Islamic revival), came to be appropriated by different kinds of political actors.

There is a difference in content, and likely in intent, between Hamza Namira's 'Ehlam Ma'aya' (Dream with me), from the debut album with the same name, and Ramy Essam's overtly political 'Irhal' (Leave). 'Ehlam Ma'aya' has lines like, 'Dream with me, about the coming of tomorrow, and if it doesn't come, we will bring it on ourselves', while 'Irhal' announces, 'We are all united as one, and we ask for just one thing, "leave"! Down with Mubarak!' While Namira's song was used by the sympathisers from both secular and more religious positions, becoming popular in all camps, Essam's became the emblematic song of the early Tahrir Square protestors managed by the secular resistance and aided by the frustrated population in general, without specific political sympathies. Regardless, the civil engagement of the lyrics of Awakening songs was taken to heart by a substantial number of people. Hamza Namira released a song in 2011 called El-Midan (The square), celebrating the moment of resistance and its spirit, in which the chorus goes, 'hold your head high, you are Egyptian, you are one of those who went to the square [i.e. Tahrir] . . . you brought back the glory of Egypt of the past'. His positive stand on the revolution and on freedom later affected Hamza Namira negatively. His songs were banned from Egyptian radio after the military coup in 2013. He now lives in London and has left the Awakening label.

This example was about Egypt, but there is a very common narrative about injustice, colonialism, suffering and political oppression that is widely shared among a great variety of Muslims. It has its heroes and villains, hopes, dreams and fears, but also ambivalence and embarrassments (that are generally avoided). Different versions – at times conflicting – are disseminated among people with very dissimilar political interests and visions, such as charity organisations, Islamo-democratic parties, resistance movements and jihadis; in other words, the shared sentiments can be tapped into by a wide variety of groups and interests. So, what is my argument? Awakening artists and their songs have a wide appeal and can be appropriated by a varied range of actors, and some of these uses are contrary to the interests of the artists themselves. Nevertheless, Awakening songs may be chosen as significant songs for movements and individuals as the songs obviously touch the hearts of many. This begs the question: in what company and contexts does Awakening want to appear?

Who Are You Musicking With?

Wanting to stress music as an act – 'to music' – Christopher Small (1998) created the concept musicking. The term is meant to be descriptive, indicating that both performance and listening are acts of musicking, and enabling the question: what are the meaning and consequences of musicking together? By following the Awakening artists on the Internet and on tour, I have been able to watch parts of a very large number of live performances. Some of these gigs are attended by well-known politicians. The symbolic claiming of an artist by one or more political leaders is obvious. Let me mention three examples from roughly the same period and then suggest an interpretation.

In May 2014, in connection with an official Ramadan celebration in Grozny, Chechnya, Maher Zain performed on stage. President Ramzan Kadyrov and a superstar Islamic cleric – the United Arab Emirates-based Yemeni scholar and Sufi Habib Ali al-Jifri – were sitting in the front row, singing along to the music. A number of other clerics whom I have not been able to identify were also in the same row. Maher Zain sings a duet with Aishat, Kadyrov's daughter, thus paying extra respect to the Kadyrov family. Kadyrov is known to seek political legitimacy through Islam and to be fiercely anti-Salafi and anti-Wahhabi.

On 2 July 2014, a week before the presidential election, Raef and Maher Zain played a gig in Jakarta for presidential candidate Prabowo Subianto. Awakening was contracted by the media group backing up Subianto's campaign. One of Indonesia's largest media groups, Awakening already had a commercial agreement with it. At the gig, members of the Indonesian Partai Keadilan Sejahtera (Prosperous Justice Party), which was supporting the candidate, were present.[9] The party supposedly drew its support from the Muslim middle class (especially in Jakarta) and is presented as moderate even though its critics suspects a hidden agenda (Rinaldo 2013: chapter 4).

In the middle of Maher Zain's song 'Mawlaya', the politicians in the front row – seated until then in wide white armchairs – and their aides, took to the stage, dancing, breaking Awakening's carefully upheld code of not having dancing on stage. This appropriating of centre stage pushed the musicians, including the singer, to the periphery for as long as the politicians liked. When I met Maher Zain in October the same year, he mentioned that he was criticised in the Indonesian press for not mixing and dancing with the politicians, but he had not wanted to because it involved dancing on stage. Towards the end of the show, Maher Zain addressed the political aspect of the meeting, politely expressing support for Prabowo Subianto who, by the way, was not elected.

During a discussion of the above with Sharif Banna, he observed that the Awakening engagement was not with the political element but with a business partner in Indonesia, meanwhile admitting that 'that's when the lines sometimes gets blurry between politics, media and art'.[10] He further stressed that Awakening consciously avoids 'political groups and Islamists' and its artists do not play for specific religious groups driven by an ideology. Awakening may engage with these, but does not want to be a vehicle for them.[11]

---

[9] Partai Keadilan had earlier engaged Indonesian *nasyid* artists such as Snada and is no stranger to the music genre (Rasmussen 2010: 203).

[10] Interview with Sharif Banna, 11 December 2018.

[11] For example, when reading about the fairly successful, London-based, cultural Sufi project 'The Rabbani Project' and going through its webpages, I find no indication that it has engaged Awakening artists. The Rabbani Project has arranged a number of public events, concerts and workshops since 2012 and has also released music. Naqshbandi Haqqani Sufism and its associated projects (like this one) has been important for many nashid artists and audiences in London; see further, Morris 2013.

At a show in Turkey, April or May 2015, Maher Zain left the stage while still performing a song and went to the first row to embrace the Prime Minister, Recep Tayyip Erdoğan, and remained with him for a while; Erdoğan later addressed the audience. The concert was arranged by UDEF, The Federation of International Student Associations. The bond between Awakening and Erdoğan has been nurtured over time (for example, Erdoğan features in two photos with Awakening founders in *the Awakening book*, p. 96) and has, among other things, resulted in a presidential campaign song celebrating Erdoğan, 'Hasat Vakti' (Harvest time), recorded by Maher Zain and released in the summer of 2018.[12] Earlier the same year, on 18 May, Maher Zain sang his song 'Palestine Will Be Free' at the rally 'Zulme lanet kudüs'e destek' (Damn the oppression, support Jerusalem) headlined by Erdoğan in support and solidarity with Palestinians.[13]

What do these three cases have in common? Political leaders and organisations searching for legitimacy through Islam are celebrated or allowed to connect to Awakening's artists, in this case Maher Zain. These are not just any contexts where some powerful people happen to be present or referenced, they are sought by political actors to give them legitimacy. Awakening is contracted to provide entertainment, accepting the possible association with open eyes and prepared praise and salutations. Does this mean that Awakening should be viewed through the prism of a certain type of political Islam? No, it really is not that simple.

To start with, Awakening organises concerts in a large variety of settings. Being a highly sought-after collaboration partner in Muslim majority contexts, the company is bound to be musicking with a wide variety of actors. Secondly, it is important to understand the breadth of the networks that people who engage themselves in Islam as an ethical empowerment discourse might connect to. Politically, culturally or, let us call it, spiritually[14] active

---

[12] For an interview with Maher Zain about this, see https://www.aa.com.tr/en/culture-and-art/singing-star-maher-zain-releases-new-song-for-erdogan/1163015 (last accessed 24 October 2018).

[13] https://www.aa.com.tr/tr/gunun-basliklari/zulme-lanet-kuduse-destek-mitingine-500-bin-kisi-katildi/1150191 (last accessed 24 October 2018).

[14] Here is not the place to sort out all the possible, reasonable objections raised to the term spiritually; see Bruce 2018; Carrette and King 2005.

Muslims are likely to have different goals and support different means, yet might belong to the same extended networks. I am writing 'might', for not having done a network analysis I can merely presume as much. Asef Bayat (2005: 898) stresses that many with strong social engagement are not really interested in meddling with party politics as they tend primarily to seek to influence 'civil society, behaviour, attitudes, cultural symbols and value systems'. Such changes may of course cause transformations in the formal political system in the long run, but those engaged are not seeking political office, merely what they experience as a better future.

Many Muslim movements, political actors, artists and intellectuals take part in this general Islamic ethical empowerment discourse, bringing people into contact with each other even though they do not necessarily share views and visions. Asef Bayat (2005) has suggested the concept 'imagined solidarity' to highlight some aspects of these networks. It has the merit of indicating shared sentiments that presume solidarity and possible collaboration, but it does not imply that actual cooperation is sought or would even be plausible. However, I am not addressing a social movement. Since the Islamic ethical empowerment discourse is global and is manifested in very different ways, I feel it would stretch the concept 'social movement' too far; it would be like labelling all those engaged in the betterment of the environment as part of the same social movement, regardless of whether they are motivated by religious, political or philosophical views, lifestyle choices or agricultural business calculations. Rather, this ethical empowerment discourse feeds into a number of different social movements and is further manifested in a multitude of social movement organisations.

Which organisations and people that are included in various arenas is dependent on factors such as networks and personal preferences. It also changes according to how someone, or an organisation, is evaluated at different times. Organisations and individuals may suddenly become politically problematic or unwanted. Most will have to take discourses other than their own into account, such as media representations, to avoid the risk of being tainted by the tarnished reputations of others, especially when acting in non-Muslim environments. This is particularly so given that the documentation of events on the Internet tends increasingly to break down the barriers between non-Muslim and Muslim environments and, further, to leave traces over time. Reinterpreted and changed positions may be haunted by prior collaborations and preferences, making it increasingly difficult to evaluate and chose collaboration partners.

When discussing the above with Sharif Banna in the final interview for this book, he agreed with this framing, emphasising that he and Bara Kherigi, when they were in their twenties, never joined any movement, rather engaging with ideas because ideas were exciting. Furthermore, instead of accepting a whole package as truth, they carved out their own space by accepting some ideas and criticising or synthesising others, regardless of where they originated.

It is tempting to connect all this to post-Islamism (Bayat 2007, 2009) but I am not entirely happy with the concept. An Islamic ethical empowerment discourse is not necessarily in a post-relation to Islamism – neither a historical one, nor an intellectual one. Post-Islamism is far too tied to the idea of social movements, rather than a broader discourse; admittedly, however, much of what Asef Bayat associates with the concept fits fairly well, especially his claim that social engagement in post-Islamist movements aims to use 'media, publications, associations, education, fashion, lifestyle, and the new discourse to bring about moral and intellectual changes in civil society' (Bayat 2009: 47). Bayat (2007: 10) also specifies that he considers post-Islamism to be a project that can be conceptualised and strategised. By engaging in social problems through an Islamic ethical empowerment discourse (or as a post-Islamist, if you will), addressing poverty, illiteracy, abuse, drugs and lack of self-esteem, social actors challenge states that show little or no interest (or ability) in improving conditions for the general population. Unfortunately, such states are in no short stock in Muslim-majority countries, making the engagement political, and in many cases politically unwanted, to those states (Olsson 2015).

Mustafa Hosny, the Egyptian superstar media *da'iya* who has collaborated with Awakening several times, fits the picture well. He promotes taking individual responsibility through personal betterment and social engagement. He is a prominent voice in the Egyptian publicness and has an international following. In his lectures he discusses, among other things, *maqasid al-shari'a*, the overall purposes of shari'a,[15] approaching Islam holistically rather than

---

[15] For example, on the programme *Fikr*. https://www.youtube.com/watch?v=eJYFFanaAuc (last accessed 22 January 2019).

through legal rulings on details. This is a very broad trend among contemporary Islamic intellectuals that complements a stress on ethics, not only *fiqh*. Yet Mustafa Hosny is not the leader of a social movement; rather, he is part of a broader Islamic ethical empowerment discourse shared with post-Islamists and others. Mustafa Hosny has a close relationship with Awakening, having used music by Awakening artists in his shows and promotion videos.

This general ethical empowerment discourse is manifested, among other things, in Islamic conferences – and at conferences you would like some entertainment, would you not? As an illustration, let us examine the guest lists of the 'Reviving the Islamic Spirit' conferences in Toronto, Canada that began in 2001. Some of the noted guests in 2009 were Habib Ali al-Jifri (the scholar who sang with President Ramzan Kadyrov), Hamza Yusuf (one of the USA's most well-known Muslim scholars), Yusuf Islam, Maher Zain, Suhaib Webb (who has released audio CDs with Awakening), Egyptian superstar 'televangelist' 'Amr Khaled (who has aired music by Awakening), theologian Tariq Ramadan (who has published books through Awakening), Abdullah bin Bayyah (Hamza Yusuf's teacher, member of the board of the European Council for Fatwa and Research, who features in a photo in *the Awakening book*) and Attallah Shabazz, oldest daughter of Malcolm X. Over the coming years, many of these returned as invited speakers and musicians and others would join, while, for several of them, this was not their first appearance. Sami Yusuf performed in 2010, as did Raihan and Zain Bhikha. In 2011, Seyyed Hossein Nasr made a speech. Sami Yusuf was at the same conference and both returned the next year. Sami Yusuf, in 2015, released a record putting Nasr's Sufi poetry to music. Outlandish, who has collaborated with Sami Yusuf, also performed at the same conference. In 2012, Mesut Kurtis, Raihan and Sami Yusuf performed, and speakers included, among others, Mustafa Ceric, at the time Grand Mufti of Bosnia, member of the board of the European Council for Fatwa and Research and a publicised – but never published – Awakening author; and journalist and Muslim celebrity convert Kristiane Backer, whose biography has been published by Awakening. Many of the earlier mentioned speakers also appeared. Mesut Kurtis sang at the 2013 conference, as did Sami Yusuf who appeared most years. In 2015, Dawud Wharnsby performed, singing one song with Yusuf Islam. Da'iya Mustafa Hosny (who has collaborated with Awakening) lectured.

The list of invited people can be continued for the coming years, and was the same before 2009, with musical entertainment having been part of it at least since 2003. For example, Mesut Kurtis sang at the 2008 convention and so did Maher Zain, who had very recently joined Awakening at that point. In 2006, Hamza Robertson was one of the artists. Outlandish performed in 2005, Raihan and Sami Yusuf in 2004. In 2003, Sami Yusuf made his first appearance. There is a large number of other speakers and artists I have not mentioned as I see no connection between them and Awakening – yet – and at every convention the Awakening staff have networked. Of course, this is not the only large conference there is, albeit one of the most prominent; according to conference arrangers' promotion videos, over 20,000 have attended the conference each year in the 2010s. Awakening artists headline a number of conferences each year, making it completely impossible for an outsider to map out contacts and networks.

The point being made here is that there are common platforms that gather Muslims engaged in an overall Islamic ethical empowerment discourse from most walks of life. The more famous speakers will socialise, they will run into Awakening artists and contacts will be made and future engagements booked. Thus, Awakening is an active part of extensive networks spanning the globe.

Awakening takes risks through its civil engagement in an Islamic ethical empowerment discourse. Being associated with Islamic political movements or leaders or social movements might backfire. Sharif Banna claims that Awakening navigated the risks fairly well up until around 2013 but, as a result of geo-political change, much has altered and it is now more important to be careful about collaboration partners, while pasts may come back to haunt you. In a discussion in 2014 with a Human Appeal employee, he pointed out that the organisation had been doing thorough background checks on potential collaboration partners in the last seven years in a way not done before, something that has become necessary as Islamic engagements have become public in a new way through the Internet. Financers and collaborating partners sensitive to public opinion might hesitate to engage or continue prior engagements due to risks of being associated with stigmatised actors.

As of now, Awakening has not been vilified by many, apart from some Sami Yusuf fans, taking his side in the contractual feud between him and the company. Rather, Awakening is a sought-after collaboration partner with which you want to be seen.

Preaching to the Converted?

Does the 'faith-based and value-driven music' reach non-Muslims? In most cases no, I would guess, but this is not a study on how the music is received so I really cannot tell. Yusuf Islam seems to be able to draw a diverse audience to his recent concert tours, probably because of his Cat Stevens songs, and is in that way reaching out, but at the concerts I have attended I have identified very few as non-Muslims apart from some of the stage crew, people working at the venues, security guards and similar. In comments to official music videos, there are typically a number of comments like 'I'm not Muslim but I love this song'.[16] However, it is impossible to draw any certain conclusions from this. As Maher Zain is one of the major stars of Islamic pop at the moment, and is a Swedish citizen, I will offer a short reflection on his outreach in Sweden.

When his first album was released in 2009, I heard about it immediately. Teaching Religious Studies and Islamic Studies at Lund University, I found it relevant to play the music video 'Insha Allah' to my students. I asked them what they thought about it. Most students liked the song and the music video (well, to be honest, few metal fans and hard-core indie rockers liked the music). Common to all students was that they had never heard of Maher Zain and they were baffled by his success and growing stardom. How could this happen outside their media-trained gaze?

During the autumn term in 2010, I had a Muslim female student with a Palestinian background who was the first to identify the man behind the music. It was her music in many respects. She loved it. It was Islamic. She was proud that Maher Zain was an Arab and Muslim who had grown up in Sweden. Actually, she went further and claimed Maher Zain as Palestinian (which he is not). The other students looked puzzled as I discussed Maher Zain's background with her. They had no clue who we were talking about.

Still, outside my classroom and outside the mp3-players of young Swedish Muslims nothing happened. Not one major newspaper wrote

---

[16] I like to thank my student Nurila Ydyrys for pointing this out to me.

about the successful artist. No radio show played Maher Zain's music. I mentioned him to journalists who contacted me to discuss the troublesome relationship of reactionary Islamist movements to music and musicians. They probably filed the information under coming projects, but never wrote about him.

Then, in late March 2013, Maher Zain played at an Islamic gathering in Stockholm and his music became the topic of two rather different state radio shows. State radio has the most influential radio channels in Sweden. The first was on one of the most acclaimed programmes on Swedish radio called 'Människor och Tro' (roughly translatable as 'People and beliefs'), a programme about all aspects of religions and beliefs, from philosophy to violent conflicts, from mysticism to dogmatic theology. Maher Zain's role was to speak about his music and its relation to his Muslim faith, and of course to mention a little about his background.[17] A week later, he was introduced in 'Musikguiden', a programme focusing on exploring the wealth of music.[18] His musical genre was introduced and discussed. I had the privilege to comment on the growth of the new Islamic music genres and on Maher Zain's artistry. This programme was not particularly interested in religion but rather in the sound and style of the music. Suddenly, and in both programmes, Maher Zain was claimed as Swedish.

The effect of the two programmes was immediate in my close circles. Colleagues where I worked at the Department of Theology and Religions Studies at Lund University in Sweden asked me about Maher Zain's music, having enjoyed it for its spiritual message. They also asked about nashid as a phenomenon. Most of my colleagues were studying Christian theology or history; none of them were Muslims. Still, the effect was very temporary.

In connection with the attention above, a few newspapers published pieces on Maher Zain but for the most part, his stardom was not felt to be a concern of the majority of society. On 3 May 2015, Maher Zain played a charity concert arranged by Islamic Relief in Malmö, the third largest city of Sweden; very

---

[17] The programme can be found on http://sverigesradio.se/sida/artikel.aspx?programid=416& artikel=5498899 (last accessed 11 February 2019).

[18] The programme can be found on http://sverigesradio.se/sida/artikel.aspx?programid=4067 &artikel=5522635 (last accessed 11 February 2019).

few non-Muslims were present (not counting staff) judging from appearances (and my gaze, of course). The concert took place in a popular venue in the middle of town. A month earlier (4 April), Sami Yusuf had played the Malmö concert hall; I was again among the few non-Muslims in the audience.

The first time[19] Maher Zain was really embraced by mainstream journalism was on 2 October 2015, when Per Sinding-Larsen – arguably the most well-known music journalist in Sweden – tweeted about him and announced on Instagram that he had interviewed Maher Zain on Swedish state television channel SVT1 on a popular morning show 'Gomorron Sverige' (Good mornin' Sweden) and that Maher Zain would perform on SVT1's charity show 'The World's Children' later that evening. He further presented Maher Zain as one of Sweden's biggest stars. The performance was Maher Zain's second on Swedish television. He chose to play 'Mawlaya', which has an Arab pop beat to it and is easy to follow. Soon after (14 October), he featured on 'Malou efter tio' (Malou after ten) at TV4 and performed 'Number One for Me'.

His second? His first performance was in an SVT2 documentary, 'Eidfirande för Alla' (Eid celebration for all),[20] about the Swedish Eid celebration in Gothenburg in late September 2009, in which he performed his song 'Insha Allah' and was interviewed. The programme was broadcast on SVT2. In this programme, the focus was not on him, although he got to perform the full song. Two of the main arrangers of that Eid celebration were Ashar Khan, some of whose music had been distributed by Awakening, and Zana Muhammad, who had introduced both Ashar Khan and Maher Zain to Awakening. In the programme, Ashar Khan and Mesut Kurtis also performed, backed by Swedish neo-folk music group Den Fule (The Ugly One). However, the programme did not generate any further media coverage.

In the summer of 2016, Maher Zain participated in the most popular radio programme in Sweden, 'Sommarpratarna', 'The Summer Talkers', a strange name even in Swedish. The show runs all through the summer and gives a number of selected politicians, artists, authors and other well-known people the possibility to host the show and say a little about their lives. Maher

---

[19] Before, Maher Zain had been interviewed for two minutes by journalist Samir Abu Eid, 1 May 2015, for SVT news in connection with his first tour in Sweden.

[20] The pronunciation of 'alla' (all) in Swedish resembles Allah in Arabic.

Zain spoke on 17 August about his youth and the transition into the status of world-famous artist.[21] The reception was very positive if reviews in newspapers are any indication. Since then, Maher Zain has appeared on the Swedish television programme broadcast on National Day 2017 (6 June) at the outdoor museum Skansen in Stockholm, singing a duet with one of Sweden's most senior jazz singers, Svante Thuresson. On Maher Zain's initiative, they sang Thuresson's 1960s song 'Hej Systrar, Hej Bröder' (Hello sisters, hello brothers) about youth celebrating international understanding and turning against quibbling tyrants who, towards the end of the song, are sent into space in a rocket ship. By now, most larger newspapers had run at least one article about Maher Zain with the angle 'Sweden's unknown star' but, still, very few non-Muslims would recognise Maher Zain in the street, one of the reasons he likes living in Sweden.

Judging from this reflection on the reception of Maher Zain in Sweden, I would argue that, while non-Muslims probably still do not know of him (yet) – although they might have heard of him or read about him – at least young people with a Muslim family background know of him, and those who like the religious message listen to him a lot, take personal pride in his success, and claim him in the way that ethnic and religious groups typically tend to do with 'their' stars in music, film and sport.

---

[21] The show can be heard in a Swedish version (http://sverigesradio.se/sida/avsnitt/758647?programid=2071) and an English one (http://sverigesradio.se/sida/avsnitt/776459?programid=2071). Last accessed 28 June 2017.

8

CAREFULLY PUSHING AHEAD

Awakening's intention was not to reform Islam, but to contemporise it. They recognised there was a collective Muslim identity crisis, and they sought to reconcile the false notion that Islam is at odds with modernity by offering an equally modern service within Islamic parameters. . . . Importantly, having a strong footing in the world of Islamic scholarship helped immensely.

the Awakening book, p. 33

This chapter aims to provide final comments on the relation between the Islamic discourses and the Awakening artists, the company, the music and the fans. It will first comment on the attitudes of Awakening to formal religious authority and then discuss ethical masculinity, new challenges for Islamic scholars and finally, creativity.

Awakening and Islamic Authorities

As already mentioned, apart from being brought up as Muslims, two of the founders of Awakening have higher education training in Islamic matters. Sharif Banna is pursuing a PhD in Islamic jurisprudence at al-Azhar University and is on the consulting board of Tariq Ramadan's CILE project. Bara Kherigi has a BA in Islamic jurisprudence from al-Azhar University.

Apart from this internal knowledge of Islam, which is both broad and vast, the Awakening founders have access to a network of scholars but, according to

Sharif Banna, they never formally consult them by asking for a legal opinion (a fatwa). As many of the scholars are senior and known for their wide learning, asking them to formally express a legal opinion could possibly hinder initiatives; rather, the founders discuss matters with several Islamic scholars including Tariq Ramadan and Abdullah Al Judai'. Sharif Banna said that some of the scholars had probably expected to be formally consulted, but instead the Awakening founders have told them that if they really think Awakening is going down the wrong path, they should pick up the phone. Awakening has also been asked whether they are going to form a shari'a advisory board, but the founders have disregarded the idea, preferring not to be bound by legal advice. 'We did not want to put arts and culture under the censorship of scholarship, but that does not mean that we do not care about scholarship', Sharif Banna claims.[1] Rather, as he modestly points out, Awakening has a foot in contemporary scholarship and knows what is happening there anyway. Yet, as he said in the same interview:

> There is more than law! . . . Does the music impact their [the listeners'] faith, does it impact their identity? . . . We [Awakening] know how, we know the emails we get. These certainly don't provide any *fiqhi* justification for anything, but it is not a *fiqhi* enterprise; *fiqh* is one part of the mosaic, but ethics is important, spirituality is important, identity is important, self-expression is important!

I had the opportunity to take part in one meeting with Islamic scholars held at St Antony's College in Oxford in 2013. It was really a part of Tariq Ramadan's CILE project, which nurtures the idea that to be able to develop Islamic ideas today – moving from 'adaptation reform' to 'transformation reform' aimed to 'change the order of things' (Ramadan 2009: 3, 33) – Islamic scholars, or scholars of text, need to engage in dialogue with scholars of other fields, scholars of context. In this case, a number of scholars of text and context were gathered to discuss the question, 'What is Islamic art and what makes art Islamic?' I was invited as a scholar of context and presented a paper published in the CILE journal where some of the other papers were also printed

---

[1] Interview with Sharif Banna, 11 December 2018.

(Otterbeck 2014b). I also participated in discussions commenting on other participants, who included Abdullah Al Judai' and Jasser Auda (who has published through Awakening). Sharif Banna took part in the discussions and, as could be expected, proved well-versed and well-informed, both about the arts in general and about Islamic jurisprudence. The two-day meeting was filled with pretty harsh discussions, and a lot of laughter and in-depth knowledge.

What was striking was the willingness and ability to discuss these issues openly in a scholarly fashion. Things were not set in stone; rather there was a shared readiness for change and development. Apart from the more theoretical issues concerning Islamic theology, the most interesting discussions revolved around beauty and morals. One *'alim* (Islamic scholar) insisted that real art must be beautiful. I and other 'scholars of text' objected, claiming that representations of the ugly may also be great art. After some confusion we realised that beautiful was actually a way of saying morally praiseworthy and of value. When art involves the morally blameworthy or even the socially destructive, it cannot claim to partake in the philosophical concept of art. This rather Platonic conviction projected onto the Qur'an in the discussion is entwined with concepts such as perfection, the good and the essence of an idea, while the opposite is associated with flaws, sins, deception, corruption of ideas and contempt for the pleasures of the people. The position of the quoted *'alim* is not unusual and can be found both in history and in our day and age (for further discussion, see Akkach 2018). Indeed, Islamised Platonic conceptions of beauty are an integral part of the discussions about *al-fann al-hadif* – art with a purpose.

Looking at the early years of Awakening, the production was clearly marked by just such an understanding of music and music videos. Both were produced in a non-stressful and appeasing fashion with few of the hard edges, such as distorted sounds or fast clips, so common in popular music and music videos. As confidence has grown, experience has increased and the limits of the possible have been pushed by a number of developments, Awakening has more or less abandoned this aspect of *al-fann al-hadif* discourse and accepted that other aesthetical palettes may be combined with the ethical ideals promoted and pursued, which opens up possibilities and leads to transformations. Wassim Malak formulated the attitude nicely in a conversation with me in 2017, claiming that every five years Awakening reconsiders a careful try to 'push ahead'.

The new music genres with the aim to come across as Islamic, 'faith-driven' and ethically sound, are developing organically, nurtured by initiatives from musicians, artists, intellectuals, business entrepreneurs and fans. The music has diversified and developed in several directions that have been difficult to anticipate, even for those involved, and it continues to do so.

Ethical Masculinity, Again

When discussing how to be an Islamic artist, Zain Bhikha commented on responsibility:

> You are mixing your faith with your creativity, two very, very powerful things. If you just did music without faith, without spirituality, without anything else and you're just an artist being creative, it would have been easy, but you're combining these two things, so who you are as a human being and who you portray yourself to be and who you think you are have to be all connected. (Zain Bhikha, interviewed by J. Otterbeck, 17 October 2017)

Zain Bhikha emphasised the reflexivity required. It is not enough to pronounce the ethical discourse; the artist will have to understand and live the part. The artists and founders of Awakening are intertwined with the ethical discourse they promote. Their songs, music videos, concerts, promotional material, social engagements and collaborations must be 'all connected'. If not, the authenticity and plausibility of the claim to be faith-driven may be questioned.

Artists are gazed upon, listened to and consumed. Since, for complex reasons, human beings have special, emotionally strong relationships to celebrities and music, often wired through sexuality, celebrity artists appealing to an Islamic ethical order must practice the art of no seduction. The masculinity of the artists is gazed upon and scrutinised. This includes the body, the discourse and the social engagement of the artists. Judging from behaviour and comments at concerts and from social media, young adult women in particular project and express admiration, love and erotic feelings onto the artists, both in an ironic, self-conscious way and most likely in a more direct, unabashed way, all rather typical of contemporary fan culture. What is particularly interesting is the controlled masculinity of the artists compared to the much less regulated behaviour of fans.

At the heart of the concert experience for many is joy and, I would propose, Muslim pride. The artists become ethical role models, but also display clothing fashion, propose normative social relations (between spouses, between offspring and mothers, between fellow humans, and so on) and celebrate central Islamic notions such as the love of the Prophet (with a capital P) and Allah, all readily consumed by attentive fans. Not everyone reacts the same way, of course. I had the opportunity to speak to a critic with a Muslim background who visited one of the concerts. He was thoroughly appalled by the message and found the music too soft, preferring metal himself, and felt that the message rang false, as his understanding of Islam rather implied intolerance and political dominance. To fans, however, it seems to be the direct opposite; the fact that Islam is portrayed as positive, contributing and sound is clearly part of the appeal. This is how they themselves comprehend Islam or would want to comprehend it. I have spoken with enough fans to maintain this.

The ethical masculinity is in a close relationship with how Islamic thought is formulated. When Islamic pop music was gaining its first incarnation in the 1990s, Islamic thought was still very character-oriented. Clearly expressed rules for conduct and virtue (*'ilm al-akhlaq*) were readily available and seldom challenged. As Islamic pop music artists have gained more confidence and as Islamic thought has been affected by a new emphasis on ethics, new opportunities have arisen.

Allow me to speculate. I suggest that the overall turn towards ethics among some Muslim intellectuals should be understood as a response to what Schreiter (1997) calls 'global theological flows', that is, intellectual discursive trends affecting not one but most intellectual expressions of religious traditions as these are situated in the contemporary conditions of the world. Schreiter gives four examples of such flows, among them ecology and human rights. The first Muslim reactions were produced by so-called liberal Islamic thinkers – the towering figure of Fazlur Rahman (d. 1988) comes to mind (see, for example, Kamrava 2009; Kurtzman 1998) – and it was later picked up by *al-wasatiyya* theologians.

I argue that the first two decades of the twenty-first century have seen an increased emphasis on ethics among rather mainstream Muslim thinkers, and a more relaxed relation to *'ilm al-akhlaq*, encouraging individualisation in expression. The turn towards ethics has caused Islamic intellectuals to examine their discursive tradition, finding the concept of *maqasid al-shari'a*, the overall purposes of shari'a, in historical sources. These contemporary intellectuals tend to particularly praise the scholar Abu Ishaq al-Shatibi (d. 1388) for his discussions on how to arrive at an interpretation of Islam aimed at avoiding hardship due to legalism and literalism (Masud 2009). The concept of *maqasid* is a smart translation and projection surface for an ethical turn in Islamic thinking, a reaction to the global theological flow insisting on the centrality of ethics. Studies of *maqasid al-shari'a*, and institutions devoted to it, have literally exploded in the twenty-first century to meet the needs of a new generation of Islamic thinkers. The focus on the meaning of norms, or ethics or *maqasid*, enables Islamic intellectuals to capture the experiences, doubts and needs of Muslims enmeshed in contemporary consumer culture who find traditional ethical rules on conduct less than helpful. Other issues regarding the environment, consumption, pluralism, pleasure and leisure, solidarity, gender, contribution and social engagement also need to be addressed, something facilitated by ethical debate. Awakening is part of this discourse, which is made visible in both the company's ethical profile and the ethical masculinity of the artists, allowing for an individual playfulness since 2014 – or, more cynically, perhaps they are required to provide a more personal, differentiated persona in order to come across as authentic and true and be marketable at the same time. But let us return to music.

New Challenges for Islamic Intellectuals

Have Islamic scholars seen it all when it comes to music? Are there new challenges around the corner? No, I don't believe they have, and yes, there are. The obvious challenges are of three kinds: the first is how to deal with norm shifts in music consumption; the second, with the plurality of norms in society in a way that is acceptable for all involved; the third, with history.

You do not have to speak to every Muslim alive to make the generalisation that most Muslims like music, and they like to listen to their chosen music. The fact that a substantial number of scholars say that music – or aspects of it – is haram (qualifying it in different ways) is problematic to many Muslims. Some will avoid music in certain periods, but most who are not impoverished will listen to music, possibly sing and dance to it, sing themselves or even play instruments; those who make the decision not to listen at all find it incredibly difficult to avoid it. This is even true for Saudi Arabia, a country where the *ulama* (the scholars of Islam) have substantial social power and most are against listening to many genres of music, at least in everyday life, and definitely against hedonistic pop music (Otterbeck 2012b).

Social philosophers call what has happened a norm shift (Green 2016: chapter 2). When moral norms among the many change, and rules and regulations – be they secular or religious – do not follow, norms risk being experienced as irrelevant at best, or oppressive and destructive at worst. In fact, rules that are thought of as oppressive or flawed can destabilise the faith of believers, provoking questions like: how can my religion demand of me to do this or abstain from that and still be good, or even relevant? In a plural society with knowledge of other worldviews, if the inherited worldview does not measure up to one's own moral standards, why stay, why accept it? Now, there are many reasons to remain attached to a religion: community, because few people want to risk being set aside by their families, a very real risk at conversion; ritual attachment may be strong; other dogma and norms may rhyme well with one's worldview; investments made in creating an identity are hard to relinquish; and so on. But very few (if any) believers appreciate the feeling of entertaining 'better', 'higher' or more morally outstanding ideals than those they perceive that their religion provides.

As shown above, the theology of purposeful art, including music, has encountered wide acceptance, finding expression in several different countries and settings. It has obviously met a need. Awakening and other actors have created the soundtrack to theological thought and, while doing so, have affected theological formulations and preferences, admittedly together with other artists. Yet musical tastes are volatile, new acts take the place of old even if old songs have become beloved evergreens; inevitably, we will see new styles and transgressions of set norms leading to new negotiations.

It is always hard for theologians to choose when to make a stand and hold their ground and when to let go and accept a norm shift. There is no shortage of interesting examples: the abolition of slavery, the introduction of democracy, gender equality, female education, and why not current discussions on gay marriages? Music is yet another interesting, currently divisive example. The Lebanese scholar Ibrahim Ramadan al-Mardini (2001) offers a kind of solution. He is permissive of music, but not anything will do. You cannot sing about illicit sex and doing drugs and still expect to be considered acceptable according to Islamic teachings, which is a fairly common position. However, al-Mardini's interesting contribution is that he claims that he is not interested in policing the believers; instead, he perceives himself as an advice-giver. If the young want to listen to music with poor morals – let them, but be there for them when they are prepared to listen to good Islamic advice about how to lead a decent life. Al-Mardini, as a devout believer, is convinced that, in the marketplace of ideas, Islam is the best option available, and quality will conquer. If I were an *'alim*, I would at least reflect on al-Mardini's insights. However, al-Mardini is marginal in both global and Lebanese Islamic thought (LeVine 2008b; Otterbeck 2008).

Another – more listened to – voice is Oxford professor Tariq Ramadan. In *Radical Reform: Islamic Ethics and Liberation* (2009), he requests more than the Islamisation of ready-made cultural expressions.

> It is urgent to invest time and thought in the now central area of culture and the arts, to devise an alternative that is altogether original, appealing, and faithful to the ethical outcomes. . . . Everywhere, people are looking for artistic expressions that are beautiful, inventive, noble, and inspiring. (Ramadan 2009: 206)

Ramadan wants to move away from the prevalent understanding of *al-fann al-hadif* and invites an art 'reconciled with the true freedom of saying everything while inviting the heart and mind to transcend the worst degradation' (Ramadan 2009: 205), thus launching criticism of commercialism and conscious vulgarity in art. As a self-proclaimed fan of French poetry, he nurtures a modernist, high-culture ideal. He continues by pitting moral art against truthful art, portraying the latter as 'expressing the realities of life', thereby challenging us to think. In Ramadan's view, art has a mission outside a role as religion's mouthpiece, an independent role that challenges routine and encourages creativity in thought, but such art, to be qualified as Islamic, must be brave and exciting without losing its moral compass.

Ramadan's call is still fairly unusual but it enables the prospect of discussing the possibility of Islamic interpretations of non-Islamic art without trying to appropriate and Islamise the art form or particular piece of art. Such a position is more equipped to open up to a plurality of art but has the possible drawback of having to be well-grounded in reflexive Islamic intellectual thought, a position not entertained by most people. However, as popular culture already affects the religious perception of the many – whether through the influence of comic books and films on the understanding of Hindu traditions (McLain 2009); the so-called 'occulture' of, for example, American popular culture, that is, the influence and normalisation of the occult in mainstream perceptions through popular culture (Partridge 2005); or pop-nashids formulating the ethics of Islam in clear, fairly simple lyrics taken to heart by many Muslims – theologians will have to come to terms with new ways of expressing Islam and how to formulate these in popular culture or in relation to it.

Creativity

The call for creativity in Islamic arts is already being met by many Muslim artists. The number of artists engaging in the arts with the explicit aim of coming across as Islamic or being understood as having an active relation to Islam is steadily growing. They are increasingly exploring new, or at least not previously used, forms of expression and communication, generally originating in the genres and cultural repertoires of contemporary consumer culture. Negus and Pickering (2004) argue that the romantic notion of creativity as 'freedom, agency and the unshackling of constraints' hampers our understanding. Instead, they argue that creativity will have to be understood in relation to communication, stating that scholars have to study the choice of form, type of media (which often involves commercial actors), copyright laws and conventions and constraints, and this without reducing creativity to mere reproduction or reassembling. Further, as noted by McClary, and quoted by Negus and Pickering (2004: 68),

> It is common to see convention only in negative terms. But conventions are enabling, for within them are inscribed 'the cultural arrangements that enable communication, co-existence, and self-awareness' within particular contexts and particular periods.

This quotation parallels Talal Asad's (1986) understanding of Islam as a discursive tradition that comprises an overall system interconnecting all the myriad complying and contradicting expressions of, for example, rituals, narratives, practices, theologies, ethics, legal practices and theories that in some way refer to Islam. Such a perspective encourages studies of how Islam is formulated, in time and space, through language and behaviour. The agency of individuals – their power or counter-power practices, authority and social positions – become important features to understand in context. Thus, creativity should be understood as in a relationship with heritage present in genres, forms and aesthetics that are prior expressions of different discursive traditions.

The artists of Awakening and the company itself have a privileged position, though it should not be ignored that they have worked hard for their success. They are listened to by audiences that are global. Awakening may offer the vision that its music is counter-cultural to the mainstream music industry, but it is also, arguably, the largest company when it comes to Islamic pop, providing it with an aura of authority and a claim to authenticity through its social engagement and ethics. This is not accepted by everyone; for example, former Awakening star Sami Yusuf and some of his fans criticise Awakening for being just a ruthless, commercial company that has lost track of Islam by not connecting actively to an Islamic heritage (that is, the established art expressions within the discursive tradition). Such is the world of claims; there is always someone to refute yours. This is precisely why I assert I study music that has the ambition to come across as Islamic; there is always resistance. But, as Sharif Banna made clear during our final interview, the Awakening founders and artists know the letters and emails they receive. They feel the emotions and engagement they receive from audiences, and are aware of scholars supporting them. The millions who follow them on social media sites, stream their music and engage with it by writing comments make up an audience that this book will never come remotely close to – not a bad social position from which to be addressing the world.

By pushing for new ways of expressing themselves, Awakening artists and founders also cause a normalisation of prior expressions; in other words, by first introducing instruments, then making use of them in new ways (for example, distorting guitars), the presence of instruments becomes normalised. Not everyone follows this route, however, and a hard-line discourse against musical instruments is upheld with remarkable persistence.

Still, without being able to prove my point, I argue that the lived practices of many Muslims, especially young adult Muslims, are considerably more progressive than general Islamic intellectual discourse allows for. The experiences of growing up surrounded by contemporary consumer culture shapes habits, values, ethics, aesthetics and the skills and styles of interpretations, and the opinion of what is morally good or bad.

The Awakening founders are now in their forties and they have orchestrated their personal, and perhaps their generation's, understanding of music and entrepreneurship for the masses. Young adults in particular have paid attention and listened, and among the youth of today are tomorrow's scholars and artists.

9

ISLAMIC DISCOURSES ON POPULAR MUSIC: A HISTORICAL FOOTNOTE

This chapter serves as an extensive footnote to the present book giving the reader a substantive background to the historical Islamic discourses on popular music. The history of Islamic discourses on music has already been described in detail many times by both Muslim and non-Muslim scholars. There is no need to repeat that feat. Therefore, this chapter will instead concentrate on what has often been scorned and unfairly treated by both sorts of scholars: popular music.

In *The Routledge Companion to Religion and Popular Culture* (2015), Lyden makes a point about how difficult it is to pin down what is referenced by popular culture. Jazz started out as a music genre of the people, detested by the societal elite for both its sound and style and its 'negro' performers (at least when writing about it), but, these days, jazz has long been taught at prestigious musical conservatories. Is jazz accurately described as popular music? History frequently teases us for inventing and imposing overly simplistic divisions.

To sort things out, Lyden (2015: 13) addresses four aspects of popular culture: (1) the elitist division between high culture and popular culture; (2) popular culture as 'folk culture'; (3) popular culture as mass-produced in modern times; and (4) popular culture as subcultural resistance to dominant culture. All aspects relate to different attitudes in the history of scholarly analyses of popular culture.

Regardless of whether Lyden's list is exhaustive or not, it provides a useful perspective when discussing Islamic views on popular culture and popular culture's relation to Islam. As will be shown below, Muslim intellectuals have made a clear division between elite music and popular forms, often expressing contempt for the latter and attaching a transcendental quality to the former (1). They have further distinguished between the music of the taverns and folk music, most authors showing more tolerance towards the latter (2). Most often, however, classical Islamic scholars have 'almost entirely ignored' folk music (Shiloah 1995: 163) even though celebration music, lullabies and songs of grief (lamentations, *nawh*) are occasionally mentioned (El Kholy 1953: part 3). While classical discourse centred on the legality of art music and Sufi *sama'* (ritual playing and listening to music), the discourse today centres on popular music. As has been addressed in Chapter 4, the discourse on mass-produced music was rather negative among Islamic scholars up until a turn slowly gained momentum in the last two decades of the twentieth century (3). In the debate, arguments about high/low and vulgarity, but also about Westernisation, are intertwined with the Islamic understanding of the allowed and the forbidden (Otterbeck 2004, 2016).

Regarding Lyden's last category, subcultural resistance (4), one finds, for at least the past five decades, that subcultural popular music has challenged dominant culture in Muslim environments: for example, different forms of rock, metal, hip-hop, sha'abi music or rai. However, the discourse among Islamic intellectuals targeting these expressions rarely rises above condemnation or moral panic about Satanism. The most permissive liberal discourse still disregards the potential value for intellectual discourse of dystopic extreme metal, politically revolutionary rap or music raising the social concerns of everyday life (Crowcroft 2017; Hecker 2012; LeVine 2008a, 2011; Otterbeck 2008, Otterbeck, Mattsson and Pastene 2018; Schade-Paulsen 1999).

To this discussion of popular music must be added the common discourse on music in classical times connecting music-making to magic and being inspired by jinn, seldom directly referred to in Islamic discourse but often mentioned in other genres of writing. Further, in the back of the minds of the scholars of Islam must have been the fact that as soon as a culture of luxury developed among Muslims as a consequence of increased riches due to conquests, the economic and political elites of society took up the practice of patronising musicians. This included holding musical soirées featuring singing, playing instruments, drinking wine and possibly dancing; musicians included both males and females, slaves, freed slaves and the elites themselves (some of the highest nobility were musicians). It was considered especially prestigious to be able to afford groups of slave women, trained in singing and playing different instruments (Shiloah 1995). It is very likely that this affected how scholars valued music. It also led to a *fiqh* discourse to the effect that professional musicians were untrustworthy because they participated in activities disruptive to the prescribed social moral order. All four Sunni law schools deny the legal value of testimonies from professional musicians, although amateur musicians involved in legal music-making were not disregarded (El Kholy 1953; al-Faruqi 1985). As Lydon points out, however, the simplistic line between the good and the bad is often blurred.

Ethnomusicologist and Islamic intellectual Lois al-Faruqi (1985) stresses that music was not an emic category of Muslim *faqih*s in classical times. Rather, they discussed a number of different categories, each carrying its specific connotations. Arabic scholars have used words like *ghina'* (singing, but also art music), *sawt* (voice, song, sound), *sama'* (listening), *ma'azif* (instruments with open strings), *'alat al-tarab* (musical instruments), *al-tarab* (music),[1] or, more slightingly, *malahi* or *lahw* (distraction, diversion) to cover specific sections of what we today refer to as a discussion on music. *Musiqa*, a loan-word from Greek probably incorporated into Arabic during the eighth or ninth century, was the philosophers' word for music when discussing music theory and cosmology (Shehadi 1995). At times, *musiqa* was used by philosophers to cover practical music, but generally other words were applied. I use music as a generic term, at times retaining the vocabulary above, so as not to distort arguments.

Below I unfold the arguments about 'popular music' in historical Islamic discourses. I have separated the arguments by philosophers, court intellectuals, Sufis and Islamic legal scholars into different sections. It is difficult to understand the positions of different writers unless they are placed in relation

---

[1] *Tarab* refers etymologically to strong feelings, literally 'enchantment', but became synonymous with music since music was considered, by definition, to awake strong emotions (Shiloah 1995: 16).

to each other, as much of the writing contains explicit or implicit criticism. I concentrate the discussion on the discourse that developed before the introduction of European music and mass culture.

Another defining aspect of popular music is whether it is participatory or presentational, to use Thomas Turino's (2008) terminology: that is, do musicians perform to an audience or with people? In folk music, understood as the music of people, participatory music is fairly common, and in the music of the taverns (a recurrent trope) it is presentational even though it is likely that audiences were active in singing and cheering, marking rhythms, dancing and the like. I return to this below, but it seems that Islamic theologians particularly disliked presentational performances.

A Language Some Could Understand: Philosophers on the Transcendence of Music

When the expanding Islamic empire took over the area today often referred to as the Middle East, it also inherited its people, along with cultures that were deeply influenced by Hellenistic or Sassanid thinking in fields such as medicine, cosmology, philosophy, astronomy and geometry, but also music. In Hellenistic descriptions of education, it is common to divide knowledge into *trivium* and *quadrivium*, the former usually consisting of grammar, logic and rhetoric, and the latter of arithmetic, geometry, astronomy and music. While *trivium* was the basic training, *quadrivium* was considered the advanced preparatory training for philosophy and later also for theology. As philosophy grew in influence in Muslim thinking from the later half of the eighth century, Muslim writers tended to divide knowledge between native sciences and foreign sciences (Shiloah 1995). The former pertained to sciences important for the understanding of religious matters, such as grammar and lexicography, in order to produce and understand Arabic correctly and, of course, the different Islamic genres such as *kalam* (scholastic theology) and *fiqh* (jurisprudence). The foreign sciences were the sciences of the *trivium* and *quadrium*, symbolised by philosophy.

Throughout the intellectual history of the so-called Muslim world, there has been tension between the proponents of philosophy and those of theology, but also creative attempts to combine and accommodate one with the other. It is important to stress that this was not a tension between believers and non-believing rationalists, as some people try to make out today (for example, the poet Adonis 2016). Philosophers like Ibn Sina (d. 1037) may have been criticised for their views on the capacity of human rationality to understand the world by supporters of the idea that the Qur'anic text as a revelation from Allah must be the starting point of all reasoning, but the philosophers were not outspoken atheists or anti-religious. For example, Ibn Sina also contributed to the religious sciences and some of his writing featured in Islamic education curricula as standard material for a long time, while the philosopher Ibn Rushd (d. 1198) was a Maliki *qadi* (judge) for a long period of his life. His harsh criticism of Asharite dogma is probably the reason why, at times, he is presented as a refuter of religion.

Many of the most well-known Muslim philosophers have written on music,[2] but, unfortunately, most of these texts are now lost.[3] Among those that have luckily survived are two written by world-renowned Abu Nasr al-Farabi (d. 950): *Kitab al-Musiqi al-Kabir* (The major book on music) and *Al-'Ilaj fi al-Musiqa* (Cure through music). In the first, al-Farabi develops music theory using mathematics and logic to explain the tonal system; in the second, he develops his thoughts on the therapeutic value of music, connecting the tonal system to the Greek allopathic system of the four humours, a common idea at the time that was also upheld by Ibn 'Abd Rabbihi (d. 940) – whose writings I return to below – and al-Kindi (d. 870) before them (Shehadi 1995: 15).

A marginal intellectual with ambition as a philosopher probably living during the eleventh century, al-Hasan al-Katib also expounded on the quality of music, clearly inspired by al-Farabi according to Shehadi (1995: chapter 5). He did not morally condemn music but, rather, aesthetically ordered it into the categories of meaningful and meaningless. According to al-Katib, the second

---

[2] Similar writing can be found in Christian philosophy, which is not surprising since the philosophers writing in Arabic had access to several tracts on music written by Greek philosophers, the very same that had an impact on Christian thought. Further, thinkers of the so-called Christian respective Islamic world had an influence on each other; see Partridge 2013; Shiloah 1995.

[3] Shiloah (1995: 46f) quotes the index of Arabic books by ibn al-Nadim (d. 995/8) that lists 104 works on music out of which only eleven are extant.

kind may be pleasing but had no depth and thus no real value and was therefore bad taste and mere amusement, going on to engage with an aesthetic discourse on (bad) taste in which he stigmatises playful frivolity. According to Shehadi, however, al-Katib does not suggest that bad taste should be regulated, instead recommending that it should not be indulged in (Shehadi 1995: 90).

Some philosophers, among them al-Farabi and the equally well-known Ibn Sina (d. 1037), refuted the commonly held idea that music had a cosmic origin, but most were prone to speculate about this cosmology (Shiloah 1995). According to Amnon Shiloah (1995), the explication by Ikhwan al-Safa' (the Brethren of Purity) is typical, and yet the finest and richest example of the affirming position in this discourse.

Ikhwan al-Safa', the famous, anonymous thinkers from Basra and Baghdad, active during the tenth century, viewed music in relation to the cosmos in their epistle on music (epistle four out of fifty-two), claiming that the origin of music should be sought in the heavens. They used music theory, mathematics, Greek medicine and the lute (*'ud*) to explicate the relationship between true music and the true use of music (Akkach 2018; Ikhwan al-Safa' 2010). 'True' is to be understood here as conditions that reflect an assumed perfect transcendent reality. The Brethren were very close to Sufism and Isma'ili Islam, and definitely inspired by Neoplatonism (Netton 1991).

The basic idea is that the philosopher who manages to understand the intricate secrets of true music will understand the structure of the creation. Philosophers have managed to transform this understanding from abstract thinking to the mathematically expressed proportions of the *'ud*, enabling the instrument to connect to the celestial music sung by angels. 'True music', played by the expert musician, will heal and complete both soul and body. Cosmological speculations may have been derived from Hellenistic thinking but they were firmly placed in an Islamic transcendent reality that included an Islamic angelology, cosmology and the supremacy of Allah (Ikhwan al-Safa' 2010).

Ikhwan al-Safa' are clear about music having correct and incorrect uses. Music is powerful and those who are not able to discipline themselves should not listen to it. Still, the Brethren write, quite explicitly, about musicians manipulating their audience through their musical skills, giving examples of how people drunk at parties or in a fit of rage may be soothed by soft melodies. While the overall moral comprises a warning against the misuse of music when pursuing worldly passions, this is not mentioned in connection with these examples of master musicians, drinking parties and noisy drunks, which merely illustrate the power of music. Still, the examples hint at the idea that even master musicians can play in such environments (Ikhwan al-Safa' 2010: 161), suggesting an ambivalent position on the performance of music.

Of course, the philosophers are not anthropologists and, as to be expected, their writings are mostly on ideas. Still, the environment in which they operated – of courts and patronage by famous families – most likely gave them rich opportunities to observe master musicians of both sexes perform the highest form of musical art. This was most certainly often part of their frame of reference as they pay little or no attention to the amateur music of the people and the (semi-)professional musicians of the taverns. Therefore, information about this sphere had to be sifted out. A richer source is provided by the courtier intellectuals who authored works on morals and the arts to which I now turn.

The Beauty, Not the Beast: Court Intellectuals on Music

Courtier intellectuals have produced another type of writing. Aiming to create a permissive attitude to music – something that they probably found a self-evident part of court life – they praise music and musicians and generally downplay the restrictions mentioned by the philosophers (and below, by the Sufis and the legal scholars). Some of these intellectuals were philosophers, Sufis or Islamic scholars in their own right, others merely referred to Islam and transcendent systems as they were part of every intellectual discourse at the time.

Ibn 'Abd Rabbihi (d. 940) was a poet and prolific intellectual at the Umayyad court in Andalusia. Among other things, he wrote a text that was to become quoted by many for centuries to come: *al-'Iqd al-Farid*, The unique necklace. The book is an edifying work on morals that features a chapter on music, arguing for its virtues and denouncing condemnatory attitudes, and is therefore quite consciously a discursive intervention in a debate. Ibn 'Abd Rabbihi is not interested in restricting music; he argues for the dominant view in society, but not necessarily in theology. Among other things, he calls music 'the spring-grass of the heart, the arena of love, the comfort of the dejected, the companionship of the lonely' and he writes that 'Often-times man will weep over his sins through [the influence of] music, and the heart will be softened from its stubbornness, and man may perceive its joys through the medium of beautiful music' (Ibn 'Abd Rabbihi quoted in Farmer [1929] 2001: 156).

It is important to note the fondness for music at most of the courts of Muslim rulers. There have been several books authored on songs and poetry in Muslim societies; others celebrate famous musicians and their musical gene-alogies (for a thorough description, see Shiloah 1995; Anderson 2018) or sim-ply the connection between romantic love and music (Ruggles 2018: 28). No book is more famous than *Kitab al-Aghani* (The book of songs), a twenty-five (at times twenty-one) volume work on songs, poems, singers, musicians and composers from pre-Islamic times up until the ninth century, by Abu al-Faraj al-Isfahani (d. 967), who was patronised by the vizier al-Muhallabi (vizier from 956) at the Abbasid court in Baghdad (Kilpatrick 2003).

A remarkable person mentioned by al-Isfahani was Jamila (d. *c.* 720), pos-sibly the most famous singer of her time (al-Isfahani 2008: VIII 134–67).[4] Born a slave in Medina, she rose to fame through her musical skills, which included singing, playing the lute and composing. Over the years, she became a reputable teacher and many musicians and singers studied under her. Even-tually she was freed and seems to have led a fairly comfortable life with her home as the centre for artistic creativity in Medina. As pertaining to religion, two stories stick out. Her spectacular hajj (pilgrimage to Mecca; al-Isfahani 2008: VIII 149–50) and the narrative about a dream she had, urging her to disassociate herself from singing (2008: VIII 160–1).

When narrating the pilgrimage of Jamila, al-Isfahani makes sure that the reader is duly impressed. Neither the people of Medina nor Mecca had seen the like of this. It was a caravan with fifty singing girls and thirty named sing-ing men. Even al-Isfahani himself doubts the plausibility of all the details but leaves it to the reader to figure out what is reliable (Kilpatrick 2003: 116). Religion is not mentioned apart from the fact that Jamila and her entourage were on a pilgrimage and that 'the Muslims' are addressed as a collective

---

[4] I am interested in Isfahani's details about Jamila's life as an argument about popular music, not for the historicity of his portrayal of her life.

noun. Yet the fact that the caravan and its entertainers and artists spread joy through song is emphasised, never questioned and not seen as incompatible with the act of pilgrimage.

Later in life, Jamila had a bad dream that scared the wits out of her. Convinced that she might die soon, she considered giving up singing to avoid being punished for it in the hereafter. She called a gathering to announce this, but a man of many years and great wisdom raised his voice, portraying music as solely positive. It heals and revives the weak and softens the heart and helps when enduring hardship. He scorned those who have a condemnatory attitude – the people of Iraq and their ilk – and warned the people of Hijaz not to take after them. Finally, he urged Jamila, rather than abandoning singing, to use it 'in the energy of worship/service (*'ala l-nashat fi 'ibadat*) of our Lord, powerful and mighty'. *'Ibadat* are the obligations that the *'abd* (worshipper/servant) has in relation to Allah. Jamila begged for Allah's forgiveness and then sang. A specialist on *The Book of Songs* asserts that this is the only lengthy argument that al-Isfahani presents for the legality of singing (Kilpatrick 2003: 254).

It needs to be pointed out that celebrated, named musicians at court and unknown bards making a living travelling around playing at festivals and taverns operated under different conditions, even though some musicians moved from one category to the other during their lifetimes. Refined musicians at court and in rich households had their protectors, while the local or travelling musicians had little protection or social status (El Kholy 1953: 230) and thus we know little about them or their craft. The narratives of al-Isfahani are not constructed around that separation, and do not moralise about music-making in more humble abodes. In fact, Jamila herself is said to have come from the humblest of backgrounds and learnt the basic part of her craft before being trained and refined.

Both Ibn 'Abd Rabbihi and al-Isfahani wrote about exceptional musicians who fulfilled the role of popular music among the elites. It was not part of their discourse to belittle, demean or to praise the folk music or the music of the taverns. Their defence of music indicates that topics like love, sadness and celebration have an important function for the human psyche and soul and, therefore, music is not forbidden by Islam – but whether this defence extended to the music of taverns is hard to tell.

If Hearing it Through the Grapevine: Sufis on Music

Generally, the Sufi positions are close to that of Ikhwan al-Safa'. Most of the writing concentrates on defending the legality of *sama'* (meaning listening, mystical audition) to critics. *Sama'* is likely to have been practiced since ninth-century Baghdad, and later spread all over the world (During 1993), and is a synecdoche for the Sufi ritual involving music, at times covering Sufi performances and concerts, although authors also write about *sama'* precisely as listening. Several Sufi masters have written treaties about *sama'*, for example Abu al-Qasim al-Qushayri (d. 1074) and 'Ali bin 'Uthman al-Hujwiri (d. 1077). The general argument goes like this. Music is a tremendous force and it must be handled with care. Only those whose higher spirit (*ruh*) is awakened (that is, have understood their role as created, and yearn for Allah) can use music for spiritual purposes and, for them, *sama'* nurtures their longing to unite with Allah, the spiritual world or some other concept signalling the assumed transcendent reality. Those who are not ready should not listen to music; it may give rise to base instincts (lust, greed, and so on), and it can even endanger their physical health. Because of this, the Sufi masters explicate, the shari'a suggests bans for listening to music with the wrong intent and in the wrong setting; it does not, however, forbid *sama'*.

The Islamic scholar and Sufi al-Ghazali (d. 1111) polemically argues about those who criticise *sama'*, claiming, 'It is like the impotent man who does not believe that there is pleasure in intercourse. That pleasure may be found in the strength of sexuality; since that sexuality has not been created in him, how may he understand it?' (al-Ghazali 2002: 13). Al-Ghazali is quite clear, using yet other examples (children, the blind): those who do not possess the spiritual experience are not qualified to judge in these matters. There are limits to al-Ghazali's acceptance, however; he scorns and disregards those Sufis whom he calls 'libertines', who, he claims, indulge in lascivious behaviour, and he takes a stance against their use of music.

Al-Ghazali (2002; MacDonald 1901–2) comments on popular music indirectly, mentioning five instances when listening to music is not allowed, two of which relate more directly to the music itself. He downright condemns music performed on stringed instruments and 'the Iraqi flute' (al-Ghazali 2002: 14), instruments that are forbidden 'because they are associated with winedrinkers' (2002: 14). Furthermore, sarcasm, satire and obscenity in lyrics are forbidden. From his reasoning, it can be deduced that obscenity includes a man singing a love song describing a woman's features to other men. The other three reasons why listening to music should be forbidden can be summarised as: being too inexperienced to handle music (other things than the love and longing for Allah are awoken in the heart); becoming reliant on music (it is only acceptable as a sporadic pastime activity); and finally, when performer and listener have the wrong social relationship (especially regarding gender). What al-Ghazali is criticising is clearly the popular music of the taverns and what he is praising is a restricted form of elite music. As an exception to the rule, al-Ghazali allows folk music in connection with occupation and family celebrations, as well as lullabies (a common exception in Islamic legal discourse; see al-Faruqi 1985). As al-Ghazali defends Sufis, he also comments on the frequent use of metaphors such as 'tavern', 'wine', 'drunkenness', 'lovers', 'hair locks' in Sufi poetry and songs. He argues against a literal understanding and explains a few metaphors to support his reading. For the actual music of the taverns, he only has contempt and writes that music in such a social setting 'is too low for us to speak of it, except to explain its lowness and that it is forbidden' (al-Ghazali quoted in MacDonald 1901–2: 706). The position of al-Ghazali is very common among Sufi intellectuals even today, as exemplified by the Iranian-American academic scholar and Sufi Seyyed Hossein Nasr (1990).

Still, at times, stories of Sufi masters finding ecstasy in the music of the taverns or at drinking parties are mentioned, often with the didactic twist that those at the gathering became so impressed that they bettered their ways: as when the Sufi master Abu Bakr al-Tamistani (d. 954) joined a gang of drunken thieves playing music and his ecstasy transformed their lives (Ernst 1985: 37). According to the narrative, the Sufi master was not above mixing with drunken thieves listening to music. This must be seen in relation to the spiritual untouchability of a Sufi master that, theoretically, implies that the master lives or has the potential to live in complete harmony with the divine, to the point of individual non-existence. The narrative is clearly structured around the juxtaposition of the holy/pure and the profane/sinful and the Sufi's ability to reveal the true way. The historical accuracy of such stories (there are many anecdotes resembling this one) is unimportant. The crucial element is that they highlight more flexible relations with popular music than al-Ghazali's more highbrow theoretical criticism, which points out that some Sufis appear not to have taken ideas about taverns, love and alcohol entirely metaphorically and rather indulged in the life of the taverns and enjoyed the music there.

Music played an especially important role in Persian Sufi poetry. The widely acclaimed poet Hafiz from Shiraz (d. 1390) repeatedly used music to conjure up associations with both the cosmological and the secular, as in the following, unusually metaphorically clear, short poem 'The Ambience of Love': 'We all sit in his orchestra, some play their fiddles, some wield their clubs. Tonight is worthy of music. Let's get loose with compassion, let's drown in the delicious ambience of Love' (Hafiz 1999: 186); or, in a phrase from a longer poem (no. 89 of the Ghazals), 'Early in the morning, after a night's drinking wine, I raise my wine cup to the music of castanet and harp' (Hafez 2006). Regardless of the frequent use of images like 'singing slave girls', music and musical instruments, the poetry seldom makes explicit references to popular music, but neither does it dismiss it.

The overall impression is that Sufi literature tends to disregard the music of the taverns but accepts certain types of folk music, or use of music in poetry and anecdotes when engaged in trying to evoke Sufi ecstasy or tell moral tales about the greatness of Sufi masters. Thus, no real defence of popular music is produced.

The Devil is Disguised: Islamic Legal Scholars on Music

It is beneficial when approaching Islamic jurisprudence (*fiqh*) to begin by making clear some of its guiding principles. First, *fiqh* is, and will always be, the outcome of interpretation. Therefore, *fiqh* is expressed through opinions by experts who base their judgements on interpretative techniques. Some techniques are general and some specific, and may become influential over time or during a certain period of time. In terms of music, some of the most important interpretative techniques are: (1) the difference between *amm* (general) and *khass* (specific); (2) finding the *'illa* (the reason behind); and (3) the halal/haram scale of five degrees. Second, *fiqh* is not merely a jurisprudence that engages intellectuals or judges; it is also communicated to the general believer as, by definition, it should be able to address and give advice on every facet of life including rituals, diet, hygiene, how to have sex and, of course, music-making and listening. Because of this, it has an elaborate discourse on sins.

When a *faqih* (a jurist) or, specifically, a mufti (a mufti gives a fatwa, a *responsum*; that is, an answer to a question about the correct Islamic way of dealing with a specified topic) tries to understand the normative texts – principally the Qur'an and the hadith collections making up the sunna, the normative custom – one of the first things that has to be decided is whether the text implies a general or a specific ruling. Of course, this is done after thorough language and grammar analyses. When it comes to music, the hadith about Muhammad and his wife Aisha standing watching a group of Abyssinians performing, dancing and singing, is discussed in these terms. Does the hadith imply a general licence for men and women to watch performances, or does it only pertain to a specific occasion, a celebration (of the Abyssinians)? This interpretative tool gives the *faqih* the possibility to restrict or expand a text and handle texts that seemingly contradict each other. Another tool that can be used is, for example, abrogation (*naskh*), the possibility to arrange both the Qur'anic text and the hadith in an order that claims that later texts replace those that precede them.

The argument about the general and the specific needs to be supported by a reason, *'illa*, the *faqih*'s claimed rationality behind a ruling in a text. Ideally, the *'illa* will have to be presented and accepted or refuted by the community of scholars; in reality, conflicting reasons and reasoning were established in the intellectual history of Islam. In the case of music, those pleading for a restrictive interpretation forbidding it claimed that the rationale behind music and musical instruments being proscribed was that music was the instrument of the Devil that led believers away from the straight and narrow path. He did this in two principal ways: first, by creating an appealing, but ultimately useless, activity (music) that requires the believer to spend time and possibly money indulging in it; therefore, amateur musicians were more favourably addressed than professionals as they spend less time on the craft. Second, the Devil has created music to function as an instigator of grave sins like fornication, the drinking of wine and ultimately unbelief. Those who looked more sympathetically on music denied that it was of the Devil and rather saw it as either cosmic or created by Allah to bring humans pleasurable experiences, like good food or objects of beauty. The ability to experience pleasure in itself is seen as created by Allah and thus good. However, over-use of any kind may be problematic, like over-eating. Instead, such *faqihs* claim that music must be judged in relation to the context – the time, the setting and the company – in which it is played or listened to. Thus, the *'illa* of the first group is refuted.

When the lawfulness of something is discussed, Islamic scholars may use a scale that is usually presented as having five categories.[5] The ingenuity of the scale is that there are four levels of halal (allowed) and one absolute category of haram (forbidden). Some things are *wajib* (a duty, obligatory), like performing daily prayers. The next category is *mustahabb* (recommended), like offering additional prayers. The next, *mubah* (neutral), pertains to things about which there are no rulings. The final halal category is *makruh* (the disliked, the reprehensible), a classic example being divorce, which is disliked but allowed. Then there are the unlawful matters – the haram – for example, fornication. Where should music be placed?

Music has been a subject of *ikhtilaf* (disagreement) all through the history of Islamic legal opinions, although all agree on two issues. The first is that tonal expressions in connection with religious rituals (like the call to prayer, pilgrim chants, and so on) are allowed. Some, but not all, have chosen not to refer to this as music. The second point of agreement is that music inciting to sin is not allowed (al-Faruqi 1985): associating 'sex and drugs' with 'rock and roll' is certainly not a new phenomenon.

The earliest extant tract written about music is Ibn Abi al-Dunya's (d. 894) *Dhamm al-Malahi* (Critical perspectives on instruments of diversion) which features a lengthy critique of music as *lahwa al-hadith* (idle tales, often shortened to *lahw*), a key concept in the discourse stemming from the Qur'anic Sura 31:6 in which people who spread *lahw* are condemned. One of Muhammad's highly respected companions, Ibn Mas'ud (d. 653), a man formative for later Qur'anic exegesis, is recorded to have claimed that by *lahw* is meant music. More moderate interpreters seldom deny this, but they claim that it is not music *per se* but diversions (like music) with a message that leads away from the message of Allah that are implied.

[5] As with most matters in Islamic theology, different versions of this scale exist. I present a common one.

When reading *Dhamm al-Malahi* it is hard to miss its edifying tone. Al-Dunya warns against the crooked path while laying out the straight path of Allah for the reader in no uncertain terms. He quotes the Umayyad caliph Yazid ibn al-Walid (d. 744), for example, saying that 'singing decreases shame, increases desire, and destroys manliness'. Further, 'it takes the place of wine and does what drunkenness does' meaning that it messes up judgement and evokes sinfulness in one's heart (al-Dunya in Robson 1938: 27). Being one of the first to have his lengthy writings on music widely disseminated, and also a prominent person in Islamic intellectual history, al-Dunya's arguments have been repeated by many after him.

It is important to understand al-Dunya's social position and his vision of theology to understand his contempt for music. He was a man of learning living in Baghdad, and was a renowned 'tutor and teacher' (Librande 2005: 12) to, among others, two future Abbasid caliphs (Mu'tadid, d. 902, and al-Muktafi, d. 908). His writing is characterised by his sincere edifying prose. The book, *Kitab al-Yaqin* (The book of certainty), carefully studied by Librande (2005), is marked by the same vision of morality: do not become attached to the diversions of life, rather, put your trust in Allah who is the provider of the created, be content with this provision and follow the sunna of Muhammad.

The Shafi'i scholar Abu l-Qasim al-Qushayri (d. 1074) presents a marked contrast with Ibn Abi al-Dunya. Al-Qushayri was both an Ash'ari scholar of the Qur'an and sunna and a master of Sufi lore, well established among the elite in Khurasan (Algar 1992). In 1045, al-Qushayri authored a Sufi manual, eventually one of the most widespread, often called *al-Risala al-Qushayriyya fi 'Ilm al-Tasawwuf* (The Qushayriyya epistle on the knowledge of Sufism; Knysh 2007). Towards the end, the epistle features a part defending *sama'* (listening) using *fiqh*-based language. He used both Qur'anic verses and hadiths to construct his arguments about music's legality, stressing the beautiful voice of Islam's messengers as proof of the value of tonal expressions. However, it is obvious that the core of his argument – where nuances are expressed – is found in his rendering of the tales and sayings of former Sufi masters. In these, music is presumed to be extremely powerful, bringing out feelings of fear, love and sadness. It has the ability to render men unconscious and even kill animals and men (it is unclear whether death is primarily symbolic or not). The stories are didactic, positioning music (and *sama'*) as a blessing for the mature Sufi, but a danger to the inexperienced. You need to consider time (*zaman*), place (*makan*) and company (*ikhwan*, lit. brethren) when evaluating what benefits or temptations music might bring (Knysh 2007).

Why the difference? After all, the texts available for both scholars are similar, they are both Sunni and they both work in the upper strata of society where music was a self-evident part of high culture. Of course, there are some structural differences: Ibn Abi al-Dunya was a moral teacher in Baghdad with wide learning who shared some intellectual similarities with Hanbali perspectives (even though his possible affiliation with this school is not proven), and al-Qushayri a Shafi'i Sufi in Nishapur two centuries later. It also seems that their personal visions of how to write theology differed. While Ibn Abi al-Dunya seems to experience his role as an uncompromised and uncompromising advisor on what is sinful and what is not, in a black and white world, al-Qushayri seems to promote reflection and the exploring of complexities. I find it reasonable to suggest that Ibn Abi al-Dunya's leaning towards moderation and ascetism (*zuhd*) and Qushayri's high culture Sufism actually formed a crucial framework of interpretation for the respective theologians.

Christopher Partridge (2013) points out the difference between those who emphasise revelation as a special historical religious event, contrasted to those who experience the whole of creation as a general revelation. While the first group tends to take a negative stance on music, the latter tends to incorporate it as a means of expressing the beauty of creation. Apart from the obvious objection that even the most closed-minded theologian stressing the uniqueness and importance of revelation also celebrates the world as created by Allah, the observation offers us a tool to notice something important about Islamic theology. For example, stern theologians will see music as competing for the attention that should be directed to the revelation, while the Sufis and philosophers often are more interested in the cosmic, transcendent origin of music. This creates an incongruent understanding of music in the two camps that can only agree on the assumed powers of music.

One must not forget the maturity of thought that Sunni scholars have shown throughout history in regard to different opinions. The fact that many scholars accepted the plurality of opinion over time and in space as a blessing – at least most theologians accepted this in theory, while not necessarily accepting a plurality of truths (Kamali 1991), just the possibility of human short-comings – is proof of a widespread acceptance in Islamic history that the individual theologian's knowledge and position in time and space mattered for the opinions expressed. This is not to claim Muslim scholars invented postmodernity or that Muslim scholars were not interested in enforcing their interpretation on students, colleagues, officials, commoners and family, merely to point out that in a scholarly discussion, this position was standard and that the position creates space for a social constructionist, historical approach.

The harshest scholars would forbid all use of music apart from the voice and the *daff* at some well-defined occasions, like a family celebration, further restricting female singing to prepubescent girls performing in front of other women, claiming that clapping and playing the *daff* is for girls and women. Admittedly, that is not a very common position but the reasons behind it are interesting. These scholars perceived music as the instigator of fornication, wine drinking and other blatant sins, and the admonishing advice is given to keep the believer on the right path according to the logic that a taste increases desire for more, thus, it is better to avoid it altogether. Shehadi (1995: chapter 6) expands on the ideas about singing and listening to music by the charismatic and controversial theologian and jurist Ibn Taymiyya (d. 1328), very much in line with the most restrictive views mentioned above. Apart from singing or using a melodic language in relation to rituals, Ibn Taymiyya thought singing was allowed to incite bravery in war, at family celebrations and in caravans. Music for pure enjoyment, particularly vulgar music, is the Devil trying to lure the faithful from the path of Allah.

The Vulgar and the Harmless

However, regardless of which historical voice one turns to, one will not find a defence of the music of the taverns. It is by definition considered vulgar, crude and outside the sphere of what Islam can tolerate. Whether these opinions were based on a firm first-hand knowledge or on stereotypes and class contempt is impossible to tell, but judging from folk tales about sexuality, wine and humour it is quite possible that taverns were not very pious places.

The popular music of the people – that is, folk music connected to family and holiday celebrations – met with wider tolerance, if not liking. Scholars who did not condemn music altogether, found folk music acceptable as harmless jocularities and recreational amusements. Lullabies and working songs, mentioned in hadiths, encountered the greatest acceptance and non-vulgar amusing songs the least. In the same spirit, amateurs were more tolerated than professionals.

These discourses continued into the twentieth century. For example, Mustafa Sabri (d. 1954) used to serve as *şeyhülislam* (the highest religious authority) in the Ottoman state. A short article by him, published in 1910 in the Turkish magazine *Beyan-ul Haq* issued by the Islamic Scholars Society, provides a good example of restrictive reactions to new conditions.[6] Sabri writes:

> Perhaps Islam does not see right to remain indifferent to music because it knows how delightful music is to our nature and how strong it is on our feelings. Our religion has an exceptionally good view in any case, in discovering the hidden dangers which might be inherent in the sweetest and most pleasurable things. (Sabri [1910] 1995)

With this warning, Sabri attaches himself to one of the main arguments of the restrictive scholars. He further explains that music awakes passion in people and makes them see reality in a more extreme way than it really is – increasing happiness for the glad and sorrow for the miserable – but the most problematic issue is that 'music has a tremendous effect in agitating the feelings of romance and love' (Sabri 1995). Thus, music opens up the uncontrollable in people by warping their perceptions, while Islamic guidance promotes control, the remembrance of Allah and listening to Qur'anic recitation, rather than admittedly skilled musicians and composers. Sabri also opines that music is a 'useless activity' and that some are led astray by Western influences and let their daughters spend time learning instruments.

Sabri wrote from the perspective of a trained Islamic scholar who was well aware of new social patterns he considered to be influenced by the West. The article bridges classical and new writing, touching on most of the themes that

---

[6] Almost a century later, Sabri's text was reprinted in translation in the journal *Anadola* – not as a historical text on music but as an authoritative text on the topic.

would be repeated during the coming century. The popular music that was made available through radio, records, concert halls and, eventually, a number of other media and technical devices was rarely appreciated and discussed from an intellectual, Islamic stand-point. It was instead debased, being called useless at best, the Devil's luring voice at worst, and popular music was also frequently seen as foreign and a result of non-Islamic cultural imperialism (Otterbeck 2004).

The more acquiescent, more recent discourse has already been discussed in previous chapters. As the more hostile discourse is not a concern at the heart of this book and largely repeats some of the discourse above, I do not dwell on it (for more detail, see Otterbeck 2008, 2012b, 2016). If further information on the subject is required, you will find an endless stream about this on the Internet, or in books like *The Music Made Me Do It: An In-Depth Study of Music through Islam and Science* by Dr Gohar Mushtaq (2011) or the well-researched book *Slippery Stone: An Inquiry into Islam's Stance on Music* by Khalid Baig (2011).

Finally, allow me to predict the future: the Islamic discussion about (popular) music will never end, but as the possibilities to create alternative popular culture are taken more and more into account, the acceptance of faith-driven music will only increase, with Awakening being acknowledged as a pioneer in creating a global, Islamic, popular-culture market.

GLOSSARY

(Primarily Arabic words)

'abd: servant, as in the name 'abdallah, servant of Allah.

adab: ethics, especially deontological ethics; also a general word for literature but not in this book.

'alim (pl. *'ulama'*): someone learned, specifically someone learned in Islamic matters.

daff: frame drum; an age-old word important for the Islamically informed discourse on music. Also spelt *duff*.

da'iya: public promotor of Islam, someone doing *da'wa*; also *da'i*.

da'wa: the promotion of Islam to Muslims as well as non-Muslims.

al-fann al-hadif: purposeful art; important terminology in contemporary Islamic discussions on music and on art in general.

al-fann al-nazif: clean art; art that is not religious, but neither morally blameworthy.

faqih: a specialist in *fiqh*, Islamic jurisprudence.

fatwa: a *responsum* by a mufti (an expert in Islamic jurisprudence), i.e. an answer to a question about Islamic knowledge, often about behaviour. Fatwas are advisory.

fiqh al-aqaliyya: minority jurisprudence. A recent concept building on classical and new legal viewpoints about how to live according to Islam when not in a Muslim-majority state.

ghina': singing.

hadith: the sayings and action of Prophet Muhammad or other people close to him among the first generations of Muslims. To many, hadith collections are as important to Islamic thought as the Qur'an.

al-hadra: the circle. In this case referring to collective Sufi rituals, but especially the music associated with such.

hajj: the annual pilgrimage to Mecca.

halal: allowed according to Islamic jurisprudence.

haram: forbidden according to Islamic jurisprudence.

hijab: the Islamic headcloth or veil.

hijabi: someone who wears the hijab.

ikhwan: brotherhood or company, depending on the context.

'illa: the proposed reason behind an Islamic rule deduced from the sources (primarily the Qur'an and the sunna),

'ilm al-akhlaq: the art, or knowledge, of the correct moral behaviour.

iltizam: commitment. Used early on in the twentieth-century discourse about moral arts; see *al-fann al-hadif.*

lahw: entertainment, with the side meaning of waste of time or even sin, at least to some.

latmiyat: lament; Shiite poetic and musical genre.

madih: praise; devotional song most often about the Prophet Muhammad.

makruh: disliked but not forbidden. In Islamic theology, one finds scales of different levels of halal (the allowed), separating between, for example, duties and the preferred. *Makruh* is the last category before the forbidden – the disliked: that which should be avoided, but that is still allowed.

maqasid al-shari'a: the purposes of shari'a, i.e. the reasons behind rulings. An Islamic legal doctrine. Often used as a parallel to applied ethics addressing the big issues of contemporary societies.

mawlid al-nabi: the Prophet's, i.e. Muhammad's, birthday.

al-mazamir: (plural) wind instruments, but also illicit music in Islamic thought critical of music.

mufti: an Islamic authority who is capable of issuing a fatwa.

munshid: a (nashid) singer.

na'at: a vocals-only genre of tonal, devotional poetry.

nashid: a song. In the context of this book, an Islamic themed song.

nay: a reed flute, particularly associated with Sufis in history and with contemplative music in contemporary recordings.

sama': listening; also a common name for music-driven Sufi ritual.

shari'a: the very varied, Islamic legal tradition.

sunna: Muhammad's normative example, at times including the examples of the first generations of Muslims.

Sunni: literally, the followers of *al-sunna*, the over-all name of the most common understanding of Islam, in itself containing a large variety.

takbir: the pronunciation of the phrase *Allahu akbar*. If someone says '*takbir*' out loud, others are supposed to say '*Allahu akbar*'. This is a way of honouring someone who has done something good.

'ud: the Arabic lute, the precursor of the acoustic, Spanish guitar.

'ulama': plural of *'alim*; the learned scholars of Islam.

al-wasatiyya: the middle way. In this book, an intellectual trend merging traditional scholarship with contemporary solutions originating in Egyptian discourse.

wird: litany. Many Muslim orders have their own set *wird* to be pronounced ritually at different occasions.

zakat: the alms, one of the pillars of Islam.

REFERENCES

Awakening Media Products

Abu Ghuddah, Shaykh 'Abd al-Fattah [2004] (2011a), *The Value of Time*, 3rd edn, Swansea: Awakening. [Book]

Abu Ghuddah, Shaykh 'Abd al-Fattah [2001] (2011b), *Islamic Manners*, 4th edn, Swansea: Awakening. [Book]

al-'Asqalani, Ibn Hajar (2004), *Preparing for the Day of Judgement*, trans. Sharif Banna, Swansea: Awakening. [Book]

Auda, Jasser (2012), *A Journey to God: Reflections on the Hikam of Ibn Ata'illah*, Swansea: Awakening. [Book]

Awakening (2014), '*The Awakening book*' [no title given], London: Awakening. [Book]

Azami, Nazeel (2006), *Dunya*, AWK05. [CD]

al-Banna, Imam Shaheed Hasan (2001), *Al-Ma'thurat*, London: Awakening. [Book]

al-Banna, Imam Shaheed Hasan (2004), *Al-Ma'thurat*, AWAKCD03. [CD]

al-Banna, Sharif M. H. [2000] (2011), *The Sirah of the Final Prophet*, 4th edn, Swansea: Awakening. [Book]

al-Banna, Sharif H. (2012), 'Spirituality and Civic Engagement: The Prophetic Model', essay at www.cilecenter.org/en/articles-essays/spirituality-and-civic-engagement-the-prophetic-model/ (last accessed 18 October 2017).

al-Banna, Sharif H. (2016), 'Halal but un-Islamic, restoring the Ethical. Core of Islam', *Islamic Institute for Development & Research*, 27 June, https://www.iidr.org/opinions/34-halal-but-un-islamic-restoring-the-ethical-core-of-islam/ (last accessed 10 December 2018).

The Best of Islamic Music, Vol. 1 (2012), AWK15. [CD]

The Best of Islamic Music, Vol. 2 (2013), unknown article number. [CD]

The Best of Islamic Music, Vol. 4 (2019), unknown article number. [CD]

Burdah of Imam al-Busairi, Selections from the (2006), performed by Ahmed Jalmam & Group, CDA AWK07. [CD]

Faris, Muhammed (2017), *The Productive Muslim: Where Faith Meets Productivity*, Swansea: Claritas. [Book]

al-Haddad, Mohammed (2011), *Malak Ghair Allah (You have no one except Allah)*, unknown article number. [CD]

Harris J (2015), *Salam*, AWK36. [CD]

Harris J (2015), 'Salam Alaikum', directed by Mike Harris. [Music video]

Harris J (2017), 'Save Me from Myself', directed by Jenson Singarajah. [Music video]

Harris J (2018), *Live in Concert*, unknown article number. [CD]

Harris J and Ward Jenkins (2017), *Salam Alaikum: A Message of Peace*, New York: Salaam Reads/Awakening. [Book]

Humood (AlKhudher) (2015), *Aseer Ahsan*, unknown article number. [CD]

Humood (AlKhudher) (2018), 'Kun Fiduliyan', directed by Anas Tolba. [Music video]

Khan, Ashar (2008), *If You Only Knew*, AWK16. [CD]

Kurtis, Mesut (2004), *Salawat*, AWKCD02. [CD]

Kurtis, Mesut (2007), 'Burdah', directed by Hani Osama. [Music video]

Kurtis, Mesut (2009), *Beloved*, AWK10 [CD]

Kurtis, Mesut (2014), *Tabassam*, AWK27. [CD]

Kurtis, Mesut (2014), 'Rouhi Fidak', directed by Uygur Akkaya. [Music video]

Kurtis, Mesut (2018), 'Ilahi', unknown director. [Music video]

Kurtis, Mesut (2020), 'Asma Allah alhusna', directed by Mesut Kurtis and his family during the 2020 lockdown. [Music video]

The Life of Muhammad (2001), unknown article number. [CD]

Makki, Irfan (2011), *I Believe*, unknown article number. [CD]

Makki, Irfan, featuring Maher Zain (2011), 'I Believe', directed by Lena Khan. [Music video]

Namira, Hamza (2008), *Ehlam Ma'aya, Dream with Me*, CDAWK07. [CD]

Namira, Hamza (2011), *Insan*, CDAWK19. [CD]

Namira, Hamza (2014), *Esmaani*, AWK31. [CD]

Raef (2011), 'It's Jumuah [Friday]', directed by Karim Shaaban. [Music video]

Raef (2014), *The Path*, CDAWK26. [CD]

Raef (2016), 'The Muslim Christmas Song', directed by Alaa Alkhateeb. [Music video]

Raef (2018), 'Ramadan is Here', directed by Ridwan Adhami. [Music video]

Raef (2019), 'Subhan Allah', directed by Abdulrahman ElAbyad. [Music video]

Raef (2019), *Mercy*. AWK22. [CD]

Ramadan, Tariq (2012), *Western Muslims: From Integration to Contribution*, Swansea: Awakening. [Book]

Robertson, Hamza (2007), *Something About Life*, AWK09. [CD]

Sanders, Peter (2008), *The Art of Integration: Islam in Our Green and Pleasant Land*, Swansea: Awakening. [Book]

Siba'i, Mustafa (2001), *The Islamic Civilization*, trans. Sharif Banna, Swansea: Awakening. [Book]

Sing Along With Friends (2013), childrens' songs by Mariam Elhiny, CD AWK24. [CD]

Usman, Azhar (2002/3), *Square the Circle: American Muslim Comedy of Distortion*, unknown article number. [CD]

Webb, Suhaib William (2003), *Mothers of the Believers*, unknown article number. [CD]

Yusuf, Sami (2004), *Al-Mu'allim*, AWAKCD01. [CD]

Yusuf, Sami (2005), 'Al-Mu'allim', directed by Hani Osama. [Music video]

Yusuf, Sami (2005), 'Hasbi Rabbi', directed by Hani Osama. [Music video]

Yusuf, Sami (2005), *My Ummah*, AWKCD04. [CD]

Yusuf, Sami (2008), *Sami Yusuf On: Camera*, MDCA014. [DVD]

Yusuf, Sami (2008), *Sami Yusuf Live at Wembley Arena*, AWKDVD02. [DVD]

Yusuf, Sami (2009), *Without You*, unknown article number. [CD]

Yusuf, Sami (2011), *The Very Best of Sami Yusuf*, CDAWK37. [CD]

Zahawy, Hussein (2008), *One Word*, unknown article number. [CD]

Zain, Maher (2009), *Thank You Allah (music version)*, CD AWK17. [CD]

Zain, Maher (2009), 'Palestine Will Be Free', directed by Andrew Morgan. [Music video]

Zain, Maher (2010), 'Insha Allah', directed by Mike Harris. [Music video]

Zain, Maher (2011), 'Ya Nabi Salam Alayka', directed by Hamzah Jamjoom. [Music video]

Zain, Maher (2011), 'For the Rest of My Life', directed by Lena Khan. [Music video]

Zain, Maher (2012), *Thank You Allah (vocals only version)*, CD AWK17. [CD]

Zain, Maher (2012), *Forgive Me*, IS 423. [CD]

Zain, Maher (2012), 'Mawlaya', directed by Hadi Chatila. [Music video]

Zain, Maher (2013), 'Ramadan', directed by Hamzah Jamjoom. [Music video]

Zain, Maher (2016), *One*, CD AWKK37. [CD]

Zain, Maher (2016), 'Close to You', directed by Amr Singh. [Music video]

Zain, Maher (2016), 'Allah ya Moulana', directed by Abdulrahman El Abyad. [Music video]

Zain, Maher, featuring Mustafa Ceceli (2016), 'The Way of Love', directed by Hasan Kuyucu. [Music video]

Zain, Maher (2017), 'Medina', directed by Lena Khan. [Music video]

Other Recordings

Ay, Mehmet Emin (1989), *Dolunay*. Beyza Yapım. [Audio cassette]

Bhikha, Zain (1994), *A Way of Life*. [Privately released. Later by Jamal Records]

Bhikha, Zain (2005), *Mountains of Makkah*, Zain Bhikha Studios. [CD]

Bhikha, Zain (2006), *Allah Knows*, Zain Bhikha Studios. [CD]

Bhikha, Zain (2006), 'Can't U See', from *Allah Knows*, Zain Bhikha Studios.

Bhikha, Zain (2009), 'Freedom will Come', from *The Beginning*, Zain Bhikha Studios.

Bhikha, Zain (2010), *A Way of Life*, Zain Bhikha Studios/Jamal Records. [CD]

Bhikha, Zain (2011), 'Better Day', Zain Bhikha Studios. [Released as a single and music video]

Bhikha, Zain (2014), *Songs of a Soul*, Zain Bhikha Studios. [3 DVD set with live, documentary, music videos]

Chappell, Heather (2007), *The Moon, A Bullethole*, Independent release. [CD]

Isam B (2018), *Lost for Words*, Warner. [CD]

Islam, Yusuf (1995), *The Life of The Last Prophet*, Mountain of Light. [CD]

Islam, Yusuf (2000), *A is for Allah*, Jamal Records. [CD]

Islam, Yusuf (2006), *Footsteps in the Light*, Jamal Records. [CD]

Jackson, Michael (1991), 'Heal the World', Epic. [Single]

Makki, Irfan (1997), *Reminisce*, Independent release.

Makki, Irfan (2006), *Salam*, Sound Vision. [CD]

Mecca2Medina (1996), *Life after Death*, Dawa Records. [CD]

Namira, Hamza (2018), *Hateer min Tany*, Namira Productions. [CD]

Outlandish (2005), *Closer than Veins*, RCA. [CD]

Phillips, Idris (2016), *Star by Moon*, Let the Change Be. [CD]

Radmanesh, Babak (2016), 'Va inak 'Eshq', Sedaye Honar. [Single release and music video]

Raihan (1996), *Puji-Pujian*, Warner Music Malaysia. [CD]

Raihan (1997), *Syukur*, Warner Music Malaysia/Zamrud Records. [CD]

Raihan (2001), *Syukur 21*, WEA/Zamrud Records. [CD]

Raihan (2001), *Demi Masa*, WEA/Zamrud Records. [CD]

Raihan (2005), *Ameen*, WEA. [CD]

Raihan (2008), *The Spirit of Shalawat*, WEA. [CD]

Robertson, Tom (2014), *What You've Become*, Andante. [CD]

Stevens, Cat (1970), 'Father and Son', Island Records. [Single]

Thuresson, Svante (1966), 'Hej Systrar, Hej Bröder', Metronome. [Single]

Wharnsby-Ali, Dawud (1995), *Blue Walls and the Big Sky*, Enter Into Peace. [CD]

Wharnsby-Ali, Dawud (1996), *A Whisper of Peace*, Sound Vision. [CD]

Wharnsby, Dawud (2004), *Vacuous Waxing*, Enter Into Peace. [CD]

Wharnsby, Dawud (2007), *Out Seeing the Fields*, Beloved Musika. [CD]

Wharnsby, Dawud (2014), *Acoustic Simplicitea*, Silk Route Media. [CD]

Young, Neil (1982), *Trans*, Geffen. [LP]

Yusuf (2006), *An Other Cup*, Ya Records/Polydor. [CD]

Yusuf (2009), *Roadsinger*, Ya Records/Island Records. [CD]

Yusuf (2014), *Tell 'Em I'm Gone*, Sony Music/Legacy Recordings. [CD]

Yusuf, Sami (2012), *Salaam*, Mazzika. [CD]

Yusuf, Sami (2015), *Songs of the Way Volume 1*, Andante. [CD]

Other References

'Abd al-Baqi, Muhammad Fu'ad (1986), *al-Mu'jam al-Mufahras li-Alfazi l-Qur'ani l-Karim* [Concordance of the Holy Qur'an]. Beirut: Dar al-Fikr.

Ackfeldt, Anders (2019), *Islamic Semiotic Resources in US Hip-Hop Culture*, Lund: Lund University.

Adonis (2016), *Violence and Islam: Conversations with Houria Abdelouahed*, Cambridge: Polity Press.

Ahmad, Salman (2010), *Rock & Roll Jihad: A Muslim Rock Star's Revolution*, New York: Free Press.

Aidi, Hisham D. (2014), *Rebel Music: Race, Empire, and the New Muslim Youth Culture*, New York: Vintage Books.

Aken, Mauro van (2007), 'Dancing Belonging: Contesting Dabkeh in the Jordan Valley, Jordan', *Journal of Ethnic and Migration Studies*, 32(2), 203–22.

Akkach, Samer (2018), 'Aural Geometry: Poetry, Music, and Architecture in the Arabic Tradition', in M. Frishkopf and F. Spinetti (eds), *Music, Sound, and Architecture in Islam*, Austin: University of Texas Press, pp. 166–97.

Alagha, Joseph (2014), 'G. Banna's and A. Fadlallah's Views on Dancing', *Sociology of Islam*, 2(1–2), 60–86.

Alagha, Joseph (2016), 'Shi'a Discourses on Performing Arts: Maslaha and Cultural Politics in Lebanon', in K. van Nieuwkerk, M. LeVine and M. Stokes (eds), *Islam and Popular Culture*, Austin: University of Texas Press, pp. 151–68.

Alazrak, Nermeen, and Alamira Samah Saleh (2016), 'The Neo-Liberal Islamic Preachers: "It is not enough to believe, but you must act on your faith"', in N. Mellor and K. Rinnawi (eds), *Political Islam and Global Media: The Boundaries of Religious Identity*, Abingdon: Routledge, pp. 219–30.

Al-Albani, Nasir al-Din (2002), *Tahrim Alat al-Tarab* [The prohibition of musical instruments]. Al-Jubail: Dar al-Sadiq.

Algar, Hamid (1992), 'Introduction', in *Principles of Sufism by Al-Qushayri*, trans. from the Arabic by B. R. von Schnegell, Berkeley: Mizan Press.

Alibašić, Ahmet (2014), 'Bosnia and Herzegovina', in J. Cesari (ed.), *The Oxford Handbook of European Islam*, Oxford: Oxford University Press, pp. 429–74.

Anderson, Glaire D. (2018), 'Aristocratic Residences and the *Majlis* in Umayyad Córdonba', in M. Frishkopf and F. Spinetti (eds), *Music, Sound, and Architecture in Islam*, Austin: University of Texas Press, pp. 228–54.

Armbrust, Walter (1996), *Mass Culture and Modernism in Egypt*, Cambridge Studies in Social and Cultural Anthropology, Cambridge: Cambridge University Press.

Armbrust, Walter (2005), 'What would Sayyid Qutb Say? Some Reflections on Video Clips', *Transnational Broadcasting Studies*, 14, https://www.arabmediasociety. com/what-would-sayyid-qutb-say-some-reflections-on-video-clips/ (last accessed 18 January 2019). [This issue is registered as issue 13/2004 in the link.]

Arnold, Gina, Daniel Cookney, Kirsty Fairclough and Michael Goddard (2017), *Music/Video: Histories, Aesthetics, Media*. London: Bloomsbury.

Asad, Talal (1986), *The Idea of an Anthropology of Islam*, Occasional Papers Series, Center for Contemporary Arab Studies, Georgetown: Georgetown University.

Asad, Talal (1993), *Genealogies of Religion: Discipline and Reasons of Power in Christianity and Islam*, Baltimore: Johns Hopkins University Press.

al-'Asqalani, Ibn Hajar (no date), *al-Munabbihat 'ala-l-Ist'adad li-Yaumi-l-Ma'ad* [Preparing for the Day of Judgement], No place: Muhammadiyya Bris. Available at http://dar.bibalex.org/webpages/mainpage.jsf?PID=DAF-Job%3A166898 (last accessed 29 September 2017).

al-Athari, 'Abdullah (2013), *Singing & Music: In Islamic Perspective*. Riyadh: Maktaba Dar-us-salam.

Auda, Jasser (2008), *Maqasid al-Shariah as Philosophy of Islamic Law: A Systems Approach*. Herndon: The International Institute of Islamic Thought.

Baig, Khalid (2011), *Slippery Stone: An Inquiry into Islam's Stance on Music*. Garden Grove, CA: Open Mind Press.

Baker, Raymond William (2003), *Islam without Fear: Egypt and the New Islamists*. Cambridge, MA: Harvard University Press.

Barendregt, Bart (2012), 'Sonic Discourses on Muslim Malay Modernity: The Arqam Sound', *Contemporary Islam* 6(3), 315–40.

Bayat, Asef (2005), 'Islamism and Social Movement Theory', *Third World Quarterly*, 26(6), 891–908.

Bayat, Asef (2007), *Making Islam Democratic: Social Movements and the Post-Islamist Turn*, Stanford: Stanford University Press.

Bayat, Asef (2009), 'No Silence, No Violence: A Post-Islamist Trajectory', in M. J. Stephan (ed.), *Civilian Jihad: Nonviolent Struggle, Democratization, and Governance in the Middle East*, New York: Palgrave/Macmillan, pp. 43–52.

Berg, Carin (2012), 'Tunes of Religious Resistance? Understanding Hamas Music in a Conflict Context', *Contemporary Islam*, 6(3), 297–314.

Berg, Carin (2017), 'The Soundtrack of Politics: A Case Study of Anashid in Hamas and Hezbollah', Dissertation, School of Global Studies, University of Gothenburg.

Berg, Carin, and Michael Schulz (2013), 'Hamas's Musical Resistance Practices: Perceptions, Production, and Usage', in M. Kanaaneh, S.-M. Thorsén, H. Bursheh and D. A. McDonald (eds), *Palestinian Music and Song: Expression and Resistance Since 1900*, Bloomington and Indianapolis: Indiana University Press, pp. 141–55.

Berkowitz, Michael (2002), 'Religious to Ethnic-National Identities: Political Mobilization Through Jewish Images in the United States and Britain 1881–1939', in S. H. Hoover and L. Schofield Clark (eds), *Practicing Religion in the Age of the Media: Explorations in Media, Religion, and Culture*, New York: Columbia University Press, pp. 305–27.

Bhikha, Zain (2018), *Allah Made Everything: The Song Book*, Markfield: The Islamic Foundation with ZeeBeeKids.

Bohlman, Philip V. (2002), *World Music: A Very Short Introduction*, Oxford: Oxford University Press.

Bourdieu, Pierre (2001), *Masculine Domination*, Cambridge: Polity Press.

Brackett, David (2000), *Interpreting Popular Music*, Berkley: University of California Press.

Brend, Barbara (2005), *Islamic Art*, London: The British Museum Press.

Brown, Jonathan (2007), 'Holy Rock Star: The Voice of Islam', *Independent*, 3 October.

Bruce, Steve (2018), *Researching Religion: Why We need Social Science*, Oxford: Oxford University Press.

Butt, Riazat (2007), 'Muslim Live8 brings home Darfur Crisis', *The Guardian*, 22 October, https://www.theguardian.com/uk/2007/oct/22/religion.musicnews (last accessed 6 January 2020).

Byrne, David (2013), *How Music Works*, Edinburgh: Canongate.

Carrette, Jeremy, and Richard King (2005), *Selling Spirituality: The Silent Takeover of Religion*, Abingdon: Routledge.

Cashmore, Ellis (2014), *Celebrity Culture*, 2nd edn, New York: Routledge.

Cloonan, Martin (2017), 'A Right Ding Dong: The Death of Margaret Thatcher and Music Censorship in the Digital Age', in A. Kirkegaard, H. Järviluoma, J. S. Knudsen and J. Otterbeck (eds), *Researching Music Censorship*, Newcastle upon Tyne: Cambridge Scholars Publishing, pp. 9–27.

Comer, Brooke (2005), 'Ruby: The Making of a Star', *Transnational Broadcasting Studies*, 14, http://tbsjournal.arabmediasociety.com/Archives/Spring05/comer.html (last accessed 11 September 2017).

Connell, Robert William (1995), *Masculinities*, Oxford: Blackwells.

Crowcroft, Orlando (2017), *Rock in a Hard Place: Music and Mayhem in the Middle East*, London: Zed.

Culler, Jonathan (1992), 'In Defence of Overinterpretation', in S. Collini (ed.), *Interpretation and Overinterpretation*, Cambridge: Cambridge University Press, pp. 109–24.

Danielson, Virginia (1997), *The Voice of Egypt: Umm Kulthum, Arabic Song, and Egyptian Society in the Twentieth Century*, Chicago: University of Chicago Press.

DeNora, Tia (2000), *Music in Everyday Life*, Cambridge: Cambridge University Press.

van Dijk, Kees (2014), 'Politicians who Love to Sing and Politicians who Detest Singing', in B. Barendregt (ed.), *Sonic Modernities in the Malay World: A History of Popular Music, Social Distinction and Novel Lifestyles (1930s–2000s)*, Leiden: Brill, pp. 291–319.

During, Jean (1993), 'Sama' [Listening]', in *Encyclopaedia of Islam*, Leiden: Brill.

Dusuki, Asyraf Wajdi, and Nurdianawati Irwani Abdullah (2007), 'Maqasid al-Shari'a, Maslaha, and Corporate Social Responsibility', *The American Journal of Islamic Social Science* 24(1), 25–45.

El Kholy, Samha Amin (1953), 'The Function of Music in Islamic Culture (in the period up to 1100 A.D.)', PhD thesis, Edinburgh University.

Ernst, Carl W. (1985), *Words of Ecstasy in Sufism*, Albany: State University of New York Press.

Eyerman, Ron, and Andrew Jamison (1998), *Music and Social Movements: Mobilizing Traditions in the Twentieth Century*, Cambridge: Cambridge University Press.

Farmer, Henry George [1929] (2001), *A History of Arabian Music*, New Delhi: Goodword Books.

al-Faruqi, Lois Ibsen (1985), 'Music, Musicians and Muslim Law', *Asian Music* 17(1), 3–36.

Fiscella, Anthony (2015), *Universal Burdens: Stories of (Un)Freedom from the Unitarian Universalist Association, the MOVE Organization, and Taqwacore*, Lund: Lund University.

Foley, Sean (2013), 'When Life Imitates Art: The Arab Spring, the Middle East, and the Modern World', *Alternatives: Turkish Journal of International Relations*, 12(3), 32–46.

Foucault, Michel [1971] (1998), 'Nietzsche, Genealogy, History', in J. D. Faubion (ed.), *Aesthetics, Method, and Epistemology: The Essential Works of Foucault, vol. 2*, New York: The New Press, pp. 369–92.

Foucault, Michel (1990a), *The Use of Pleasure: Volume 2 of the History of Sexuality*, New York: Vintage.

Foucault, Michel [1980] (1990b), 'About the Beginning of the Hermeneutics of the Self', in J. R. Carrette (ed.), *Religion and Culture by Michel Foucault*, Manchester: Manchester University Press pp. 158–81.

Foucault, Michel (2000), 'Self Writing', in P. Rabinow (ed.), *Michel Foucault: Ethics – Subjectivity and Truth. Essential works of Foucault 1954–1984, Volume 1*, London: Penguin, pp. 207–21.

Frishkopf, Michael (2000), 'Inshad Dini and Aghani Diniyya in Twentieth Century Egypt: A Review of Styles, Genres, and Available Recordings', *Middle East Studies Association Bulletin*, 34(2) (Winter), 167–83.

Frishkopf, Michael (2002), 'Islamic Hymnody in Egypt: Al-Inshad al-Dini', in V. Danielson and Dwight Reynolds (eds), *Garland Encyclopedia of World Music, vol. 6: The Middle East*, New York: Routledge, pp. 165–76.

Frishkopf, Michael (2014), 'Social Forces Shaping the Heterodoxy of Sufi Performance in Contemporary Egypt', in K. Salhi (ed.), *Music, Culture and Identity in the Muslim World: Performance, Politics and Piety*, Abingdon: Routledge, pp. 35–56.

Funch, Johnny (2000), '"Vi saluterar Ahmad Yassin" – En diskussion kring "Hamasmusik"' ['We salute Ahmad Yassin': A discussion about 'Hamas music'], unpublished BA dissertation in Islamic studies, Lund University, Sweden.

al-Ghazali, Abu Hamid Muhammad ibn Muhammad (2002), *On Listening to Music*, trans. from Persian by M. N. Abdus Salam, Chicago: Great Books of the Islamic World.

al-Ghazali, Muhammad [1984] (1997), *Mustaqbal al-Islam Kharij Ardih: Kayfa Nufakkiru Fih* [The future of Islam beyond its main region: How do we think about it], Al-Qahira: Dar al-Shuruk.

Gilsenan, Michael (1992), *Recognizing Islam: Religion and Society in the Modern Middle East*, London: I. B. Tauris.

Green, Duncan (2016), *How Change Happens*, Oxford: Oxfam.

Gruber, Christiane (2014), 'The Rose of the Prophet: Floral Metaphors in Late Ottoman Devotional Art', in D. J. Roxburgh (ed.), *Envisioning Islamic Art and Architecture*, Leiden: Brill, pp. 227–54.

Guettat, Mahmoud (2002), 'The Andalusian Musical Heritage', in V. Danielson and Dwight Reynolds (eds), *Garland Encyclopedia of World Music, vol. 6: the Middle East*, New York: Routledge, pp. 441–54.

Hafez (2006), *The Poems of Hafez*, trans. Reza Ordoubadian, Bethesda: Ibex Publisher.

Hafiz (1999), *The Gift: Poems by Hafiz, the Great Sufi Master*, trans. Daniel Ladinsky, New York: Penguin Compass.

Harvey, Graham (2004), 'Performing and Constructing Research as Guesthood in the Study of Religions', in L. Hume and J. Mulcock (eds), *Anthropologists in the Field: Cases in Participant Observation*, New York: Columbia University Press, pp. 168–82.

Hashas, Mohammed (2019), *The Idea of European Islam: Religion, Ethics, Politics and Perpetual Modernity*, London: Routledge.

Hecker, P. (2012), *Turkish Metal: Music, Meaning and Morality in a Muslim Society*, London: Routledge.

Hedin, Christer (1988), *Alla är födda muslimer: Islam som den naturliga religionen enligt fundamentalistisk apologetik* [Everyone is born Muslim: Islam as natural religion according to Fundamentalist apologetics], Stockholm: Verbum.

Hirschkind, Charles (2006a), 'Cassette Ethics: Public Piety and Popular Media in Egypt', in B. Meyer and A. Moors (eds), *Religion, Media, and the Public Sphere*, Bloomington: Indiana University Press, pp. 29–51.

Hirschkind, Charles (2006b), *The Ethical Soundscape. Cassette Sermons and Islamic Counterpublics*, New York: Columbia University Press.

Hodgson, Marshall G. S. (1974), *The Venture of Islam, part 1*, Chicago: University of Chicago Press.

Hoffman, Valerie J. (1995), *Sufism, Mystics, and Saints in Modern Egypt*, Columbia: University of South Carolina Press.

Høigilt, Jacob (2010), 'Rhetoric and Ideology in Egypt's Wasaiyya Movement', *Arabica* 57(2–3), 251–66.

Ikhwan al-Safa' (2010), *Epistles of the Brethren of Purity: On Music. An Arabic Critical Edition and English Translation of Epistle 5*, ed. and trans. Owen Wright, Oxford: Oxford University Press.

'Imara, Muhammad (1991), *al-Islam wa-l-Funun al-Jamila* [Islam and the belle arts], Al-Qahira: Dar al-Shuruq.

Irwing, Robert (1997), *Islamic Art in Context*, New York: Abrams.

al-Isfahani, Abu al-Faraj (2008), *Kitab al-Aghani* [The book of songs], vol. VIII, Beirut: Dar Sader.

Islam, Yusuf (2007), 'Music a Question of Faith or Da'wah', published online on http://www.mountainoflight.co.uk/talks.html (printed 1 July 2007).

Islam, Yusuf (2017), *Why I Still Carry a Guitar: The Spiritual Journey of Cat Stevens to Yusuf*, Wakefield: Sakinah Media.

Janmohamed, Shelina (2016), *Generation M: Young Muslims Changing the World*, London: I. B. Tauris.

Janson, Torsten (2003), *Your Cradle is Green: The Islamic Foundation and the Call to Islam in Children's Literature*, Stockholm: Almqvist & Wiksell International.

Janson, Torsten, and Jonas Otterbeck (2014), 'Islamiska bilder' [Islamic images], in M. Fahlén (ed.), *Bildens kraft: Religion och samtida utmaningar* [The power of images: Religion and contemporary challenges], Lund: Studentlitteratur, pp. 61–94.

Jarar, Husni Afham, and Ahmad al-Jada (1988–90), *Anashidi l-Da'watu l-Islamiyya* [The nashids of the Islamic Da'wa movement], Amman: Dar al-Diya'.

Jargy, Jean (2002), 'Sung Poetry in the Arabian Peninsula', in V. Danielson and Dwight Reynolds (eds), *Garland Encyclopedia of World Music, vol. 6: the Middle East,*. New York: Routledge, pp. 663–9.

Jouili, Jeanette S. (2015), *Pious Practice and Secular Constraints: Women in the Islamic Revival in Europe*, Stanford: Stanford University Press.

Al Judai', Abdallah bin Yusif (2007), *al-Musiqa wa-l-Ghina'a fi Mizana l-Islam* [Music and song in the rulings [lit. balance] of Islam], Beirut: Mu'assasatu l-Riyyan.

Juul Petersen, Marie (2012), 'Islamizing Aid: Transnational Muslim NGOs After 9.11', *Voluntas*, 23(1), 126–55.

Juul Petersen, Marie (2015), *For Humanity or for the Umma? Aid and Islam in Transnational Muslim NGOs*, London: Hurst & Company.

Kamali, Mohammad Hashim (1991), *Principles of Islamic Jurisprudence*, Cambridge: Islamic Texts Society.

Kamali, Mohammad Hashim (2015), *The Middle Path of Moderation in Islam: The Qur'anic Principle of Wasatiyyah*, Oxford: Oxford University Press.

Kamrava, Mehran (ed.) (2009), *The New Voices of Islam: Reforming Politics and Modernity – A Reader*, London: I. B. Tauris.

Kapchan, Deborah (2007), *Traveling Spirit Masters: Moroccan Gnawa Trance and Music in the Global Marketplace*, Middletown, CT: Wesleyan University Press.

Khabeer, Su'ad Abdul (2016), *Muslim Cool: Race, Religion, and Hip Hop in the United States*, New York: New York University Press.

Khaled, Amr (2005), 'Culture: The Distinguishing Feature of a People', *Transnational Broadcasting Studies*, 14, https://www.arabmediasociety.com/culture-the-distinguishing-feature-of-a-people/ (last accessed 18 January 2019). [This issue is registered as issue 13/2004 in the link.]

Kilpatrick, Hilary (2003), *Making the Great Book of Songs: Compilation and the Author's Craft in Abu l-Faraj al-Isbahani's Kitab al-aghani*, London: Routledge.

Kirkegaard, Annemette, Helmi Järviluoma, Jan Sverre Knudsen and Jonas Otterbeck (eds) (2017), *Researching Music Censorship*, Newcastle upon Tyne: Cambridge Scholars Publishing.

Knysh, Alexander D. (2007), *Al-Qushayri's Epistle on Sufism*, trans. A. D. Knysh (Great Books of Islamic Civilization), Reading: Garnet.

Kraidy, Marwan M., and Joe Khalil (2009), *Arab Television Industries*, Basingstoke: Palgrave.

Kubala, Patricia (2005), 'The Other Face of the Video Clip: Sami Yusuf and the Call for al-Fann al-Hadif', *Transnational Broadcasting Studies*, 14, https://www.arabmediasociety.com/the-other-face-of-the-video-clip-sami-yusuf-and-the-call-for-al-fann-al-hadif/ (last accessed 18 January 2019). [This issue is registered as issue 13/2004 in the link.]

Kubala, Patricia (2010), 'The Controversy over Satellite Music Television in Contemporary Egypt', in M. Frishkopf (ed.), *Music and Media in the Arab World*, Cairo: The American University in Cairo Press, pp. 173–224.

Kurtzman, Charles (ed.) (1998), *Liberal Islam: A Sourcebook*, Oxford: Oxford University Press.

Kvalvaag, Robert W. (2015), '"Ya Habib ya Muhammad" – Sami Yusuf of framveksten av en global muslimsk ungdomskultur' ['Ya Habib ya Muhammad': Sami Yusuf and the growth of a global Muslim youth culture], *Kirke & Kultur*, 1, 50–72.

Lahoud, Nelly (2017), 'A Cappella Songs (*anashid*) in Jihadi Culture', in T. Heghammer (ed.), *Jihadi Culture: The Art and Social Practices of Militant Islamists*, Cambridge: Cambridge University Press, pp. 42–62.

Larsson, Göran (2004), 'Don't Believe the Hype: Musik, identitet och religion bland unga muslimer' [Don't believe the hype: Music, identity and religion among young Muslims], in A. Häger (ed.), *Tro, pop och kärlek* [Faith, pop and love], Åbo: Åbo Akademi, pp. 81–92.

Larsson, Göran (2011), 'The Return of Ziryab: Yusuf Islam on Music', in T. Bossius, K. Kahn-Harris and A. Häger (eds), *Religion and Popular Music in Europe: New Expressions of Sacred and Secular Identity*, London: I. B. Tauris, pp. 92–104.

LeVine, Mark (2008a), *Heavy Metal Islam: Rock, Resistance, and the Struggle for the Soul of Islam*, New York: Three Rivers Press.

LeVine, Mark (2008b), 'Heavy Metal Muslims: The Rise of a Post-Islamist Public Sphere', *Contemporary Islam*, 2, 229–49.

LeVine, Mark (2011), 'How a Music About Death Affirms Life: Middle Eastern Metal and the Return of Music's Aura', in I. Peddie (ed.), *Popular Music and Human Rights, vol. II*, London: Ashgate pp. 55–71.

Lewis, Reina (2015), *Muslim Fashion: Contemporary Style Cultures*, Durham, NC: Duke University Press.

Lia, Brynjar (1998), *The Society of the Muslim Brothers in Egypt: The Rise of an Islamic Mass Movement 1928–1942*, Reading: Ithaca Press.

Librande, Leonard (2005), 'Ibn Abi al-Dunya: Certainty and Morality', *Studia Islamica*, 100/101, 5–42.

Lyden, John C. (2015), 'Definitions: What is the Subject Matter of "Religion and Popular Culture"?', in J. C. Lyden and R. M. Mazur (eds), *Routledge Companion to Religion and Popular Culture*, London: Routledge, pp. 7–20.

MacDonald, Duncan Black (1901–2), 'Emotional Religion in Islam as Affected by Music and Singing. Being a translation of the Ihya 'Ulum ad-din of al-Ghazzali with Analysis, Annotation, and Appendices', *Journal of the Royal Asiatic Society of Great Britain and Ireland*, Parts I and II (1901), III (1902).

Mahmood, Saba (2005), *Politics of Piety: The Islamic Revival and the Feminist Subject*, Princeton: Princeton University Press.

Malm, Krister, and Roger Wallis (1992), *Media Policy & Music Activity*, London: Routledge.

al-Mardini, Ibrahim Ramadan (2001), *al-Tibyan fi Ahkam al-Musiqi wa-l-Alhan* [Treaties on the regulations of music and melodies], Beirut: Markaz Beiruti li-l-Dirasat wa-l-Tawthiq.

Masud, Muhammad Khalid (2009), *Shatibi's Philosophy of Islamic Law*, 2nd edn, New Delhi: Kitab Bhavan.

Matusky, Patricia, and Tan Sooi Beng (2017), *The Music of Malaysia: The Classical, Folk and Syncretic Traditions*, 2nd edn, Abingdon: Routledge.

McDonald, David A. (2013), *My Voice is My Weapon: Music, Nationalism, and the Poetics of the Palestinian Resistance*, Durham, NC: Duke University Press.

McLain, Karline (2009), *India's Immortail Comic Books: Gods, Kings, and Other Heroes*, Bloomington: Indiana University Press.

Michot, Jean R. (1991), *Musique et danse selon Ibn Taymiyya* [Music and dance according to Ibn Taymiyya], Paris: J. Vrin.

Mitchell, Richard P. [1969] (1993), *The Society of the Muslim Brothers*, New York: Oxford University Press.

Moll, Yasmin (2009), 'Screening Faith, Making Muslims: Islamic Media for Muslim American Children and the Politics of Identity Construction', in Y. Y. Haddad,

F. Senzai and J. I. Smith (eds), *Educating the Muslims of America*, Oxford: Oxford University Press, pp. 155–77.

Morgan, Simon (2011), 'Celebrity: Academic "Pseudo-event" or a Useful Concept for Historians?', *Cultural and Social History*, 8(1), 95–114.

Morris, Carl (2013), 'Sounds Islamic? Muslim Music in Britain', PhD thesis in Religious and Theological Studies, Cardiff University. [Published online.]

Mostyn, Trevor (2002), *Censorship in Islamic Societies*, London: Saqi.

Müller, Dominik M. (2014), *Islam, Politics and Youth in Malaysia: The Pop-Islamist Reinvention of PAS*, London: Routledge.

Müller, Dominik M. (2015), 'Islamic Political and Popular Culture in Malaysia: Negotiating Normative Change between Shariah Law and Electric Guitars', *Indonesia and the Malay World*, 43(127), 318–44.

Mushtaq, Gohar (2011), *The Music Made Me Do It: An In-Depth Study of Music Through Islam and Science*, Riyadh: International Islamic Publishing House.

Najmabadi, Afsaneh (1991), 'The Hazards of Modernity and Morality: Women, State and Ideology in Contemporary Iran', in D. Kandiyoti (ed.), *Women, Islam and the State*, London: Macmillan, pp. 48–76.

Nasr, Seyyed Hossein (1990), *Islamic Art and Spirituality*, Oxford: Oxford University Press.

Negus, Keith, and Michael J. Pickering (2004), *Creativity, Communication and Cultural Value*, London: Sage.

Nelson, Kristina (2001), *The Art of Reciting the Qur'an*. Cairo: The American University of Cairo Press.

Netton, Ian Richard (1991), *Muslim Neoplatonists: An Introduction to the Thought of the Brethren of Purity*, Edinburgh: Edinburgh University Press.

Nietzsche, Friedrich [1887] (2017), *On the Genealogy of Morality*, 3rd edn, Cambridge: Cambridge University Press.

Nieuwkerk, Karin van (2011), 'Of Morals, Missions, and the Market: New Religiosity and "Art with a Mission" in Egypt', in K. van Nieuwkerk (ed.), *Muslim Rap, Halal Soaps and Revolutionary Theater: Artistic Developments in the Muslim World*, Austin: Texas University Press, pp. 177–205.

Nieuwkerk, Karin van (2012), 'Popularizing Islam or Islamizing Popular Music: New Developments in Egypt's Wedding Scene', *Contemporary Islam*, 6(3), 235–55.

Nieuwkerk, Karin van (2013), *Performing Piety: Singers and Actors in Egypt's Islamic Revival*, Austin: University of Texas Press.

Oliver, Anne Marie, and Paul Steinberg (2002), 'Popular Music of the Intifada', in V. Danielson, S. Marcus and D. Reynolds (eds), *Garland Encyclopedia of World Music, vol. 6: the Middle East*, New York: Routledge, pp. 635–40.

Olsson, Susanne (2015), *Preaching Islamic Revival: 'Amr Khaled, Mass Media and Social Change in Egypt*, London: I. B. Tauris.

Ostovar, Afshon (2017), 'The Visual Culture of Jihad', in T. Hegghammer (ed.), *Jihad Culture: The Art and Social Practices of Militant Islamists*, Cambridge: Cambridge University Press.

Otterbeck, Jonas (2000), *Islam på svenska: Tidskriften Salaam och islams globalisering* [Islam in Swedish: The journal *Salaam* and the globalization of Islam], Stockholm: Almqvist & Wiksell International.

Otterbeck, Jonas (2004), 'Music as a Useless Activity: Conservative Interpretations of Music in Islam', in M. Korpe (ed.), *Shoot the Singer! Music Censorship Today*, London: Zed Books, pp. 11–16.

Otterbeck, Jonas (2008), 'Battling over the Public Sphere: Islamic Reactions on the Music of Today', *Contemporary Islam*, 3(2), 211–28.

Otterbeck, Jonas (2010), *Samtidsislam: Unga muslimer i Malmö och Köpenhamn* [Contemporary Islam: Young Muslims in Malmö and Copenhagen], Stockholm: Carlsson.

Otterbeck, Jonas (2012a), 'The Issue of Music in Islamic Theological Discourse', *Contemporary Islam*, 6(3), 228–33.

Otterbeck, Jonas (2012b), 'Wahhabi Ideology of Social Control versus a New Publicness in Saudi Arabia', *Contemporary Islam*, 6(3), 341–53.

Otterbeck, Jonas (2014a), 'Records & Representation', in Awakening, *the Awakening book*, published by Awakening.

Otterbeck, Jonas (2014b), 'What is Islamic Art? And What Makes Art Islamic? The Example of the Islamic Discourse on Music', *CILE Journal*, 1(1), 223–47.

Otterbeck, Jonas (2015), '"I Wouldn't Call them Muslims!": Constructing a Respectable Islam', *Numen*, 62(2–3), 243–64.

Otterbeck, Jonas (2016), 'The Sunni Discourse on Music', in K. van Nieuwkerk, M. LeVine and M. Stokes (eds), *Islam and Popular Culture*, Austin: University of Texas Press, pp. 151–68.

Otterbeck, Jonas (2017), 'Maher Zain och den nya islamiska popmusiken' [Maher Zain and the new Islamic pop music], in *Riksbankens Jubileumsfonds Årsbok 2017*, Stockholm: Makadam.

Otterbeck, Jonas, and Johannes Frandsen Skjelbo (2020), '"Music Version" versus "Vocals-Only": Islamic Pop Music, Aesthetics and Ethics', *Popular Music and Society* 43(1), 1–19.

Otterbeck, Jonas, Douglas Mattsson and Orlando Pastene (2018), '"I am Satan!" Black Metal, Islam and Blasphemy in Turkey and Saudi Arabia', *Contemporary Islam*, 12(3), 267–86.

Partridge, Christopher (2005), *The Re-enchantment of the West. Vol. 2: Alternative Spiritualities, Sacralization, Popular Culture and Occulture*, London: T&T Clark International.

Partridge, Christopher (2013), *The Lyre of Orpheus: Popular Music, the Sacred, and the Profane*, Oxford: Oxford University Press.

Pieslak, Jonathan (2015), *Radicalism and Music: An Introduction to the Music Cultures of al-Qa'ida, Racist Skinheads, Christian-Affiliated Radicals, and Eco-Animal Rights Militants*, Middletown: Wesleyan University Press.

Pieslak, Jonathan (2017), 'A Musicological Perspective on Jihadi *anashid*', in T. Heghammer (ed.), *Jihadi Culture: The Art and Social Practices of Miltant Islamists*, Cambridge: Cambridge University Press.

Poljarevic, Emin (2012), 'Exploring Individual Motivation for Social Change: Mobilization of the Muslim Brotherhood's Youth in Pre-revolutionary Egypt', PhD thesis, European University Institute, Florence.

della Porta, Donatella, and Mario Diani (2006), *Social Movements: An Introduction*, 2nd edn, Oxford: Blackwell.

al-Qaradawi, Yusuf [1960] (1997), *al-Halal wa-l-Haram fi-l-Islam* [The allowed and the forbidden in Islam], Al-Qahira: Maktaba Wahba.

Qutb, Muhammad [1960] (1983), *Minhaj al-Fann al-Islami* [A programme for Islamic art], Beirut/Cairo: Dar al-Shuruq.

Ramadan, Tariq (1999), *To be a European Muslim*, Leicester: Islamic Foundation.

Ramadan, Tariq (2004), *Western Muslims and the Future of Islam*, Oxford: Oxford University Press.

Ramadan, Tariq (2009), *Radical Reform: Islamic Ethics and Liberation*, Oxford: Oxford University Press.

Rasmussen, Anne K. (2010), *Women, the Recited Qur'an, and Islamic Music in Indonesia*, Berkeley: University of California Press.

Rice, David T. (1985), *Islamic Art*, London: Thames & Hudson.

Ridley, Yvonne (2006a), 'Pop Culture in the Name of Islam', https://www.islamicboard.com/general/22051-pop-culture-name-islam-yvonne-ridley.html (last accessed 5 July 2021).

Ridley, Yvonne (2006b), 'Post Script to Pop Culture in the Name of Islam', http://www.therevival.co.uk/forum/general/1721 (last accessed 5 July 2021).

Riis, Ole, and Linda Woodhead (2010), *A Sociology of Religious Emotion*, Oxford: Oxford University Press.

Rinaldo, Rachel (2013), *Mobilizing Piety: Islam and Feminism in Indonesia*, Oxford: Oxford University Press.

Roald, Anne-Sofie (1994), *Tarbiyya: Education and Politics in Islamic Movements in Jordan and Malaysia*, Stockholm: Almqvist & Wiksell International.

Robson, James (1938), *Tracts on Listening to Music*, Oriental Translation Fund vol. XXXIV, London: The Royal Asiatic Society.

Ruggles, D. Fairchild (2018), 'Listening to Islamic Gardens and Landscapes', in M. Frishkopf and F. Spinetti (eds), *Music, Sound, and Architecture in Islam*, Austin: University of Texas Press, pp. 19–34.

Sabri, Mustafa [1910] (1995), 'A Topic of Dispute in Islam: Music', *Anadolu* 5(4), 1–5. [Original published in *Beyan-ul Haq*]

Said, Behnam (2012), 'Hymns (*Nasheeds*): A Contribution to the Study of the Jihadist Culture', *Studies in Conflict & Terrorism*, 35(12), 863–79.

Sakr, Naomi (2001), *Satellite Realms: Transnational Television, Globalization & the Middle East*, London: I. B. Tauris.

Salamandra, Christa (2016), 'Ambivalent Islam: Religion in Syrian Television Drama', in K. van Nieuwkerk, M. LeVine and M. Stokes (eds), *Islam and Popular Culture*, Austin: University of Texas Press, pp. 224–41.

Salvatore, Armando (2007), *The Public Sphere: Liberal Modernity, Catholicism, Islam*, New York: Palgrave Macmillan.

Sarkissian, Margaret (2005), '"Religion Never Had It so Good": Contemporary Nasyid and the Growth of Islamic Popular Music in Malaysia', *Yearbook for Traditional Music*, 37, 124–52.

Sawa, George. (2002), 'Theories of Rhythm and Meter in the Medieval Middle East', in V. Danielson and Dwight Reynolds (eds), *Garland Encyclopedia of World Music, vol. 6: the Middle East*, New York: Routledge, pp. 395–400.

Sayigh, Yezid (1997), *Armed Struggle and the Search for the State: The Palestinian National Movement, 1949–1993*, Oxford: Clarendon Press.

al-Sayyid, Mazan (2017), 'Saut al-Jihad: Min al-Nahdati ila-l-Dawla' [The voice of jihad: From the (Islamic) renaissance to the state], https://ma3azef.com/ صوت-الجهاد / (last accessed 28 June 2018).

Schade-Paulsen, Marc (1999), *Men and Popular Music in Algeria: The Social Significance of Raï*. Austin: The University of Texas Press.

Schielke, Samuli (2009), 'Being Good in Ramadan: Ambivalence, Fragmentation, and the Moral Self in the Lives of Young Egyptians', *Journal of Royal Anthropological Institute*, 15(1), 24–40.

Schielke, Samuli (2015), *Egypt in the Future Tense: Hope, Frustration, and Ambivalence Before and After 2011*, Bloomington: Indiana University Press.

Schimmel, Annemarie (1985), *And Muhammad is his Messenger: The Veneration of the Prophet in Islamic Piety*, Chapel Hill: University of North Carolina Press.

Schreiter, Robert J. (1997), *The New Catholicity: Theology between the Global and the Local*, Maryknoll: Orbis Books.

Shahid, Omar (2011), 'Maher Zain: "My Music is a Message of Islam"', *The Guardian*, 15 December.

Shannon, Jonathan Holt (2006), *Among the Jasmine Trees: Music and Modernity in Contemporary Syria*, Middletown: Wesleyan University Press.

Shehadi, Fadlou (1995), *Philosophies of Music in Medieval Islam*, Leiden: Brill.

Shiloah, Amnon (1995), *Music in the World of Islam: A Socio-Cultural Study*, Aldershot: Scolar Press.

Siamdoust, Nahid (2017), *Soundtrack of the Revolution: The Politics of Music in Iran*, Stanford: Stanford University Press.

Small, Christopher (1998), *Musicking: The Meanings of Performing and Listening*, Middleton: Wesleyan University Press.

Snir, Reuven (2006), *Religion, Mysticism and Modern Arabic Literature*, Wiesbaden: Harrassowitz Verlag.

State of Global Islamic Economy Report 2019/20, https://ceif.iba.edu.pk/pdf/state-of-global-islamic-economy-report-2019-20.pdf (last accessed 7 January 2020).

Stenberg, Leif (2012), '"Nedsändelserna", *al-Ma'thurat*, – en handling i konsten att vara en from muslim' ['Supplications', *al-Ma'thurat*: a document in the art of being a pious Muslim], in J. Otterbeck and L. Stenberg (eds), *Islamologi: Studiet av en religion*, Stockholm: Carlssons, pp. 40–61.

Stjernholm, Simon (2011), *Lovers of Muhammad: A Study of Naqshbandi-Haqqani Sufis in the Twenty-First Century*, Lund: Lund University.

Stokes, Martin (2014), 'New Islamist Popular Culture in Turkey', in K. Salhi (ed.), *Music, Culture and Identity in the Muslim World: Performance, Politics and Piety*, Abingdon: Routledge, pp. 15–34.

Street, John (2012), *Music and Politics*, Cambridge: Polity.

Tammam, Husam, and Patrick Haenni (2004), 'De retour dans les rythmes du monde: Une petite histoire du chant (ex)islamiste en Égypte' [The return to the rhythms of the world: A short history of (ex)Islamist singing in Egypt], *Vingtième siècle: Revue d'histoire*, 82, 91–102.

Tan, Sooi Beng (2007), 'Singing Islamic Modernity: Recreating Nasyid in Malaysia', *Kyoto Review of Southeast Asia*, 8–9.

Turino, Thomas (2008), *Music as Social Life: The Politics of Participation*, Chicago: University of Chicago Press.

TRTWorld (2016), Interview with Maher Zain and Mustafa Ceceli on the programme 'Showcase', 24 June, https://www.trtworld.com/video/showcase/showcase-exclusive-maher-zain-mustafa-ceceli/5a40bcc441736a1f528aca4d (last accessed 11 February 2019).

Waardenburg, Jacques (2007), 'Can the Science of Religion Render Service to the Study of Islam?', in J. Waardenburg, *Muslims as Actors*, Berlin: W. de Gruyter, pp. 25–39.

Waugh, Earle H. (1989), *The Munshidin of Egypt: Their World and Their Song*, Columbia: University of South Carolina Press.

Weintraub, Andrew N. (2008), '"Dance Drills, Faith Spills": Islam, Body Politics, and Popular Music in Post-Suharto Indonesia', *Popular Music*, 27(3), 367–92.

Wensinck, Arent Jan (1967), *Concordance et indices de la tradition musulmane, tome VI* [Concordance and index of the Muslim traditions, vol. VI], Leiden: Brill.

Werbner, Pnina (2003), *Pilgrims of Love: The Anthropology of a Global Sufi Cult*, London: Hurst & Company.

Wharnsby, Dawud (2009), *For Whom the Troubadour Sings: Collected Poetry and Songs*, Markfield: Kube Publishing.

van Wichelen, Sonja (2012), 'The Body and the Veil', in B. S. Turner (ed.), *Routledge Handbook of Body Studies*, London: Routledge, pp. 206–16.

Wiegers, Gerard (2011), 'Dr Sayyid Mutawalli ad-Darsh's Fatwas for Muslims in Britain: The Voice of Official Islam?' in G. MacLean (ed.), *Britain and the Muslim World: Historical Perspectives*, Newcastle: Cambridge Scholars Publishing, pp. 178–91.

Winegar, Jessica (2016), 'Islam at the Art School: Religious Young Artists in Egypt', in K. van Nieuwkerk, M. LeVine and M. Stokes (eds), *Islam and Popular Culture*, Austin: University of Texas Press, pp. 187–203.

Winston, Diane (2002), 'All the World's a Stage: The Performed Religion of the Salvation Army, 1880–1920', in S. M. Hoover and L. Schofield Clark (eds), *Practicing Religion in the Age of the Media: Explorations in Media, Religion, and Culture*, New York: Columbia University Press, pp. 113–37.

Wise, Lindsay (2006), 'Meet Islam's biggest Rock star', *Time Magazine*, 31 July, http://content.time.com/time/world/article/0,8599,1220754,00.html (last accessed 6 January 2019).

Yusuf, Sami (2006), 'Open Letter from Sami Yusuf to Yvonne Ridley', https://turntoislam.com/community/threads/open-letter-from-sami-yusuf-to-yvonne-ridley.4215/#post-20713 (last accessed 5 July 2021).

INDEX